Managing Artists in the Music Industries

Managing Artists in the Music Industries

An Examination of the Key Role in Music Creator Development

Allan Dumbreck and John Williamson

With contributions from Jayne Stynes, Brendan Moon and Clare K. Duffin

CABI is a trading name of CAB International

CABI
Nosworthy Way
Wallingford
Oxfordshire OX10 8DE
UK

CABI
200 Portland Street
Boston
MA 02114
USA

Tel: +44 (0)1491 832111
E-mail: info@cabi.org
Website: www.cabi.org

T: +1 (617)682-9015
E-mail: cabi-nao@cabi.org

© Allan Dumbreck and John Williamson 2026. All rights, including for text and data mining, AI training, and similar technologies, are reserved. No part of this publication may be reproduced in any form or by any means, electronically, mechanically, by photocopying, recording or otherwise, without the prior permission of the copyright owners.

The views expressed in this publication are those of the author(s) and do not necessarily represent those of, and should not be attributed to, CAB International (CABI). Any images, figures and tables not otherwise attributed are the author(s)' own. References to internet websites (URLs) were accurate at the time of writing.

CAB International and, where different, the copyright owner shall not be liable for technical or other errors or omissions contained herein. The information is supplied without obligation and on the understanding that any person who acts upon it, or otherwise changes their position in reliance thereon, does so entirely at their own risk. Information supplied is neither intended nor implied to be a substitute for professional advice. The reader/user accepts all risks and responsibility for losses, damages, costs and other consequences resulting directly or indirectly from using this information.

CABI's Terms and Conditions, including its full disclaimer, may be found at https://www.cabidigital-library.org/terms-and-conditions.

A catalogue record for this book is available from the British Library, London, UK.

ISBN-13: 9781836992332 (hardback)
9781789245301 (paperback)
9781789245318 (ePDF)
9781789245325 (ePub)

DOI: 10.1079/9781789245325.0000

Commissioning Editor: Claire Parfitt
Editorial Assistant: Emma McCann
Production Editor: James Bishop

Typeset by Exeter Premedia Services Pvt Ltd, Chennai, India
Printed in the USA

Contents

Contributors		vii
Interviewees		ix
Acknowledgements		xiii
Methodology		xv
Prologue		xvii

Part 1: In Context: The Manager within the Music Industries

1	**Introduction to Artist Management** *John Williamson and Allan Dumbreck*	1
2	**The Manager: A Selective History (1926–2024)** *John Williamson*	12
3	**Organizing Music Managers** *Allan Dumbreck*	27

Part 2: The Manager's Voice: Interviews and Analysis

4	**Getting Started** *Allan Dumbreck*	51
5	**Growing the Business** *Allan Dumbreck*	73
6	**External Factors and Conflict** *Allan Dumbreck*	89

Part 3: The Changing Environment: Current Developments and Possible Futures

7	**Finance and International** *Brendan Moon*	104

8	**Equality, Diversity and Inclusion (EDI)** *Clare K. Duffin*	119
9	**Mental Health** *Jayne Stynes*	131
10	**Outcomes, Conclusions and Further Research** *Allan Dumbreck*	143

Appendices – Questionnaires and Further Possible Research 159

Index 161

Contributors

Allan Dumbreck is a musician and educator with over 35 years' experience of the music industries. As a keyboard player with several Scottish acts, including The Big Dish, Horse the Band, and Autumn 1904, he has performed and recorded internationally, supporting, amongst others, BB King. As a music educator he has developed a series of university and college music programmes, teaching across the UK and Europe, and is currently Senior Lecturer at the University of the West of Scotland where he established the BA (Hons) Commercial Music in 2001. He is the co-author of *Music Entrepreneurship*, published by Bloomsbury, and Editor of the *Music Education Directory*, published by UK Music (previously by the BPI).

John Williamson is a Lecturer in Music at the University of Glasgow. He has previously written on issues surrounding musical work, the music industries and the history of popular music in Scotland. He recently co-edited *Made in Scotland*, part of Routledge's Studies in Popular Music series. Prior to this he managed the Glasgow-based bands Bis, and Belle and Sebastian, worked as a freelance music writer for the *Herald* newspaper, and was press agent for the T in the Park music festival.

Clare Duffin is a Lecturer at the University of the West of Scotland, where she leads the MA Music programme. As a drummer, she has performed on BBC Scotland, Canadian TV and in David Mackenzie's feature film *You Instead*, as well as at festivals including RockNess and Princes Street Gardens. Her PhD examined the development of the conceptual framework she termed 'gender gapping', which explored freelance music practices among women in Scotland. This innovative research has since informed book chapters published by Cambridge University Press and Palgrave Macmillan.

Brendan Moon has managed a diverse range of artists including Paolo Nutini, The View and GUN. He is an Associate Lecturer at the University of the West of Scotland and at Glasgow University. He has held pivotal roles at Neil O'Brien Entertainment, Mercury Records/Universal Music London, and DF Concerts. As the Managing Director of Morsecode Management Ltd, founded in 2003, he has led the company in arts and event management. He is currently completing his PhD on funding and government policies in popular music, at the University of Glasgow.

Jayne Stynes is a Lecturer in Commercial Music at the University of the West of Scotland and a PhD researcher in the Department of Media and Communications at the University of Leeds. Her research examines gender equality initiatives in the UK music industries. She spent over five years as a manager at Eleven Management (Blur, Gorillaz, The Clash, Kano, Róisín Murphy) before taking on the role of General Manager at the UK Music Managers Forum (2019–2021). She currently chairs the Equalities, Diversity, Inclusion and Access Advisory Committee for the Scottish Music Industry Association, helping to develop an EDIA strategy for Scotland's music industry.

Interviewees

Denise Allan
Denise Allan is the founding partner and Director of 677 Media Management, an independent artist management company based in Glasgow. She manages a series of artists including Glasvegas, who achieved a No. 2 UK album chart position and a nomination for the Mercury Prize with their platinum-selling eponymous debut album. Other acts signed to 677 include Plasticine and Lamaya.

Steven Braines
Steven Braines is the co-founder of the international event series and record label HE.SHE.THEY, which promotes diversity and inclusion in electronic music. He also founded the talent management company The Weird & The Wonderful, which manages artists such as Maya Jane Coles, Emily Nash, SYREETA and Wax Wings. Previously, he managed Tricky, Tale of Us and Magda, amongst others. He is a qualified occupational psychologist. He serves on the board of NTIA and MMF and was previously a board member of AFEM.

Chris Chadwick
Chris Chadwick is the founder and Director of Famous Friends Management. Over the last ten years, he has assisted artists in growing from demos and debut shows to international touring platforms, festival performances, TV and radio appearances, and global audiences. He currently manages Anna B. Savage, Guy Sigsworth, Harvey Grant, LVRA, Puma Blue and Rosie Lowe, amongst others.

Annabella Coldrick
Annabella Coldrick started her professional life at the Design Council where she was involved in helping to shape the UK government's policy on creative industries. Annabella has also worked in advocacy in Brussels, as well as in government communications and public affairs roles at major organizations such as Cadbury and Which?. She is now the CEO of the Music Managers Forum UK, which is the representative body for artist managers in the UK.

Polly Comber
Polly Comber started her career as a record label A&R, moving into artist management with the band Ghosts, which went on to sign with Atlantic Records. She then co-founded Black Fox Management in 2013 with Josh Smith. Their management roster includes Ghostwriter and Balcony. Previously, they managed Bastille and Rag'n'Bone Man, amongst others.

Bruce Findlay

Bruce Findlay started his career working in the music section of a department store and later opened his record shop Bruce's in the 1960s, which went on to become the largest independent record chain in the UK. He established his own record label in the late 1970s and, later, managed a series of artists including China Crisis and Simple Minds, taking the latter to international success, including a US No. 1 ('Don't you forget about me'). Based in Scotland, he has had advisory roles and has been an advocate for education in the music industries. In 1992 he was part of a group of artist managers who initiated the first Music Managers Forum in the UK.

Ellie Giles

Ellie Giles started in the music industry as a promoter at Barfly and then had a successful stint as an A&R rep, developing artists such as Ellie Goulding and White Lies at Polydor Records. She has a passion for helping artists strategically co-ordinate and build their careers. Ellie's artists include Matty Green, who is the mix engineer for Ed Sheeran and U2, amongst others, and Billy Ryder-Jones, an artist and producer. She is based in the UK.

Virpi Immonen

Virpi Immonen is the CEO of the Helsinki-based artist management company Fullsteam Management. She is the Chair of the Music Managers Forum in Finland. She has managed artists such as KUUMAA and worked as a music supervisor on animated television. Her company represents a wide variety of artists, ranging from hip-hop and pop acts to some of Finland's most interesting indie and alternative bands. Virpi has also served as a board member of the International Music Managers Forum (IMMF) and has won awards for her role in management, including the Finnish Industry Awards for 2011, 2021 and 2013.

Chris Hardin

Chris Hardin is an artist manager and founder/owner of the music management firms Hardin Bourke Entertainment and Music Mgmt Inc. He has guided the careers of such artists as LIVE, Robert DeLong, The HU, Starship, Indigenous, Los Amigos Invisibles, Galactic, Rahzel (of the Roots), Si*Se, Yerba Buena, Tom Tom Club, Lou Gramm, Sweet and Ed Kowalczyk, amongst others. He has produced multiple tours for his clients in over 16 countries and has helped artists achieve gold and platinum sales awards and Grammy nominations.

Keith Harris

Keith Harris has extensive experience in the music industries. He joined EMI Records in 1976 and worked in promotions. He worked for Motown in the USA for two years and became a general manager for the label. During this period he worked with artists such as Marvin Gaye, Diana Ross, Smokey Robinson, Rick James and Stevie Wonder. Returning to the UK in 1982, he formed his own management company working with artists such as Junior Giscombe, Junior Tucker and Lynden David Hall. He is now a music consultant, still working closely with Stevie Wonder. He was the Director for PPL and a former Chairman of the MMF UK. He is also a founding member of the European Music Managers Alliance.

Scott Kirkwood

Scott Kirkwood is a Glasgow-based artist manager and A&R consultant. Having completed his BA in Commercial Music, Scott was also the project manager on the youth music project 'Hit the Road', at the Scottish Music Centre. He spent five years with Sony Music UK, later creating his own management company, SKMGMT, in 2014. He also helped develop KLOE and later signed her to Columbia Records UK. He currently heads up Kingdom Management and was responsible for the discovery and early development of Lewis Capaldi.

Steijn Koeijvoets
Steijn Koeijvoets has over 20 years' experience in the music industry. He began his career with independent label PIAS and later worked at Strictly Confidential as General Manager. He established the Dutch office of the international streaming company Deezer in 2012. He is now a partner at 3S Music Management where he applies his expertise in launching, marketing and promoting artists, and developing their careers. He is also a board member of EMMA.

Per Kviman
Per Kviman is a music industry executive who has worked in the industry for 43 years. He is currently the CEO of Stockholm-based management company Versity Music and Chair of European Music Manager Alliance. Versity was founded in 2003 with Andy Farrow and currently represents Watain, Backyard Babies, Takida, Stiftelsen and Bright Black. Versity Music artists has been awarded platinum and gold records.

David Martin
David Martin was the booker and director at the Dimensions Festival until 2018. He also held roles in government. He is now CEO of the Featured Artists Coalition (FAC), the UK trade body representing the rights and interests of music artists. FAC is a not-for-profit organization serving a diverse global membership of creators at all career stages. Formed by artists *for* artists, FAC focuses on advocacy, education, collaboration and research, providing a strong collective voice within the industry and to government.

Mark Melton
Mark Melton is an entertainment lawyer with P. Russell & Co. Solicitors and has over 25 years' experience in copyright law and negotiating music business agreements. He also served as an advisor to the Musicians' Union. He has expertise in negotiating international music and entertainment agreements. He previously worked as an MU official and as artist manager for Charlotte Church, and has been executive producer for three series of TV shows for Channel 4.

Cara Mills-McLaughlin
Cara Mills-McLaughlin is an event manager with considerable experience in artist and tour management and is a box-office specialist. Skilled in communication, event management, artist management and social media, she previously worked for Kingdom Management alongside Scott Kirkwood. She gained a first-class BA (Hons) in Commercial Music from the University of the West of Scotland and a postgraduate degree in marketing from the Glasgow Caledonian University.

Brendan Moon
Brendan Moon has managed artists such as Paolo Nutini, The View and GUN. He is an Associate Lecturer at the University of the West of Scotland and Glasgow University. He has held pivotal roles at Neil O'Brien Entertainment, Mercury Records/Universal Music London and DF Concerts. As the Managing Director of Morsecode Management Ltd, founded in 2003, he has led the company in arts and events management. He is currently completing his PhD in funding and government policies in popular music, at Glasgow University.

Karl Nielson
With over 30 years' experience in the music industry, Karl Nielson has undertaken a number of successful music ventures – most recently AEI Media – including labels, music brands and live events such as Drum & Bass Arena, UKF and SubSoul. He was a founder of the Video Interactive TV Group, home to Fizz TV and Channel U. He also held a senior marketing position at British Airways and was Global Marketing Communications Director at Dr. Martens. His management experience includes reintroducing Goldie to the world with three new albums, a UK tour and live performances with a

64-piece orchestra. He currently manages William Orbit and Maeve and serves on the BPI/MEGS Board.

Ross Patel
Ross Patel is the founder, CEO & Consulting Advisor of Whole Entertainment. He has over ten years' diverse experience in music, entertainment, sustainability & technology. He has a passion for team and talent management, creating platforms to launch and support artists, talent, brands and events with social impact. He is committed to making the company climate-positive by developing low-impact practices, implementing company initiatives and funding carbon-offset projects. He was a board member of the Music Managers Forum UK and was the chief strategy officer at UMA Entertainment. He also holds licences such as ClimateEQ certification and membership of the MMF UK.

Neeta Ragoowansi
Neeta Ragoowansi is President of Music Managers Forum – US (MMF-US) and President of International Music Managers Forum (IMMF). She has been an attorney and music business professional for over 30 years, serving as strategic advisor, business development resource and legal counsel to entertainment and tech industry clients. She is also co-founder of NPREX (National Performing Rights Exchange), Global Co-Chair for Women in Music, and Chair of the Diversity & Inclusion Task Force of the American Bar Association's forum on the entertainment and sports industries. She serves on the advisory boards of Gritty in Pink/In Pink and All About Music Conference (India).

Lyle Scougall
Lyle Scougall began his career in Glasgow, performing in bands, and later completed a BA (Hons) in Commercial Music and an MA in Music (Industries). He founded management company Manana Music Management in 2017 with Nathan Dunphy, benefitting from the MMF UK's 'accelerator' support programme for emerging managers. He has signed developing artist Joesef, who won best breakthrough artist at the Scottish Music Awards 2019 and was also nominated for the SMIA Scottish Album of the Year Award in 2021.

Horace Trubridge
Horace Trubridge was a founding member of the R&B doowop band Darts. He had a string of top 10 hits and had two gold and a platinum albums in the 1970s. In 1990, he began working with the Musicians' Union as a career advisor, and in 1997 he became the London official negotiating for the members of the Royal Opera House, English National Opera and the West End theatres. He became Assistant General Secretary of the MU and then General Secretary in 2017.

Acknowledgements

The authors/contributors would like to thank all those who participated in the interviews and the following organizations for their assistance in the research and creation of this document:

Music Managers Forum (UK)
Music Managers Forum (US)
Music Managers Forum (Canada)
European Music Managers Alliance
Featured Artists Coalition
Musicians' Union

Thanks go to Jack McAuley, Emmy Leishman, Hannah Thorne, Chris Piechowiak and Lily Connell, for additional research and transcription.

Thanks also go to all of our interviewees; Claire Parfitt, Lucy Pritchard and everyone at CABI; Amie Therrien at MMF Canada; Sharon Tapper at MMF US; Kenny Forbes; Mike Jones; and Martin Cloonan.

Methodology

Our primary research consisted of a series of semi-structured interviews (SSI) conducted with artist/creator managers and industry personnel. As defined by Adams (2015):

> Conducted conversationally with one respondent at a time, the semi-structured interview (SSI) employs a blend of closed- and open-ended questions, often accompanied by follow-up why or how questions. About one hour is considered a reasonable maximum length for SSIs in order to minimize fatigue for both interviewer and respondent.

We conducted 22 interviews with 14 individual artist/creator managers and an additional 9 interviews with 8 industry personnel (from key representative organizations) over the period March 2020–January 2025. In order to gain some balance in the responses, five of the industry personnel worked for manager representative organizations (MMFs) while two worked for bodies representing artists and musicians (FAC/MU). This gave us a total of 31 interviews with 22 different professionals.

The original interview questionnaire consisted of 13 questions which the authors felt were fundamental to a clear comprehension of the sector and the activities of the manager within it. The interviews were conducted by video link and typically lasted between 45 minutes and one hour. These were recorded (audio), transcribed and distributed to the authors/contributors for analysis. As per the description above, some questions were intentionally constructed to be open-ended, allowing the interviewer or interviewee to digress in the case of a particularly interesting but incomplete initial response.

The first round of interviews (March 2020) was curtailed due to the COVID pandemic as many interviewees told us that they did not have a clear vision of how their work would (or could) progress while the lockdown continued. This resulted in us halting the process until 2022 when restrictions had been lifted and work within the music industries was returning to a new, altered normal. The second round of interview responses raised some interesting additional issues (notably in relation to AI and equality/diversity), which we felt required further investigation, and so a second, shorter set of four follow-up questions (again, as per the definition above) was devised and a final set of interviews (6 managers and 1 industry representative agreed to respond) were undertaken. Both questionnaires are reprinted in the Appendices of this book. It is hoped that we can make the complete transcripts available online at a future date.

These primary data therefore capture an unfolding situation over a five-year period in which the music industries, and artist management in particular, experienced unprecedented change due to significant external pressures (notably the pandemic and the implementation of the EU withdrawal agreement). While this means that we are not examining a single 'snapshot' in time (which was the original intention), what we have instead is a catalogue of changing experiences and opinions as the impact of these key factors became apparent. This in turn provides us with a unique perspective on an industry in flux, responding to significant change brought about by agents and events beyond the control of those most directly affected. In many respects we believe that this delivers a more realistic and informative body of outcomes and a more accurate understanding of the ever-changing world of artist management.

Note

[1] Throughout this book we use the term 'artist management' or 'artist manager' to mean the activities involved in managing any musical creator (musician, songwriter, vocalist, producer, DJ, composer, etc.). Other terms (e.g. 'music manager', 'creator manager') do exist, but it was felt that 'artist manager' gave the clearest explanation for the majority of readers of this document.

Reference

Adams, W. (2015) Conducting semi-structured interviews. In: Newcomer, K.E., Hatry, H.P. and Wholey, J.S. (eds) *Handbook of Practical Program Evaluation*, 4th edn. Wiley, Chichester, UK. DOI: 10.1002/9781119171386.ch19

Prologue

For music fans, it is common to have a song which runs around our head all day, an album that transports us to another time, usually by an artist we love. We hear their music on our playlist, go to the concert, buy the T-shirt, follow them on social media, but rarely pause to wonder how they became successful.

How did they get that critical record deal? How did they negotiate the breakthrough single release or TV appearance? How were they accelerated from playing in bars in their hometown to writing that movie song? How exactly did they go viral and who, apart from the artist, were part of the process?

One of the often invisible links here is the manager. Variously, they are a combination of talent-spotter, financer, therapist and general dogsbody, working closely with the artist and driving their career forward. But who are these people? Where do they come from? What is their role? What do we know about them? And why should we care?

When we do hear about them, more often than not, it is in a negative light. Among contemporary managers, fame (or infamy) usually is a result of a combination of dubious business practices, Svengali-like behaviour and the breakdown of the relationship between them and their more famous clients.

Every year sees press reports and litigation of this type, where the artist manager is often presented in the media as unscrupulous, syphoning off their clients' profits or simply being negligent. Examples of this in the recent past have involved Leonard Cohen (Michaels, 2012), The Killers (Lindvall, 2009), Coldplay (Music Week, 2023) and Madlib (Tencer, 2024), whose respective managers – Kelley Lynch, Braden Merrick, Dave Holmes and Eothen Alapatt – have been accused of a mixture of financial mismanagement and incompetence that has come to light through court proceedings. Perhaps more seriously, the duty of care that managers have in relation to their artists has been called into question, with the parents of Avicii (Williams, 2018) and Lil Peep (Aswad, 2019) holding their former managers partly responsible for their premature deaths.

Other recent examples of artist managers acquiring a public profile or celebrity status involve their extracurricular activities. Thanks to the tabloid attention paid to Louis Walsh (former manager of Boyzone and Westlife) and Sharon Osbourne (manager of her husband Ozzy, and others) and as a result of their roles on TV talent shows, their previous successes in the music business have been either overlooked or traduced. Similarly, by purchasing the rights to Taylor Swift's Big Machine masters, enraging both the singer and her fans, Scooter Braun (best known for managing Justin

Bieber and Ariana Grande) was catapulted to a level of attention well beyond that which he achieved through his many prior successes in the music industries (Mercuri, 2021).

A longer historical lens (as explored in Chapter 2) only further blackens the reputation of the artist manager thanks to some of those who have developed an overblown public persona through a mixture of biographies, memoirs and interviews detailing excessive, manipulative and sometimes violent behaviour. In this respect, the legacies of the likes of Peter Grant, manager of Led Zeppelin (Blake, 2018) or Don Arden, manager of the Small Faces and Black Sabbath (Cartwright, 2007), both in their prime half a century ago, fall within this category.

But how do these stories and perceptions relate to the everyday world of a contemporary artist manager? Are these high-profile individuals truly the tip of a wholly unappealing iceberg or are they part of a Dickensian minority? Is this still the approach required to make your clients successful in the 21st century or are they anachronisms, evidence of the dark underworld of the music industries of the past? Or is it simply the case that 'good news is no news' and the only time managers come to the fore is when something bad has happened or someone has something derogatory to say about them?

Either way, is it a picture that ignores thousands of highly skilled managers who work under the radar, at all levels, protecting their charges, negotiating the most advantageous contracts for them and propelling them to greater success?

It is this final group of artist managers that this book is about, and its aim is to produce an accurate and sober perspective that speaks to the lived experience of management within the wider context of the music industries.

References

Aswad, J. (2019) Lil Peep's mother sues managers over his death. *Variety*, 8 October. Available at: https://variety.com/2019/music/news/lil-peeps-mother-sues-managers-over-death-1203363212/ (accessed 1 May 2025).

Cartwright, G. (2007) Don Arden. Obituary. *The Guardian*, 26 July. Available at: www.theguardian.com/news/2007/jul/25/guardianobituaries.musicnews (accessed 19 September 2024).

Lindvall, H. (2009) Behind the music: when artists and managers fall out. *The Guardian*, 19 March. Available at: www.theguardian.com/music/musicblog/2009/mar/19/artist-manager-relationship (accessed 19 September 2024).

Mercuri, M. (2021) The Taylor Swift and Scooter Braun drama explained. Forbes, New York. Available at: www.forbes.com/sites/monicamercuri/2024/06/21/the-taylor-swift-and-scooter-braun-drama-explained/ (accessed 28 September 2024).

Michaels, S. (2012) Leonard Cohen's ex-manager sentenced to 18 months in jail. *The Guardian*, 19 April. Available at: www.theguardian.com/music/2012/apr/19/leonard-cohen-manager-sentenced-jail (accessed 19 September 2024).

Music Week (2023) Coldplay and former manager Dave Holmes in high court legal battle. Available at: www.musicweek.com/management/read/coldplay-and-former-manager-dave-holmes-in-high-court-legal-battle/088635 (accessed 19 September 2024).

Tencer, D. (2024) Madlib sues former manager for alleged 'rank self-dealing' and 'pervasive mismanagement'. Music Business Worldwide, 1 November. Available at: https://www.musicbusinessworldwide.com/madlib-sues-former-manager-for-alleged-rank-self-dealing-and-pervasive-mismanagement/ (accessed 1 May 2025).

Williams, H. (2018) Avicii's step-father reportedly blames the artist's manager for his death. *Mixmag*, 8 August. Available at: https://mixmag.net/read/aviciis-step-father-apparently-blames-the-artists-manager-for-his-death-news (accessed 1 May 2025).

1 Introduction to Artist Management

John Williamson and Allan Dumbreck

Supreme juggler! You become the de facto *CEO, running the artist's business.*
Karl Nielson (2024), UK artist manager

The origins of this book can be traced back to approximately 2015 when we began to contemplate the vague notion of developing some of our previous work on the music industries generally and the role of managers specifically. What was initially a somewhat loose idea slowly evolved into something more concrete and has resulted in what you are reading now. At the start, our hunches were that managers had historically played a much more important role in the music industries than they were given credit for; that role was far more nuanced and three-dimensional than was generally represented and, most importantly, it was becoming more critical and more distinctive as the industries in which they operate have been disrupted by technology, politics, economics and geography (to list but a few factors) in the last two decades.

The book's period of gestation has highlighted both the problems of trying to capture a profession in flux, where the challenges of 2015 only slightly resemble those of 2025. We began conducting interviews with managers from around the world in 2020 before, as in many sectors of the music industries, work was placed on hold by the COVID-19 pandemic. When we returned to complete these, the narratives were different and more urgent: loss of income during the global pandemic was exacerbated by a global recession; nativism (for example, with the consequences of Brexit for UK artists and tighter visa requirements for touring artists in other parts of the world); and more music specific concerns surrounding the downward pressure on both concert and streaming revenues (to varying degrees).

Though this forced a considerable degree of rethinking on our part, it strengthened rather than diminished our rationale for writing in the first instance – that the manager within the music industries matters; that their role is poorly understood; and that their importance has grown as the music industries have changed fundamentally in recent years.

This introduction will provide some orientation for the remainder of the book. It begins with an explanation of why we chose to embark on this project, before providing a more rounded explanation of why artist management and managers matter. It will then consider some definitions of the role, and will end by setting out exactly how we are going to build on that existing knowledge, both methodologically and structurally.

Why Write This Book?

All the contributors to this book have shared interests in and perspectives on artist management that span the music industries and academia. These include experience as a musician who was managed (Dumbreck), a manager who was employed by a large management company and industry organization (Stynes) and self-employed artist managers (Williamson, Moon, Duffin). The book is undoubtedly a product of these experiences and others across several decades, good and bad. With all the authors having been in and around universities for a number of years, it is perhaps unsurprising that

© Allan Dumbreck and John Williamson 2026. *Managing Artists in the Music Industries: An examination of the key role in music creator development* (eds Allan Dumbreck and John Williamson)
DOI: 10.1079/9781789245325.0001

we have an interest in reflecting on what we did (and in some cases still do) and, perhaps less explicably, why we did it, or do it.

The book is not a string of tired anecdotes and is something of a negation of the many music business memoirs of this ilk, which tend to portray managers hanging out with their more famous clients and their associates, surrounded by drink and drugs, where a combination of mismanagement and often misplaced entrepreneurial bravado results in everything ending badly. Nor is it an attempt on our part to instruct anyone in how to manage an artist in the music industries. Apart from the fact that none of us has the conceit to suggest that our efforts in the field are necessarily examples of great practice, as will become clear, artist management is not a field where the rules that apply to one apply to all. Experiences of artist management vary hugely based on several factors: age and experience, social class, gender, genre, sexuality, history and geography, to name but a few.

If that outlines some of what we are *not* doing, it is important to set out clearly what we *are* attempting to do and why. First, it takes artist management seriously, as an increasingly important part of the wider music industries and, hopefully, makes the case for it being worthy of this type of study. Secondly, it seeks to portray the nuance of the role through the various career stages of managers and artists, with the accompanying industrial and personal challenges this presents. Finally, it seeks to contextualize and understand artist management in the contemporary music industries, casting new light on both.

Throughout, our aim is to do this primarily using the voices of artist managers themselves, drawing on 22 interviews with managers and industry personnel at various levels managing different types of artists and enjoying varying degrees of success in a range of countries. This will be supplemented with our own analysis and some insight from trade bodies and artists to provide a more rounded picture of the profession.

We will now outline our rationale for conducting the research and some of the starting points within existing literature, before explaining how we are going to develop these and structure the book.

Why Artist Management Matters

How can you differentiate your artists within the very crowded landscape? That's the key challenge.

Stein Koeijvoets, Dutch artist manager

Beyond our personal experiences, there are four main reasons that make an in-depth study of artist management of wider interest. The first is to place artists at the centre of an account of the wider music industries, where historically their importance has been neglected relative to the large corporations that dominate. In doing so, we are also highlighting the importance of the artist manager within this wider ecosystem, thanks to their proximity to the artist. We will then contend that the artist manager is the only individual within the industries to have a holistic view of the music industries due their role as a conduit and connector between the artist and all the others involved in their business activities, potentially including record labels, concert promoters, agents, publishers, marketers, lawyers, accountants, and so on. Lastly, we argue that the expansion and professionalization of artist management is a key reason for investigating and critiquing it more thoroughly as a profession.

This part of the argument does not need too much justification, and it is somewhat stating the obvious that without the artist, the composer and the songwriter there would be no music to commercialize. The artist is the root of all musical developments in every direction; without them, there is no music, no performance, no songs, no videos, no events, no streaming, no merchandise, no sponsorship, no music industries. The part which is perhaps less obvious is that, in many instances, without the manager the talent would often remain hidden, unpromoted, undeveloped and unknown. The historical role of the artist manager is to identify the unique voice, the advanced ability, the hit song, the essence of a great artist, and then devise the best way to grow and harness that art in a business sense. Chas Chandler, the 1960s/70s manager of Jimi Hendrix and Slade, regarded his job as 'to look for material, work with the group, advising on songs they write, on the stage act, seeing them as often as possible on stage so that you can advise them as often as possible' (quoted in Frith, 1978, p. 81).

Of course, this conception of the music business relates to a different and simpler era, during which its economics were dominated by the still-growing recording industry. By way of contrast, it has been reported, variously, that 99,000–120,000 new songs are being uploaded to Spotify every day (Ingham, 2022; Ross, 2024; Schmahl, 2025). This highlights three developments: that it is virtually impossible to quantify both the number of artists who are trying to make themselves heard in music; that a tiny percentage of these can do so professionally (see Osborne, 2021); and that those who achieve the latter almost always engage several intermediaries.

Frith (2000) and Negus (2011) have referred to these intermediaries as 'gatekeepers' in selecting who progresses into professional music, with managers being central to such a grouping. Elsewhere, these roles have been theorized as either impresarios or cultural intermediaries, following in the tradition of Becker's *Art Worlds* (1982) and Bourdieu's *Distinction* (1984), respectively. Regardless of how they are described, these are the personnel in the music industries who influence which artists get radio play, festival slots and recording contracts. The role of the manager, initially as a radar/filter and later as a catalyst/alchemist in locating and growing the creative talent, is perhaps not properly understood nor fully appreciated, and one of the aims of this research is to assess the artist manager's work and show how important they are in this role, initially as a gatekeeper, intermediary and talent developer.

The position of the artist manager, however, needs to be viewed more holistically in relation to the music industries. To this end, we generally follow Williamson and Cloonan's (2007) view of music being classed as a series of related industries rather than the singular industry that lobbying organizations have historically succeeded in popularizing. Within this, the three largest component industries economically are the recorded music industry, the music publishing industry and the live-music events industry, though the importance of each has fluctuated over time.

Mike Jones offers a similar definition of the music industries, but expands this conceptualization to include 'the music industry', a term he uses to refer to the 'practices and perspectives' (Jones, 2012, p. 10) that each of these industries have in common, and 'music industry', by which he means 'the actions taken by the people who comprise the record companies, the publishers, the live agencies and all of the networks of companies they engage with' (Jones, 2012, p. 11). This helps to illustrate that although the three major industries can be viewed as a distinct area of operation, there remains considerable overlap and interaction between those working in different parts of the industries.

As Jones goes on to point out, it is here that an artist manager has the unique perspective brought about by having to deal across *all*, and not merely some, parts of the industries. By his account, the manager is 'the only position in the Music Industry which interacts with all other areas of activity' (Jones, 2012, p. 91). Similarly, Anderton et al. (2022) locate the manager at 'the centre of a network of relationships' (p.14), meaning that while each sector has an individual function within music, like organs in the same body, they are close to each other but do not necessarily interact in meaningful ways. The artist manager, on the other hand, is more akin to the blood supply or nervous system, linking all theatres of music in a coherent and constructive manner, which aligns and activates them structurally or chronologically to suit the development process of a particular creator on their roster.

This makes the artist manager unique in having a clear awareness and overview of different roles within each sector or industry in order to gain best leverage for their artists. By examining the role of the manager we gain a broad perspective of the overall functioning of the music industries in a way that no other role would provide. Therefore, we argue that a detailed study of the work of the manager is vital as it allows greater insight into the overall operation of the music industries.

The final part of our case for the study of artist management relates to thinking of it as a profession or even distinct industry within the music industries, rather than as an adjunct to them. Our argument is that artist managers are, rather than peripheral actors, the most important part of the music industries. However, until relatively recently, this has barely been recognized, as shown by the lack of trade and representative organizations for managers, who were historically seen as part of a shadowy, solitary, individualistic and unregulated fringe of the music business. This has changed substantially alongside the growth and professionalization of the music industries coupled with a sizeable (though hard to quantify) increase in the number of people working in artist management.

By way of comparing the trajectory of these industries, the first representative body for artist managers, the Music Managers' Forum (MMF), was formed in the UK in 1992, whereas the other parts of the music industries have been organized in different ways as far back as the mid-19th century. The music publishing industry was the first to have formal representation, with royalty collection societies dating back to 1851 when the Société des Auteurs, Compositeurs et Éditeurs de Musique (SACEM) was set up in France. Other national bodies were set up, subsequently, to collect royalties and support music publishers and composers, like the Music Publishers' Association (MPA), which was founded in 1881, and the Performing Right Society (PRS), which was founded in the UK in 1914. While these were specific to the UK market, the Confédération Internationale des Sociétés d'Auteurs et Compositeurs (CISAC), the global agency for music publisher representation, was founded in 1926.

The arrival and development of the recording industry in the early 20th century was formalized by the creation of the International Federation of Phonographic Industries (IFPI) in 1933 (see Fleischer, 2015) with national organizations following, like the Recording Industry Association of America (RIAA) in 1952 and the British Phonographic Industry (BPI) in the UK in 1973. Comparatively, the live music industry has been the slowest of the three major industries to organize. The Association of British Orchestras (ABO), formed in 1948, was predominantly, but not exclusively, concerned with live performance; but it was not until 1986 that the Concert Promoters Association (CPA), representing the British commercial promoters, came into being. Subsequently, organizations such as the Association of Independent Festivals (AIF), formed in 2008, and the umbrella body LIVE (Live music Industry, Venues and Entertainment), set up in response to the COVID pandemic, in 2020, have provided a representative voice and lobbying mechanism for what the latter calls 'the UK's contemporary live music sector' (LIVE, 2023).

This will be tracked in greater detail in Chapter 3, but each of these bodies is an indicator of the increasing formalization of the music industries and the need for representation to governments and policy-makers in negotiations for trade and regulatory agreements. While we have focused on the UK and global bodies, similar groupings exist in most major markets. That artist management is relatively late to the party is noteworthy, and given that other key areas of music activity (recorded music, music publishing and live events) have had representation over a longer period of time and have had more opportunity to evaluate and assess the economic, cultural and employment impact of their work, there is a strong case to examine the work of artist managers in more detail and to clarify the nature of the work they undertake, as it is only recently that this group has been organized collectively.

We will now turn to the extent of the profession and how its organization has changed. Central to this is the MMF, which was established by a group of UK managers in 1992 with the explicit aim of providing a collective voice for music managers and to 'educate, innovate, advocate' (MMF UK, 2023). According to the founder and inaugural Chairperson, Dennis Muirhead:

> Until the formation of the Music Managers Forum, music managers were the only part of the industry that did not have their own association. They had to work alone, make mistakes alone and negotiate with powerful multinationals on their own. There were no means of sharing and learning from the experiences of other managers, no forum for discussing common concerns.
> (MMF Canada, 2023)

Other manager-focused organizations have subsequently been established, including the US MMF in 1993 (whose original purpose was lobbying government and the recorded music industry, though now operates as a looser network of local chapters), MMF Canada in the year 2000, as well as a range of European management organizations who now act collectively under the umbrella organization known as the European Music Managers Alliance (EMMA), founded in 2018. In Australia, the Australian Association of Artist Managers (AAM) and the Australian MMF have an active presence, and beyond these examples there is an array of organizations around the globe providing some form of networking opportunities or representation for music managers, ranging from the International Music Managers Forum (whose membership includes certain national MMFs and individual members) to smaller groups operating through social media such as MMF LatAM or MMF Zimbabwe.

Despite this proliferation of managers' organizations, gathering a clear picture of the extent of the profession is difficult. While some organizations are open about their membership data (e.g. according to their respective websites, the UK currently has 1500 members, the AAM has 300+, EMMA states that it has 2000, but includes UK figures within its total), the picture can become muddled quite quickly. In some cases, a lack of transparency around membership data is the norm, especially for the organizations who do not operate on a paid membership model basis. For those that do, there can be difficulty convincing music managers of the value of paying an annual membership fee, especially considering how transient and precarious the profession can be. In addition, such organizations will only represent those who know of their existence, approve of their ethos and have the resources to pay a membership fee, potentially excluding many managers, particularly at the outset of their career.

This speaks to the wider point that artist management exists at many levels – from informal partnerships, where little or no money is involved, via a plethora of small businesses, to transnational corporations involving artists generating millions of dollars. Within these there are a range of business relationships and ways of working, meaning that many artist managers will often exist outside the sphere of these trade-body or network-focused organizations, for a range of practical, economic and ideological reasons. Furthermore, within each of these, the definition of what constitutes a professional or economically active manager will vary. Individuals may also not self-identify as artist managers despite taking on many aspects of the role, perhaps through having multiple business identities and professions. So any attempt to calculate the number of artist managers globally would be speculative due to these exclusions, the lack of reliable data and an absence of representative organizations in large swathes of the world (including some major markets like South Korea and Japan).

While the existence of various music management organizations or MMF-related groups might not provide us with enough detail to establish a clear figure in terms of the total number of artist managers in existence, it does give us a picture of how the role of artist manager has become increasingly professionalized. Established organizations like the MMF UK and the AAAM have a formal code of practice, which outlines the norms and expectations of what an artist manager does, subsequently demystifying the role and ensuring neither artists nor managers are exploited. In a similar manner, most MMFs or management organizations provide training opportunities, as well as acting as a connector between commercial music organizations and their members. While the specific offerings and influence of certain MMF branches will be discussed in more detail in subsequent chapters, this section provides some introductory context around the connectivity, community building and business opportunities provided by artist management organizations, through their meet-ups and online forums.

As the attention given to artist management grows (this book included) it is inevitable that the identifiable and quantifiable number of artist managers will expand, alongside the roles of the organizations we have described. Although the MMF's aims of educating, informing and advocating have not fundamentally changed, the extent of these roles has, with an expanding membership, staff and range of issues at the heart of its operation (notably around mental health, inclusivity and equality, education, and streaming royalties), and will continue to do so. Examining the issues that are important to artist managers in 2025 – alongside the role of management organizations and how they interact with their members and the wider music industries – makes up the core tenets of the original contribution this book seeks to make. Artist manager organizations will be further analysed in Chapter 3.

By positioning the artist manager alongside the artist as an integral and under-examined part of the music industries, taking into consideration the extent to which other 'sectors' of music have been organized in positions of political, economic and cultural influence and the more recently established artist management organizations, these four reasons are why we believe that the individuals who seek, locate and identify the creative talent which supplies the music industries and essentially feed the raw materials to the rest of the active sectors are intrinsic to our understanding of how the commerce of music works, and we will expand on each of these throughout the course of the book. In the remainder of this introduction we outline relevant definitions and provide some context around the existing terminology relating to artist management.

Defining the Role

> The artist–manager relationship is a business marriage, where you share all the ups and downs in your life; you need to have complete trust in each other.
>
> Virpi Immonen, MMF Finland/EMMA
>
> It is a strange relationship, isn't it?
>
> Annabella Coldrick, MMF

Embarking on this journey requires some initial investigation and explanation of the role of the manager of an artist or creator within the music industries. For consistency and ease from this point we will refer to these collectively as 'artist managers' and to the profession as 'artist management', though colloquially and in some other contexts, including by some of our interviewees, they will at various points be referred to as music managers, business managers or just managers.

Put at its most simple, we consider the artist managers to be those who are assigned some responsibility for the career of an individual artist or group of artists in the context of the music industries. Throughout the remainder of the book, we will add layers of complexity to these definitions, noting the different types of artists and artist managers that are working at various levels and the multitude of formal and informal relationships between the parties.

We have adopted a necessarily broad definition of both throughout. The artist is taken, in this context, to mean any creative individual generating or contributing to the production of the music itself. This includes vocalists, songwriters, performers, musicians/instrumental players, DJs, producers, programmers, lyricists, rappers, re-mixers, MCs, composers and arrangers. The term 'artist' used throughout this book should then be taken to mean any individual directly involved in the creation of original compositions, recorded audio and/or live performance of music. This, of course, is not the extent of the creative personnel with which an artist manager will engage. Many others contribute to the peripheral activities and products associated with music (for example, video producers, influencers, social media content generators, dancers, stylists, designers, marketing personnel, choreographers), and while we are increasingly seeing artist managers taking some of these on as clients, they are not associated directly with the production of the song, audio track or live music performance and are only in the peripheral view of this book.

Secondly, but perhaps more importantly, we need to begin to expand what we consider we mean by the term artist manager and what the role entails. There is, inevitably, no singular or set definition of what an artist manager is or what *exactly* the role involves, though many from academic, business and journalistic perspectives have tried to narrow this down with varying degrees of insight. Anderton et al. (2022) argue that the artist manager is 'a key figure who negotiates within the music and media industries', the aim being to 'develop and represent artists by finding, creating, and developing strategic goals and opportunities' (2022, p. 14). Allen (2022) sees artist managers as directing 'the career success of an artist' and 'developing meaningful interpersonal [business] relationships' (Allen, 2022, p. 17) and the MMF variously notes that the role involves helping 'steer the business of the artist', requiring them to take a 'holistic approach' and be 'entrepreneurial' (Webb et al., 2022, p. 3). If these offer a slightly general overview, Passman (2021), US lawyer and writer on the music industries for some three decades, distinguishes two key roles within artist management – the personal and the business. In most instances, the one individual or company will take on these overlapping roles, though Passman is correct to point out that in others, the roles will be discrete, with the financial management being in the hands of a separate company (usually an accountancy firm). Perhaps it was the journalist Alex Pappademas, in an article on the septuagenarian management stalwart Irving Azoff, who most succinctly described the artist manager role as 'somewhere between consigliere and concierge' (Pappademus, 2020).

These relatively recent definitions variously characterize the artist manager as an entrepreneur, a project manager, a negotiator, a confidante, a bookkeeper and even a gofer. Yet while these accounts and definitions are accurate as far as they go, they also leave little space for nuance. Through this book we seek to explore the very different experiences of the artist–manager relationship and how this is dependent on (among other things) the age, experience, genre, talents, career goals and ambitions of the artist and how these align with the skills of the individual manager or managers.

Indeed, much of the book is less about the artists and their managers *per se* and rather about the nature of the relationship between them. In this respect, it is also important to note both the frequent lack of hierarchy (in either direction) and the importance of the working relationship between the parties. Most involved see the success of the artist manager role as being down to the strength of the partnership with the artists rather than in a traditional employer–employee relationship. For example, the MMF likens the manager–artist relationship to chief operating officer and chief executive working together, stating that the 'manager–artist relationships are as individual and bespoke as can be, but the key thing to remember is that this is a partnership and should be based on mutual respect' (Webb *et al.*, 2022, p 3).

The extent to which a manager can support their client depends on the clarity of vision and business acumen of the individual artist, and while some artists are predominantly creatively focused with little or no interest in the brand or business development, others will see this as integral to their artistic endeavours and lead accordingly. In either instance, the role of the artist manager is either advising on the creation of a plan or the implementation of an existing one, but, more usually, the artist manager's role can be seen as filling in the gaps in the business processes where the artist is lacking in a combination of time or knowhow to do everything. For such a relationship to succeed requires a combination of creative and commercial abilities, but regardless of the portions in which these are provided, a mutual respect, understanding and emotional intelligence in relatively equal amounts are required. Throughout the book, we consider examples of how different managers working with different types of artists may have significantly different responsibilities and experiences of the role.

Some Historical Context

While it is perhaps self-evident that recent changes in the recording, live music and music publishing industries have made the job of artist managers more complicated and significant, we would suggest that it has become, simultaneously, less understood. In the same way that the advent of rock'n'roll and the evolution of the recording industry in the 1950s and 1960s completely reconstituted what was involved in managing an act, so too have the 21st century changes.

In noting the importance of pioneers in the field of that era, e.g. Colonel Tom Parker and Larry Parnes, Mike Jones argues that they 'did not entirely invent artist management' but instead were compelled to 'radically rethink the role' (Jones, 2012, p. 84). For all their innovations, which saw them much more integrally involved in the creation of a star and propelling their career in the wider entertainment industry (notably in film and television), Parker and Parnes also contributed to the other prevailing narrative about the early managers of the rock'n'roll era – that of the dubious, rogue entrepreneurs who would stop at nothing to rapaciously exploit their artists.

While the picture was inevitably much more complicated than this (as we will examine in Chapter 2), the portrayal of the music manager has usually fallen somewhere between the self-mythologizing of the managers themselves and the media portrayal of them as fraudsters, gangsters and crooks, with an element of comedy thrown into the mix. Spinal Tap's fictional manager, Ian Faith, a combination of hapless and hopeless, remains a cautionary example for many managers, and, extraordinarily, the likes of Parnes and some of his contemporaries (for examples, see Goodman, 2015; Blake, 2018; Bullock, 2021) remain sources of fascination and detailed biography some 50 or 60 years after their managerial heyday. Furthermore, the string of memoires by former artist managers also shows no sign of slowing down, with some examples from the last ten years including books by Napier-Bell (2007), Summers (2013), Gordon (2016), McGee (2014) and Lisberg (2023); though it is telling that most of these have been marketed heavily on the back of the major artists with whom they worked. A cursory glance shows that these accounts mostly relate to a pre-millennium music business (albeit many of those mentioned continued to work afterwards) and that they almost exclusively feature and focus on white men of a certain age.

When we last tried to contextualize the place of artist managers – specifically as *petite bourgeoisie* entrepreneurs in the music industries – we noted that previous accounts of the profession were limited in scope and depth, leaving 'a considerable gap in the literature to attempt a serious, contemporary account of what is an increasingly important, economically significant and professional occupation' (Williamson, 2015, p. 88). So it is also important to note – and we will examine this more closely in the next chapter – that considerable strides have been made subsequently and more nuanced theorizations and accounts of the processes involved in artist management have begun to emerge in the last decade. Reflecting the industrial changes of the period, writing about artist management has, at least partially, moved on from personal reflections, mythologizing and instruction manuals (e.g. Riches, 2012; Allen, 2022) that have dominated previous work.

This is the case in both industrial and academic approaches, which overlap with increasing frequency. In short, not only is artist management being taken more seriously, but its changing nature and complexity are increasingly recognized. The change is visible in the most recent guide published by the MMF, where Chief Executive Annabella Coldrick recognizes that 'the role of the music manager has become far more pivotal, far more complex and far more demanding' and that, crucially, within that, 'there are no rules' (Webb et al., 2022, p. ix). Elsewhere, a number of authors (e.g. Morrow, 2018; Anderton et al., 2022) have gone some way to locate the practice of artist management within wider spheres of management studies and the music/creative industries, while another welcome shift has been a growth in the amount of writing that focuses on pastoral and well-being elements of both the music industries generally (Gross and Musgrave, 2020; Jones and Heyman, 2021) and the role of managers within them specifically (MMF, 2021).

It could be argued that these make an academic book about artist management somewhat superfluous, but, as we outline below, we aim to further fill the previously identified gaps with an account that takes an overview of different types and levels of artist management, where the focus is on the experiences of the managers themselves and those artists and organizations that work most closely with them.

A Note on Methods

As well as drawing on the varied music industries experiences of the authors (detailed in the introduction), the methodological underpinning of the book was a combination of an extended literature review and a series of semi-structured interviews conducted over a period spanning five years (2019–2024).

The former is mainly dealt with in the opening two chapters, where we attempt to locate the work within previous accounts of artist management. While Flick notes the importance of both theoretical and empirical literature to 'contextualise, compare and generalise the findings' (Flick, 2014, p. 66), it is worth noting that while the role of the manager has been written about in many locations and contexts, it is not an area, with a few notable exceptions, that has been greatly theorized. Instead, most accounts are of the empirical and, in some instances, anecdotal variety, taking the form of memoirs, autobiographies, reports and manuals. Nevertheless, as will become apparent, these are important in establishing what (via Flick) is already known about the topic, which concepts are discussed, and, most importantly, what 'questions remain' and 'what has not yet been studied' (Flick, p. 67).

At the outset, our approach was neither to theorize artist management nor attempt to explain on a practical level how to do it. Both, to varying extents, are fools' errands and likely to end in a manner that satisfies no one. Instead, we identified that the gap in the existing literature was a holistic account of artist management as a profession that drew heavily on the experiences and stories of those working across it, at different levels, in a variety of management contexts.

Twenty-two semi-structured interviews were conducted to build on existing accounts and add colour and detail. Specifically, the focus of these was aligned to the second and third parts of the book. The second aims to give a detailed, empirical account of management as a career and business within the wider music industries and economy while the third identifies a few recurring themes, notably around the current political context, well-being of artists and managers, and equality and inclusion.

The interviewees were drawn by a process of snowballing, beginning locally and using some industry contacts that were already known to us (particularly via Jayne Stynes' work with the MMF (UK), before asking these initial interviewees to 'suggest relevant friends or colleagues to interview'. During this process we were cognisant of the likelihood that this would yield 'others who were broadly similar to themselves' (Byrne, 2018, p. 230) and sought to balance the range of perspectives by age, gender, ethnicity and geography within the limitations of the project. In total, interviews were conducted with 14 artist managers and eight others from representative bodies and industry organizations, and with differing backgrounds, experiences and perspectives on management (a full list of interviewees appears in the preliminary pages of this book).

The interviews were predominantly conducted on Zoom and took the form of semi-structured interviews where a series of set, general questions were asked, leaving the interviewer 'some latitude to ask further questions in response to what are seen as significant answers' (Bryman and Bell, 2015, p. 213). As well as seeking life history and biographical details, questions centred around attributes of managers, training and qualifications, changes and developments in the wider music industries, and their analysis of contemporary issues (e.g. Brexit, COVID and mental health) that were impacting the role (a copy of the questionnaire appears in Appendix 1). These were transcribed and themes picked out using Nvivo, which were used as the basis for some of the later chapters of the book.

Inevitably, given the time constraints on the project and despite our best efforts, we can make no definitive claims for how representative our sample of interviewees was, an occupational hazard of qualitative research. As Bryman and Bell observe, 'the people who are interviewed in qualitative research are not meant to be representative of a population' and it is, in fact, the theoretical reasoning and analysis of the data that 'is decisive in considering the generalizability of the findings' (Bryman and Bell, 2015, p. 414). Nevertheless, we hope that our combined backgrounds and the theoretical groundings of the work provide, nevertheless, a basis for its findings to be resonant across different genres and geographical contexts.

How Are We Going to Do It?

The outcome of the research is a book in three parts. The first part is predominantly contextual; the second examines the interview responses and details the activities and issues managers are engaging with; and the third part focuses on the broader environmental and societal challenges currently facing managers in the contemporary music industries.

More precisely, Chapter 2 locates managers historically within the music industries and evidences the substantive changes in the period since 1999. In doing so, it will add to the portrayal of managers in both existing academic and other media contexts, setting out what is missing from existing literature on artist management. In Chapter 3, we complete the background to the research by considering artist management from an organizational perspective, investigating the growth of industry organizations (notably the MMFs) and analysing their achievements to date and the possible futures of artist/creator representation.

Part 2 looks at the different stages of the closely intertwined careers of the artists and their managers, and the business models that underpin them, predominantly using the interviews with individual managers and relevant industry representatives. Chapter 4 considers the starting points for managerial careers, and the musical and educational backgrounds that lead them to mount the bottom rungs of a musical/music business career ladder. It discusses the importance of experience and perseverance in routes into management and how relationships between artists and managers are built – personally, financially and contractually. Chapter 5 examines how management businesses grow alongside artistic success and discusses the role of artist managers in developing careers, especially via social media and live music, noting the blurred boundaries between the roles of artists, managers, record labels, music publishers and agents. Chapter 6 considers how broader factors, not specific to the music or creative industries, are affecting managers (the role of government, artificial intelligence and adapting to change) as well as investigating sources of conflict in the artist–manager relationship, as well as possible solutions.

Part 3 uses examples from the recent past to look forward, questioning what will and will not change in artist management (and, by extension, in the wider music industries) during the next ten years. All three chapters in this part are written by authors bringing the practical experience of managing artists themselves. Chapter 7 considers the economic and political context post-COVID, with inflation, supply chain issues and increasing restrictions on travel all impacting elements of the music industries, creating problems for managers at all levels. It also examines some of the ways in which these challenges have been circumnavigated by artists and their managers. Chapters 8 and 9 deal with the often entangled issues of inequalities, and health and well-being, the former exploring how these are being recognized and addressed among managers and industry organizations and the latter considering how managers deal with both their own and their artists' physical and mental health, and the support available to them in doing this. To end the book, Chapter 10 draws together the various strands to present a holistic picture of contemporary artist management, reflecting on the personnel, skillsets and global variations that characterize the role while considering the future and challenges facing those embarking on it.

References

Allen, P. (2022) *Artist Management for the Music Business: Manage Your Career in Music, Manage the Career of Others*, 5th edn. Focal Press, Oxford, UK.
Anderton, A., Hannam, J. and Hopkins, J. (2022) *Music Management, Marketing and PR*. Sage, London.
Becker, H. (1982) *Art Worlds*. UCLA Press, Berkeley, California.
Blake, M. (2018) *Bring it on Home: Peter Grant, Led Zeppelin and beyond: The Story of Rock's Greatest Manager*. Omnibus, London.
Bourdieu, P. (1984) *Distinction: A Social Critique of the Judgement of Taste*. Harvard Press, Cambridge, Massachusetts.
Bryman, A. and Bell, E. (2015) *Business Research Methods*. OUP, Oxford, UK.
Bullock, D. (2021) *The Velvet Mafia: The Gay Men Who Ran the Swinging Sixties*. Omnibus, London.
Byrne, B. (2018) Qualitative interviewing. In: Searle, C. (ed.) *Researching Society and Culture*, 4th edn. Sage, London.
Fleischer, R. (2015) Protecting the musicians and/or the music industry. On the history of 'neighbouring rights' and the role of Fascist Italy. *Queen Mary Journal of Intellectual Property* 5(3).
Flick, U. (2014) *An Introduction to Qualitative Research*, 5th edn. Sage, London.
Frith, S. (1978) *The Sociology of Rock*. Constable, London.

Frith, S. (2000) Music industry research: Where now? Where next? Notes from Britain. *Popular Music* 19(3), 387–393.
Goodman, F. (2015) *Allen Klein: The Man Who Bailed Out the Beatles, Made the Stones and Transformed Rock & Roll*. Eamon Dolan/Houghton Mifflin Harcourt, Boston, Massachusetts.
Gordon, S. (2016) *They Call Me Supermensch: A Backstage Pass to the Amazing Worlds of Film, Food and Rock'n'Roll*. HarperCollins, London.
Gross, S.-A. and Musgrave, G. (2020) *Can Music Make You Sick*. University of Westminster, London.
Ingham, T. (2022) It happened: 100,000 tracks are now being uploaded to streaming services like Spotify every day. *Music Business Worldwide*. Available at: www.musicbusinessworldwide.com/its-happened-100000-tracks-are-now-being-uploaded/ (accessed 16 October 2022).
Jones, M. (2012) *The Music Industries: From Conception to Consumption*. Palgrave MacMillan, Basingstoke, UK.
Jones, R. and Heyman, L. (2021) *Sound Advice: The Ultimate Guide to a Healthy and Successful Career in Music*. Shoreditch Press, London.
Lisberg, H. (2023) *I'm into Something Good: My Life Managing 10cc, Herman's Hermits and Many More*. Omnibus, London.
LIVE (2023). Available at: livemusic.biz/ (accessed 12 May 2023).
McGee, A. (2014) *Creation Stories: Riots, Raves and Running a Label*. Pan, London.
MMF (2019) *Managing Expectations*. MMF, London.
MMF (2021) *The MMF Guide to Mental Health 2021*. MMF, London.
MMF (2023). Available at: themmf.net/ (accessed 12 May 2023).
MMF Canada (2023). Available at: mmfcanada.ca/ (accessed 24 May 2023).
Morrow, G. (2018) *Artist Management: Agility in the Creative and Cultural Industries*. Routledge, London.
Napier-Bell, S. (2007) *Black Vinyl, White Powder*. Ebury, London.
Negus, K. (2011) *Producing Pop: Culture and Conflict in the Popular Music Industry*. Originally published 1992. Edward Elgar, London. Available at: research.gold.ac.uk/id/eprint/5453/1/Producing_Pop.pdf
Nielson, K. (2024) Nielson, K. (2024) Questions on artist management. Interview by Allan Dumbreck on Zoom, 25 January.
Osborne, R. (2021) I am a one in ten: Success ratios in the recording industry. In: Osborne, R. and Laing, D. (eds) *Music by Numbers: The Use and Abuse of Statistics in the Music Industries*. Intellect, London, pp. 387–393.
Pappademus, A. (2020) He's our Satan: Mega music manager Irving Azoff, still feared, still fighting. Los Angeles Times, 5 November. Available at: www.latimes.com/entertainment-arts/music/story/2020-11-05/irving-azoff-eagles-manager (accessed 12 May 2023).
Passman, D. (2021) *All You Need to Know about the Music Business*, 10th edn. Penguin, London.
Riches, N. (2012) *Music Management Bible*, revised edn. Music Sales, London.
Ross, G. (2024) More music released in a single day in 2024 than the entirety of 1989, study shows. *Mixmag*. Available at: https://mixmag.net/read/more-music-released-single-day-2024-than-entirety-1989-study-streaming-news
Schmahl, M. (2025) Spotify streaming report 2024 reveals: 50 million songs with no listeners – 175 million under 1000 streams. gear news. *Gear News*. Available at: https://www.gearnews.com/spotify-streaming-report-2024-tech/ (accessed 1 June 2025).
Summers, J. (2013) *Big Life*. Quartet Books, London.
Webb, A., Bonham, P., Harmon, A., Coldrick, A. and Dethekar, M. (2022) *Essentials of Music Management*. Music Managers Forum, London.
Williamson, J. and Cloonan, M. (2007) Rethinking the music industry. *Popular Music* 26(2), 305–322.
Williamson, J. (2015) Artist management. In: Dumbreck, A. and McPherson, G. (eds) *Music Entrepreneurship*. Bloomsbury, London.

2 The Manager: A Selective History (1926–2024)

John Williamson

Introduction

This chapter purports neither to be a comprehensive discussion of scholarly literature – of which there is relatively little devoted to artist management – nor a complete history of the profession. Instead, it seeks to provide some historical foundations and some starting points for the wider discussion of the recurring issues associated with it – notably around organization, contracts, the artist–manager relationship, inequalities and well-being – that make up the remainder of the book.

It begins with a general discussion of the role, highlighting some key definitions, characteristics and representations of the role before embarking on a thumbnail, chronological account of how artist management has changed in several overlapping eras alongside the music industries over the last century. It will do this by matching examples of managers and artists, illustrating the changing dynamics of the relationship between managers, artists and the associated industries. Predominantly, this will focus on what is widely considered to be the period of peak historic growth in the recording industry in the late 20th century, bookmarked by the emergence of rock'n'roll *c*.1955 (Peterson, 1990) and the end of the boom period in 1999 (as detailed by Forde, 2024).

To provide further context, it also offers a short prologue covering management in the pre-rock'n'roll era and concludes with an epilogue that links this to some contemporary examples to highlight both the stagnant and dynamic elements of artist management in the last 100 years. In short, it provides a series of snapshots to locate the manager through the prism of different decades and a selection of genres, from Duke Ellington to Last Dinner Party, via early rock'n'roll and beat groups; the biggest pop stars of the 1960s; rock bands in the 1970s; independent artists in the aftermath of punk; post-Live Aid stadium rock; and manufactured pop. It concludes by using these examples to offer some wider reflections on some of the key trends and points of disruption in both management and the music business more generally throughout the period.

Starting Points

Before embarking on this journey, it is important to consider more holistically what exactly is being discussed when terms like 'artist manager', 'music manager' and 'manager' are used in the specific context of the music industries. As noted in Chapter 1, there is a long history of unflattering representations of managers across a range of media. In films, fictional characters, from the less than reputable Johnny Jackson in *Espresso Bongo* (1959) via Ian Faith in *This Is Spinal Tap* (1982) to Curtis Taylor Jr in *Dreamgirls* (2006), have often rarely deviated from the depictions of real managers like Colonel Tom Parker in *Elvis* (2022), Malcolm McLaren in *Pistol* (2022) and John Reid in *Rocket Man* (2019). Regardless of the variable quality of the acting, the managers, reality or otherwise, are all larger than life, manipulative and exploitative, in volatile relationships with their charges. Similarly, on television, managers have been either fictionally comedic and incompetent (Eddie Clougherty in *Tutti Frutti* (1988)) or part of a documentary series that draws on the more sensational life stories of pre-millennium managers, as in Channel 4's *Mr. Rock'n'Roll* (1999). By 2020, when candidates on the UK version of *The Apprentice* were given a task that simulated being music managers, reality merged with fiction, and comedy with reality when it came to the way managers were portrayed in popular media forms. This, however, is to only scratch the surface of the superficial and generally dated picture of these representations.

Notwithstanding these portrayals, more nuanced accounts of what artist management involves began to emerge with some of the first academic studies of the music business in the 1970s. Simon Frith was one of the few researchers of the time to look beyond the recording industry; and in doing so, he provided the most durable account of the role, describing it as 'a personal manager who manages all affairs of the artist they represent', and adding that the job involved doing 'everything for their artiste' apart from getting 'up there and singing (Frith, 1978, p. 80). If this definition of the role is suitably all-encompassing, Frith was also astute enough to recognize a hierarchy of priorities for the artist manager in the 1970s, arguing that their primary task was 'to win their client the highest possible income... to organise finances, to negotiate the best deals' (Frith, 1978, p. 106). Frith's account identifies that the artist manager juggles creative, personal and business aspects of their clients' careers, with the latter, in most instances, being the highest priority.

In his subsequent work, Frith developed this account, placing the manager as a buffer or intermediary between the record company and the artist when he claimed that managers had the unenviable task of 'keeping everyone happy; keeping the costs down and the spirits up; preventing freak-outs and piss-abouts; papering over group cracks... turning them into good pros' (Frith, 1983, p. 105). If this was the main job of the manager by the 1980s, he also identified that a career in management was often one with serious financial risks as well as rewards, observing that they were often investors, too, 'a source of capital' at an early stage in an act's career, in return for 'a percentage (20–25% most commonly) of all his clients' earnings', meaning that 'a group can be as much an investment for the manager as for the record company (Frith, 1983, p. 106). If this scenario offered a crude version of the more complex accounts of the role that would be developed some 40 years later in both industry (e.g. Allen, 2022; Webb *et al.*, 2022) and academic accounts (Morrow, 2024), they did, nevertheless, broadly lay solid foundations for subsequent explanations of the underpinning issues in artist management.

Latterly, Mike Jones has presented a more refined explanation of the job, reflecting not only the expansion of the music industries in the subsequent period but also the accompanying complexity of the arrangements and roles surrounding them. He argues, importantly, that 'artist managers occupy the only position in the Music Industry which interacts with all the other areas of activity and the individuals involved in them' (Jones, 2012, p. 91), and that to do so on behalf of the artist requires 'access to the total of the act' (Jones, 2012, p. 90). It is in the latter relationship that Jones unpicks the dilemmas and potential conflicts between the contractual relationship where the 'usual structure is for the artists to employ the manager' (Bagehot and Kanaar, 1998, p. 1) meaning that the manager is primarily 'a service provider to musicians. . . a servant hired to effectively be a leader' (Jones, 2012, p. 91).

If this presents a cynical but realistic view of many of the relationships between artists and their managers, as Jones goes on to identify, it is also a source of conflict for a few reasons, not least a consequence of the entrepreneurial ambitions of the managers themselves. As the historical overview that follows will show, artist managers have tended to emerge from a range of business and creative backgrounds, meaning that while this can be leveraged to the advantage of their clients, it can also produce tensions where the aims of the managers and the artists diverge. As Jones puts it, being 'alert to potential cultural purchase in musicians' (Jones, 2012, p. 92) is a characteristic that lends itself to competition among artists for the attention of managers and a magnet for managers becoming engaged in other related or competing business activities to further their own ambitions.

This, however, is another characteristic of artist management that is far from universal:

while many of the more fabled examples are often cut from the same cloth as the early entertainment and music industries impresarios, Negus correctly identified that for most managers, the reality of the role is more prosaic, bureaucratic and administrative than the image portrayed suggests. For him, the manager is not only involved in the 'moulding and manipulating' of their acts but also guiding rather than manipulating' them (Negus, 1992, p. 41).

So, having established that the nature of artist–manager arrangements is historically fluid and intrinsically linked to changes in both the music industries, specifically; and in society, the economy, taste and technology more generally, the remainder of this chapter will attempt to unpack this, drawing primarily on examples from the UK and USA to evidence and illustrate how the role has evolved, and personnel involved have changed.

The bulk of the story that follows is in six parts, mostly focusing on the period between 1955 and 1999. After a prelude that highlights some management practice in the pre-rock'n'roll era, it briefly considers the roles of Colonel Tom Parker and Larry Parnes, the traditional starting points for the discussion of managers in Anglo-centric accounts of the music industries, before considering the managers of the 1960s as impresarios and entrepreneurs. The penultimate part takes contrasting examples of the individuals managing hugely successful artists at the height of the recording industry's success in the latter part of the twentieth century, while the after-history in the final part offers some examples that both confirm elements of the historical narrative, while also suggesting some more fundamental changes that will be discussed elsewhere in the book.

Prologue: In the Days Before Rock'n'Roll

To begin a study of artist managers in the post-rock'n'roll era requires a broader historical context, and to recognize that the role long predated 1955, with entrepreneurs from a range of backgrounds hitching themselves to the fortunes of artists in the formative years of the music business. Two illustrative cases here are Irving Mills, the manager of Duke Ellington between 1926 and 1939 and and Hank Sanicola, who managed Frank Sinatra from 1936 until 1962. Of particular interest are their backgrounds (which raise pertinent issues of race and gender), their unplanned involvement in management, and the way in which they monetized their involvement with the respective artists. Their timing is also important as both had lengthy careers in the music business spanning a period of huge change. Significantly, their work straddled the period of changes in technology, law, the record industry and media that Richard Peterson depicts as where the 'rock aesthetic' displaced the 'jazz-based aesthetic in American popular music. As he notes, 'the stars of the era like Frank Sinatra, Perry Como and Nat King Cole were supplemented, and superseded by a new breed that included Elvis Presley, Bill Haley, Little Richard and 'the growing legion of rockers' (Peterson, 1990, p. 97). In this light, the careers of both men are illuminating when considering the origins of contemporary artist management, especially Sanicola who straddles two distinct eras.

Mills, described by Tosh Berman as 'one of the architects of the music business' (Berman, 2019), was also involved across the industries in several roles and entrepreneurial ventures, including as a musician, songwriter, music publisher, record label owner, president and (briefly) film producer. He worked in music publishing – a pathway already pursued by his older brother – from the end of the First World War and it was in this capacity that he first saw Duke Ellington play in 1925. While managing Ellington, Mills owned 50% of Duke Ellington Inc. and was credited as a co-writer on many of Ellington's compositions.

Sanicola was also involved in the music business before he met Sinatra in the 1930s, by which time he was working as a promotions man for Warner Bros, but he had also played piano and had been an amateur boxer, arguably ideal qualifications for the American music business of the 1930s and 1940s. His role with Sinatra was not always formally constituted though he fulfilled managerial functions in the widest senses, acting as everything from gopher to bodyguard as well as co-writer. Latterly, he became increasingly involved in Sinatra's business affairs, as both his publisher and taking a role in diversifying Sinatra's career and investments (Kaplan, 2016). Like Mills, the involvement in their artists' careers was deep, but the rewards high and lasting. Both had similar immigrant backgrounds (Mills was born in Ukraine; Sanicola came from a Sicilian family), enjoyed considerable success and shared interests in the personal and creative parts of their clients' work. But it is worth noting that, of the two, Mills was generally considered to be the more innovative and sensitive manager. He crossed racial boundaries, not only working with Ellington and other black musicians and being involved in the formation of multiracial bands but, as Berman puts it, 'truly respected Ellington's art and treated him as an artist. Mills wanted Ellington to obtain riches, attention and work on pretty much whatever he wanted' (Berman, 2019).

1955 and All That

Arguably, these types of background and business arrangements were the precursors of the more famous relationship between Elvis Presley and his manager, Colonel Tom Parker. This has been widely problematized and discussed (e.g. Guralnick, 1995, 2000), usually focusing on the latter's background, as a Dutch (illegal) immigrant working in carnivals before moving into music promotion, his business practices, and his hold over Presley's career and, following his death, his estate.

Parker's relationship with Presley was one that, at best, had mixed outcomes for the artist. While Parker could claim many successes in his exploitation of Presley's image via films and merchandise, other decisions, such as selling off all the rights to Presley's pre-1973 recordings to RCA in the same year for a lump sum of $5.4 million (Hilburn, 1989) showed a distinct privileging of short-term gain over more strategic thinking that might have ultimately benefitted the artist to a greater extent. These kinds of deals, coupled with the over-exploitation of Presley's value as a live act in his later years, generated unprecedented revenues but came at a high price health-wise. Tellingly, Simon Frith framed the relationship between the two men as one where 'it was obvious that Elvis Presley worked for Tom Parker' (Frith, 1983, p. 109) even by the time when many successful artists were 'employing managers or management companies to work for them' (Frith, 1983, p. 109). Like Mills and Sanicola before him, Parker charged a 50% rate of commission on most of Presley's income, though Berman describes the difference in approach between Mills and Parker by claiming that while the former treated his client as an artist, 'Parker started his career as a carnival worker and con artist and always remained one. He promoted Elvis as some sort of side-show freak' (Berman, 2019).

If these selective examples show anything, it is that from the very origins of artist management, though some of the backgrounds and demographics were similar, the approaches and business models of those involved diverged considerably: the rules, as much as there were any, were being made up as they went along. In the short term, the success of Parker meant his all-controlling approach prevailed as the more popular across the industry, with at least a decade passing and many changes in the music industries taking place before a more sympathetic (artistically and financially) type of manager became more prevalent.

The 1960s: Svengalis and Impresarios

In the UK, the emergence of new and commercially successful forms of popular music (initially skiffle, rock'n'roll and, later, beat groups) brought with it a range of opportunities for managers to make large amounts of money, often at the expense of the impressionable teenagers. A similar profile of (almost exclusively) men came to the job, offering investment and access in return for complete control over the careers of their protégés, for whom, mostly, the financial returns were generally low and the career spans short. Yet, it would again be wrong to characterize all the first wave of UK-based managers in the same way, as the following examples show both innovation and degrees of understanding of personal, financial and artistic issues that would be beyond some of the more opportunistic of their number.

The most prominent British manager of the early rock'n'roll era was Larry Parnes, who had been managing Tommy Steele (with John Kennedy) since the 1950s with considerable success. According to Bullock, Parnes based 'his style of management on Colonel Tom Parker' but was still an innovator, as unlike the Colonel, he would not be satisfied with having just one act to fuss over, pamper and exploit. He wanted a clutch of would-be pop idols; a stable of stars (Bullock, 2021, p. 17). As part of this operation, Parnes described his work as 'seeking out talent. I'm at it every hour of the day, interviewing, testing, auditioning' (Bullock, 2021, p. 20), and his reward was handsome. Parnes' and Kennedy's business model was one that involved large commissions and prodigious work rate on the part of their artists, which by the end of the 1950s included not only Steele but also Joe Brown and Marti Wilde. Parnes and Kennedy took 40% of Steele's income but the latter argued that this was justified as 'we pay publicity expense, necessary entertaining and business deals as well as for the fan club'. Perhaps in a nod to Parker, he added that, 'It's nothing to what American managers take, or even what some British artists have to pay their managers' (Bullock, 2021, p. 21). Bullock further describes the relationship between artist and management as being inequitable in other ways beyond the financial, describing how Parnes and Kennedy worked 'their cash cows into the ground' (Bullock, 2021, p. 22) and putting some clients (e.g. Vince Eager and Joe Brown) on a weekly wage instead of paying royalties. The inevitable consequences of this upscaling of the Parker model of management were litigation and burnout on the part of the artists and wealth and notoriety for the managers. Where the artists were largely dispensable and replaceable waged labour, Parnes rapidly became 'as famous as his young charges (Bullock, 2021, p. 30).

Although many of what Bullock describes as 'the gay men who ran the swinging sixties' in London's entertainment industries, notably Joe Meek and Robert Stigwood, shared his appetite for close control and an extensive roster of acts, they did not hold a monopoly in terms of approach. For example, their contemporaries, Chris Blackwell (who was based in Jamaica but increasingly working in the UK), Marion Massey (a rare example of a woman managing in the early sixties) and Brian Epstein (whose success with the Beatles fundamentally changed artist management), all shared elements of the entertainment industry background and entrepreneurial flair of Parnes, Parker et al., but were able to add considerably in terms of empathy towards the artists they worked with, in the case of Blackwell and Massey being especially sensitive to the age of their charges and the problems this posed.

Blackwell saw himself as something of a talent-spotter, using his newly formed record label, Island, as a means initially of exporting the music of Jamaica to an international audience. In 1960, he signed the 15-year-old, Millie Small, who, 3 years later, was to become the first musical superstar to emerge from the Caribbean when 'My Boy Lollipop' went on to sell seven million copies worldwide. Initially, Blackwell had to convince both the producer, Coxone Dodd, and her parents to allow him to manage her career. In his autobiography, *Islander*, he notes that her mother was initially reluctant to allow her to go to London with him, but that he 'promised her that I would look after Millie and that no harm would come to her daughter' (Blackwell, 2022, p. 87). Blackwell was true to his word but had the awareness of and was shocked at the side effects of Millie's success, describing both the separation from her family and hard work Millie put in as a teenager travelling the world. When she returned to Jamaica, seeing her mother step back and curtsy in front of her superstar daughter ended his aspirations in management. He recalls that 'I was mortified. In her family's eyes Millie had become someone else, almost royalty. What had I done? I vowed then and there that I was finished with straight pop music and the idea of making and marketing stars. I didn't want to be a pop svengali (Blackwell, 2022, p. 97).

Around the same time that Millie was becoming a global superstar and Blackwell was leaving the ranks of managers to develop Island Records, Marion Massey was visiting Glasgow to see a band called The Gleneagles playing at the Lindella club. Tipped off by her brother, who owned a chain of clubs in Scotland, about them, Massey is an intriguing, atypical and little discussed example of an artist manager from this era. Not only were very few women involved in the music business at the time (not least in management), but she was also, uncommonly among the svengalis and impresarios, willing to admit that 'I doubted myself. I was not a businesswoman. I didn't even understand what a so-called manager was – but I knew I had to help those youngsters some way' (quoted in Lulu, 1985, p. 170). For Massey, taking on the management of the band, and ultimately shaping the career of its singer, Marie Lawrie (Lulu) was about 'extending my interests outside the home...to be useful in the world; to take part, to learn more about it and what makes it all work' (Lulu, 1985, p. 170). Initially, Massey's main consideration was Lulu's well-being, noting how 'pale and unkempt' (p. 171) she was and how 'my maternal instincts rose to the surface and overcame all other considerations' (p. 171). This distinctly non-monetary association turned out to be the basis of a 25-year working association, which Lulu put down to Massey's age and nature, attributing the success of the relationship to the fact that 'she didn't manage anyone else, which was very unusual then and still would be today', and 'because I was managed by this older woman who I had to answer to. Had I been managed by a different group of young guys, things may well have turned out very differently.

Massey's holistic approach was later summarized by Lulu as 'for a long time she guided every aspect of my life; she discovered, nurtured and masterminded my career (Judd, 2008), a marked contrast to the 'different group of young guys' managing artists in the mid-1960s. By the time Lulu released her first single, 'Shout', in 1964, Parnes had stepped back from the frontline of the music business, predicting that 'the beat groups as we know them, will start to wane. Yet, from this perspective, he saw the need to organize and to push back against this very narrative as it was portrayed in the media. To do this, he set up the British Impresarios' Guild, 'made up of ten men, including Stigwood, Epstein, David Jacobs and Don Arden, who controlled around nine-tenths of the country's pop acts between them, the majority of the members of the guild were either gay or Jewish, or both' (Bullock, 2021, p. 201).

The short-lived organization was initially put together to protest the Performing Right Society's (PRS) efforts to increase its share of box-office takings, something that would directly impact their artists' (and their own) revenues. Its significance at the time was limited but it provides a useful historical prism through which to view the nascent management profession and how it saw itself.

Three important things emerge from this period in UK artist management. First, the demographics of the profession show how out-of-sync Massey and Blackwell were at the time. Second, the British Impresarios' Guild was arguably the first lobbying body within the post-1955 music business and it showed the ability of managers, who were often in competition with each other, to act collectively on the occasions it suited them. Third, it showed that these managers saw themselves as impresarios in the classic showbiz/theatre tradition that long predated rock'n'roll, but which would gradually erode as artist management found its own, more distinct identity.

Perhaps the most interesting and well-known member of the Guild, Brian Epstein, in his management of The Beatles (see Coleman, 1990) was the most obvious bridge between the two approaches and a starting point for modern artist management. In one sense, he was very much part of the 'velvet mafia' described by Bullock but was also innovative and committed to his artists in ways that were less evident among most of his peers. He noted the sometimes difficult relationship with them caused by the Beatles' huge success, saying that 'there may be quite a lot of envy about, and I'm aware of that and it's for that reason that I think that it's up to me to try personally to make up for that, because it isn't a nice thing for people to feel (quoted in Bullock, 2021, p. 202).

Portrayals of Epstein tend to exaggerate his weaknesses, not least because, untrained, he was having to adapt to such a rapidly evolving business and set of circumstances. As Johnny Rogan points out, 'it is not hard to pinpoint Epstein's deficiencies', but his occasional lack of business acumen (notably around the Beatles' publishing and merchandise deals) is generally offset against his fastidiousness, fairness and the fact that he 'loved the Beatles as though they were his own children (Rogan, 1988, p. 119). By the mid-1960s, the first changing of the guard could be seen: as Parnes bemoaned the limited amount of disposable funds available to teenagers, the oversupply of artists competing for their attention and an influx of "agents, managers, groups – and television – [who] all jumped on the [beat group] bandwagon" (quoted in Bullock, 2021, p. 203). The likes of Epstein, Massey and Blackwell were taking a more longsighted view (albeit in different ways) of the possibilities afforded in working with and managing artists whose careers were likely to last more than a couple of years.

Long-Term Careers and the Rise of the Album Band: Commander Cody, Joy Division and the 1970s

The second epochal change in relation to artist management came in the 1970s, by which time the possibility of these longer, more substantive careers became more apparent, the amounts of money at the top end of the industry increased (not least as a result of the growth of album sales and larger-scale concerts), and the perception that rock'n'roll and the beat groups were a short-lived fad that had passed. These developments attracted not only a new type of artist, but also a new industry infrastructure around them, including advances and multi-album, long-term recording deals. With these came a new cadre of manager, which perhaps lacked the charisma of the 1960s impresarios like Epstein, Andrew Loog Oldham (with the Rolling Stones), Albert Grossman (with Bob Dylan) and Allen Klein, whose life stories have been revisited subsequently and extensively across a range of media formats (see, for example, Oldham, 2000, 2003, 2012; Goodman, 2015; McDonald, 2023). Typically, these focus on a combination of the business and personal management skills (or lack thereof), the financial issues and conflicts, and the creative contributions of the manager.

Of course, as this history will show, this type of larger-than-life manager remained prominent among the management community, but as Simon Frith was relatively quick to observe, 'the typical 1970s rock manager was a lawyer, not a showman' (Frith, 1983, p. 109). For him, a crucial transition had taken place whereby 'the hucksters have become bureaucrats' (Frith, 1983, p. 101), where managers moved from being risk-takers to legally and numerically astute risk-avoiders. However, the truth of such a transition and the response of managers to the changes in the scale and nature of the music industries may have been slightly more complex as three further examples from the period – Joe Kerr, Rob Gretton and Steve Dagger – illustrate.

Kerr was the LA-based manager of the Grateful Dead offshoot, New Ryders of the Purple Sage and the less well-known Commander Cody and his Lost Planet Airmen, the latter being the subject of Geoffrey Stokes's *Star Making Machinery* (1977), one of the best and most detailed accounts of the US music business in the 1970s. His description of Kerr's role within the business of the band to some extent supports Frith's characterization but also highlights the changing nature of both the artist–manager relationship and the music business at the time.

Stokes places Kerr as being responsible for the band's long-term development, while the manager is quoted as saying that his job 'is pretty much like any other businessman's job; it is just that my clients are a little weirder than theirs. But it is all the same thing. I pay the bills, make sure the cheque books are balanced, and handle any hassles with the record companies. None of it is any big deal.' This plays into the narrative of the bureaucratic manger, conforming to neither of the stereotypes of the time as presented by Stokes, as either a 'minor-league Las Vegas mafioso in double-knit slacks, a shirt open to his navel and a flashy medallion nestling among his exposed chest hairs', or a variation of Bob Dylan's famed manager, Albert Grossman. In this account, Grossman is portrayed as operating with the sole aim of maximizing revenues for his charges, 'in whom he deals unemotionally as though they were commodity futures' (Stokes, 1977, p. 71) whereas Kerr is described as spending 'the bulk of his days attached to the telephone, talking endlessly in an attempt to win friends and influence music business people throughout the country' (p. 72) in an effort to 'keep the bands from worrying about anything but their music' (p. 71).

A few years later, and on the other side of the Atlantic, the career of Rob Gretton is similar in some senses but more complex in others. Like Kerr, his *modus operandum* focused on the minutiae of management and allowing the bands he was most synonymous with (Joy Division and New Order) to focus on recording and performing live. Similarly, both managers were largely solo operations who worked with a small number of acts, neither of whom had plans to take up a career managing artists (although it had been in their peripheral vision), and both acquired the role largely by happenstance.

Partly due to the interest in the acts he worked with, Gretton's managerial and entrepreneurial career has retrospectively been well documented, notably in the posthumous publication of a collection of his notebooks, *1 Top Class Manager* (2008) which covered the years 1979–1980. Though far from a traditional biography, scholarly account or how-to manual, these offer the best document of management tasks and practices of the era. In the book's introduction, Jon Savage describes the contents as including 'the financial logistics of releasing a record, the minutiae of stage-snatched meals, petrol, hotel costs, PA hire and all the other accoutrements of moving young men and electrical equipment around the country' (Savage, 2008). Gretton's work is presented in a manner that perhaps over-emphasizes the mundane – a world of organizing insurance, carnets and paying *per diems* – but it also speaks to a more idiosyncratic and DIY way of doing things on behalf of his artists. As far removed from the world of Grossman as imaginable, Gretton writes of his interest in 'a new underground outside of the system – I would rather adopt a different role with regards to everything – try to approach everything from a different viewpoint – not having everything dictated by money' (Savage, 2008). For him, these ideals manifest themselves in more practical ways, arguing that, for Joy Division, 'the key was more control over production: doing as many different gigs as possible, making sure that any contract signed left them free to choose their producer; no extras or gimmicks (like coloured vinyl); no long tours and no TV and press interviews unless we agree' (Savage, 2008).

While Gretton was pursuing a visionary route that diverged from the more traditional understanding that managers existed purely to extract maximum revenue on behalf of their clients, it is worth noting that him and others like him, with fierce ideology underpinning their business strategy, would remain the exception rather than rule. Frith, writing just a few years after Gretton scrawled in his notebook, reasserted the manager's primary task as being 'to win his client that highest possible income...the basic concern is always to organise finances, to negotiate the best deals', noting that 'the earliest involvement of a manager with an act is often, in fact, as a banker, a source of the capital that enables a group's members to buy their equipment, to support themselves while they rehearse' (Frith, 1983, p. 106). However, this offers a somewhat limited view of the role of the artist manager in the 1980s, as financial concerns and contracts take up disproportionately large (or small) parts of the manager's wider concerns depending on a whole host of factors, not least the stage of the career at which the artist finds themselves.

For example, Steve Dagger, the manager of Spandau Ballet during their rise to global stardom in the early 1980s, noted the changing requirements and responsibilities of the role as the stakes became higher. Originally, managing the band was something he 'fell into' while a student at the London School of Economics, and not something that was undertaken for immediate financial gain. He noted that, 'I found myself doing things for the group because they were friends' and that 'rather than being a business thing for me it was rather just an extension of what was my social life'. As is often the case for artist managers, rapid success resulted in a change of outlook, and Dagger went on to admit that 'it is only in the last 2 years, when the band has broken on a massive international scale that I have had to become more professional'. In the same interview, he also pointed out that 'lots of people want to be managers now – before they were purely accountants. It has become a more attractive job' (Dagger, quoted in Glanville, 1984, p. 74), something that speaks to the wider changes in the later part of the 20th century music industries that undoubtedly impacted on artist management as a career. The decade's technological advances saw music being reproduced and generating financial reward on a scale that was previously unthinkable. At the top end of the market, this could be seen in the boost given to the recording industry by the advent of the compact disc and the emergence of MTV, giving rise to multi-million-selling albums by the likes of Michael Jackson, Madonna, Prince and Lionel Richie. Simultaneously, the 1985 Live Aid concert had prompted a similar (and related) exponential growth in the live music industry while also reviving the careers of 1970s superstars like Elton John, David Bowie, Queen and

The Who; as well as confirming the arena- and stadium-filling appeal of more contemporary acts like U2, Madonna and Dire Straits. These successes filtered through and down the music industries with the recording industry reporting substantial gains in revenue every year between 1983 and 1999.

Pre-Millennial Tension

One outcome of this growth was a trickle down of money from the record companies to artists as investment and risk taking on the part of record labels; another was that as more artists were signing long-term contracts with them, there was a corresponding uptick in the number of gainfully employed managers. For the first time, artist management was a sustainable business for more than just those associated with established and successful acts. Yet for all the increasing quantity and profile of managers, in the era when the recording industry was dominant, working practices and issues remained much as in the previous eras. Two further examples – Gail Colson and Tom Watkins – working with rock and pop acts, respectively – are good illustrations of how this played out.

Colson's remarkable career in the music industries spanned six decades, beginning in 1966 when she co-managed the Rockin' Vicars, before she went to work with Genesis manager, Tony Stratton-Smith and headed the Charisma record label during the 1970s. Leaving her role at the label in 1978, like Dagger, she 'fell into management as it were: it wasn't planned'), going on to manage Peter Gabriel and Peter Hammill in their solo ventures as well as the Pretenders, Morrisey and Whipping Boy at various points over the following 35 years. Spanning at least two different eras of artist management, she was a pioneer as both one of a small number of successful female managers active in the 20th century, but also one of the few who, even towards the end of her career, chose to operate without contracts.

On retiring in 2011, she questioned both 'how a manager makes a living in the industry nowadays. Gone are the days when a band's mate could do it. There are so many things that a manager needs to know about now and there is not enough time to learn them as you go along!'; but she acknowledged that with this had come several changes, particularly in relation to gender and contractual arrangements. She noted that 'there is absolutely no reason for there not being more female managers. I discuss this with my son, and I realise that for his generation there is no difference between male and female agents, managers, etc., which is fantastic and as it should be'. But she also cautioned future managers to 'make sure you have a good contract with your artist from the start. I was lucky but I wouldn't recommend anybody else do what I did and not work with a contract' (Easlea, 2016). For one of her clients, Hammill, Colson represented a throwback to a simpler time, noting that

> Gail and I come from that far off planet, the Sixties. That place where music was both its own reward and its own justification. I don't mean to over-romanticise, because obviously music is a business and if you don't – eventually – make the numbers add up then you'll go under. But back when the UK Music Biz was located in just a couple of streets in Soho piling up the cash was emphatically not the overriding motivation. The links to that world are going fast now but some of us remember it still.
>
> (Hammill, 2011)

By way of contrast, Tom Watkins' career spanned a shorter period but was an important bridge between two distinct eras and styles of artist management. His success in the latter part of the 20th century was partly down to being something of a throwback to the impresarios of the Larry Parnes era, where an autocratic and controlling approach to managing pop acts was a template not just for his own artists' commercial success, but also for other managers (e.g. Simon Cowell and Simon Fuller) who were able to apply a more professional and lucrative twist while extending their interests well beyond music management into television, film and sport in the shape of shows like Pop Idol and X Factor. A graphic designer, Watkins began managing pub bands in South London in the 70s but enjoyed his biggest successes in the subsequent decades with multi-million-selling acts Pet Shop Boys, Bros and East 17. Each of these relationships were as short-lived as they were successful, with disputes over artistic control and money leading to dissatisfaction on both sides. By the time East 17 imploded and his latest boy band, North and South, failed to replicate the success of his previous clients, Watkins recalled that:

> ...as ever, I wanted them to just shut up, put up, smile and mime. The problem was that I felt I had the secret formula to build the perfect pop sensation. For a while it seemed like I did. But as soon as it becomes just that – a formula – it becomes tired and cynical. My acts had become increasingly uninspired. Here was the basic problem: I was trying to make chicken soup out of chicken shit.
> (Watkins, 2017, p. 317)

For all his self-diagnosed and much reported flaws as a manager, Watkins had the self-awareness to 'get out of London and the music biz' (Watkins, 2017, p. 319) at the end of the last century, having been a product of and beneficiary from what Fred Goodman describes as 'a period of greed and self-interest that was exceptional even for the record industry' (Goodman, 2010, p. 35). Watkins had the foresight to see the end of record industry's glory days and, perhaps, that the age and cultural differences between him and his predominantly young pop acts was too great. For all his achievements, the sense that Watkins belonged to an era that had passed was highlighted when he was the subject of one of the episodes of a Channel 4 series on artist managers in 2001 called *Mr Rock'n'Roll*. The other episodes featured Tom Parker, Don Arden and Peter Grant, no doubt chosen for the vivacity of the accompanying narratives as much as for their business acumen.

The point where Watkins decided 'I'm quitting this crap and going down to the seaside full time' (Watkins, 2017, p. 318), of course, coincided with another tipping point for the music industries which was to have a significant impact on how the role of the manager evolved in the following decades. The crisis in the recording industry precipitated by music being shared online (see Witt, 2015) and the growing need for artists to extract revenue from songs and performances to offset declining recording revenues (see Williamson and Cloonan, 2007; Jones, 2012; Wikström, 2019) had inevitable consequences for artist managers trying to navigate these changes. Forde argues that 1999 saw the recording industry 'plump on profits, haughtily believing it was destined for even greater power – would never have changed unless it was forced to' (Forde, 2024, p. 48), and, arguably, the same could be said for many of the older, established and successful managers. The new century may have heralded the end of the 'borderline-psychotic old blokes wielding cricket bats' (Sutherland, 2016, p. 10) to be gradually replaced by a younger, more diverse, precarious and even more disparate workforce, but, as the examples in the rest of this book show, this is only part of the story.

Coda: Managing in the 21st Century

The final examples of artist managers in this chapter serve to illustrate both how things have changed in the new music industries of this century, but also how other fundamentals have remained relatively unchanged. To do this, it will reflect on the careers of Tara Richardson, who has worked as a manager throughout the period, and Dakota Hoven, a younger manager at the outset of her career. In doing so, it will focus on three key elements of change: the greater presence of women within artist management; the changing priorities of managers more generally and how they embrace these; and the consolidation of the artist management business in line with the changes in the music industries more generally.

In some respects, Richardson is an excellent exemplar of the cyclical nature of some of these changes. Having previously worked for Sony, she has spent the last 20 years working with major artists at two large-scale management companies, Big Life and Q Prime. Both companies managed a plethora of artists and were fronted by managers of a previous generation, Jazz Summers at Big Life (see Summers, 2013) and Cliff Bernstein and Peter Mensh at Q Prime. At Big Life, Richardson worked with acts including Snow Patrol, while Q Prime is the business owned by Bernstein and Mensh, whose management operation began managing metal acts like Def Leppard, AC/DC and Metallica in the 1980s. As of 2024, the latter comprises nine managers representing 30 acts, including Gillian Welch, Muse, Pantera and Metallica. While working for the latter, between 2007 and 2024, Richardson worked with (among others)

Foals, Declan McKenna and, most recently, Last Dinner Party and Nell Mescal. She left Q Prime to set up her own management company/creative agency, T-Time, in 2024 (Paine, 2024).

Though Dakota Hoven is younger and has worked in management for a shorter period, she has also worked, initially as an intern, for an already established management company, Chosen Music, which describes itself as 'a boutique management company in Central London with a global footprint representing a chosen roster of best-in-class artists, producers and writers' (www.chosenmusic.com [accessed 2/7/25]). It is much smaller than Q Prime with four managers and 11 acts in 2024 (www.rostr.cc [accessed 2/7/25]), within which Hoven manages Nathan Evans and Caity Baiser. Despite presenting itself as a 'boutique' company, it is part of a larger operation. Chosen's directors are Alistair Galbraith and longstanding music and theatre impresario, Jonathan Shallit. Chosen Music is a partnership between Galbraith and Shalit's InterTalent agency.

A notable aspect of both management careers has been Richardson's and Hoven's ability to both find and develop acts in recent years, even though how this happened also speaks to the changing nature of the music industries. Richardson's partnership with Last Dinner Party at Q Prime began in a relatively traditional manner: going to see the band play live and pursuing them in the face of much competition subsequently. Abigail Morris, of the band, told *Music Week*: 'As soon as we sat down with Tara, we thought, 'oh shit, this is the one. She has a great attitude: one that is simultaneously empathetic and nurturing and kind and supportive and funny – she is the funniest person I know. But also, so tough and impossible to f**k with' (Gunn, 2024, p. 24). By way of contrast, Hoven describes her route into artist management via discovering Caity Baiser 'on TikTok. Her catchy lyrics and the way she is unapologetic caught my eye.' For her, Chosen Music 'have been Caity's partners from the start, and it's that kind of relationship that I think is going to be more normalised, especially in a world where the choices of label and distribution partners that artists and managers have continue growing' (Gunn, 2024, p. 15).

As both women note, these choices have become increasingly (if not entirely) equitable on grounds of gender in recent years. Richardson points to the #MeToo movement as a relatively recent turning point, reflecting on the last 20 years in management, wishing that, 'I had known that I wouldn't be the only woman in the room', and remembering that, 'there was a point when I was doing Women in Music seminars and me and Mairead Nash (managing Florence and the Machine) were the only female managers. When I met Declan McKenna to try and manage him, he met forty-two managers, and I was the only woman. That was only 8 years ago (quoted in Jones, 2024, p. 26). For Hoven, her role at Chosen Music represents an opportunity to amplify the voice of her artists, acknowledging that for both her and Baiser, 'being a woman has never been easy in music but I'm just proud of what Caity stands for. Her authenticity really cuts through online; my role is just to make that as loud as possible', something she notes is made easier by the presence of women all round Baiser's career, notably at her record company, EMI (Jones, 2024, p. 15).

For Richardson, the gradual move towards a gender balance is both a factor in and reflection of the changing nature of the role itself in the last two decades. She notes a change in both the needs of artists and the approach of the managers. As she puts it:

> With this generation of artists you need to work differently. They don't like 'football managers' who go in like an ox. They like managers who are calm and collected. When problems do arise, or someone does something wrong, we come to the best conclusion and figure it out. We don't end up in a row, we don't end up parting ways.
> (Richardson, 2024)

With this comes a willingness on the part of both artists and managers to discuss and share their own anxieties and vulnerabilities – something that would have been unthinkable in the 'starmakers and svengalis era of 20th century management. For Richardson, this is a two-way process between artists and managers, noting when discussing her own panic attacks that 'within every company I think that there should be wellbeing classes or a group that meets once a week. The younger bands have taught me to be more mentally aware and not to run and hide, they don't see it as a weakness. I've learned from them – and the industry can, too' (quoted in Jones, 2024, p. 27).

If Richardson and Hoven offer a couple of positive examples from many of the 21st century managers successfully developing both their own and artists' careers, it is worth making a few brief and final, cautionary points about some of the wider themes discussed in this section, all of which will be expanded with more specific instances and examples later in the book. These relate to the scope of artist management and some of the challenges that remain for managers more generally, and for women in artist management more specifically.

As the recording industry contracted in size (not just in economic terms, but via redundancies and consolidation), both labels and managers were largely having to increase their reach and workloads. In the case of the former, this was visible, in the moves by companies like Sanctuary and Warners in the early part of the 21st century towards the 360-degree model, described by Marshall as a deal 'where the label participates in and receives income from a range of musical activities beyond the sales of recordings' (Marshall, 2013, p. 77). And while this was implemented with varying degrees of success, it did result in a blurring of the lines between roles that had previously been considered the domain of the record labels and those of managers; for example, around promotion of both recordings and concerts. To add a further disruption, other players within the music industries sought to adapt to the industrial changes by similarly embarking on the process of acquiring rights and expanding horizontally and vertically. Famous examples of this included Warner Music setting up a management division to look after artists signed to the label, and the concert promoter Live Nation signing 360-degree-style deals with major artists. In doing so, they set up a management company largely by buying out existing managers and management companies. The scale of this is such that they note in their most recent Annual Report that, 'we managed more than 380 artists in 2023 (Live Nation, 2024, p. 3).

Along with others, Live Nation accelerated and took the business of artist management to unprecedented levels. One of their main competitors, Red Light, lists 236 managers and 484 acts under its umbrella in 2024 (www.rostr.cc [accessed 2/7/25]) including Sabrina Carpenter, Lady A, Sugababes, Lionel Richie and Franz Ferdinand, and operates as a transnational management firm, involved in all aspects of the music industries (including various label partnerships). For its UK managing partner, James Sandom, this type of superstructure is an inevitable consequence of these industrial changes and the greater importance of managers. He told Music Week:

> I would say that managers are more important than ever. By and large, we are handling the artist development and their direction. As the needle has shifted, the importance of guidance on careers and the intelligent route to market has empowered the managers even more – and most importantly empowered the artists.
>
> (Paine, 2023)

While this is arguably true, the shifts of the last 20 years may also have resulted in a less creative, more organized and less entrepreneurial approach on the part of managers. It is, however, also significant that an experienced and successful manager like Richardson is reversing such a trend and setting up in her own right in 2024. This needs to be seen in the light of both broader historical change in the music industries and some more nuanced discussion of gender balance in the business of artist management. First, it is important to note that consolidation and integration and disintegration are recurring aspects in all of the creative industries (see Lash and Urry, 1994, pp. 113–120) and that within these recent changes there are also important historical continuities, not least when it comes to representation at the top level of artist management. While the most recent MMF data reports that 43% of managers identify as women and 29% as black, Asian or from an ethnic background, it also notes a gender pay gap where 29.6% of male managers earn more than £30,000 per year, but only 22% of women (Bonham et al., 2024). Though this supports the idea of a much more diverse workforce than at the turn of the century, even a cursory look at the ownership, boards and management of Live Nation, Q Prime, Red Light and Chosen Music show that these remain largely the preserve of older, white, middle-aged men. Indeed, seven out of nine directors of Live Nation are men, and all the directors of Red Light, Q Prime and Chosen Music.

Conclusion

This account of the historical development of artist management in the UK and USA through the 20th century to the present day has sought to provide a range of examples from the UK and beyond to consider both what the profession involves and how this has changed spanning almost a century of music from Duke Ellington to Last Dinner Party. However, with a small sample size and often contradictory examples, it would be justified in concluding that it is impossible to either neatly categorize different styles of management or explain how *exactly* these have changed. Yet, there are still some useful lessons from this potted history that underpin the discussion and first-hand experiences of contemporary managers that follows.

The history does nevertheless show the evolution of artist management as an industry or career in its own right, from the earliest entertainment entrepreneurs who saw an opportunity afforded by big-band singers, to early rock'n'roll stars and beat groups, through to a younger cadre of 21st century managers, many of whom come from different and more varied backgrounds, albeit with a similar range of routes into management and often via higher education as well as the tried-and-tested 'friend of the artist' path. Whereas learning on the job was integral to most 20th century experiences (and remains so to a point given the amorphous nature of the role), increasingly, new managers have the benefit of mentoring schemes, such as those organized by MMF UK and EMMA, industry-specific education or training courses, and a range of literature and how-to guides from industry organizations and beyond. If this levels the playing field and diversifies the profession to a degree, all of these require access to finance and knowledge that are not necessarily widely available. Of course, the rapid growth of both music streaming and the live music industry in the last decade has also created more opportunities within music management, albeit ones that are offset by the increasingly high number of qualified potential entrants and the generally low salaries for most participants: in the MMF's most recent survey, the prospects were as grim for managers as for musicians themselves with 76% of those surveyed earning less than £30,000 per year, 12% earning nothing and 72% not having a pension (Bonham et al., 2024, p. 11).

It may also be reasonable to expect that a history of the role would help clear up both the precise nature of the artist manager's job and the approaches taken to it, though this chapter suggests that it remains at least a little opaque to non-participants. The combination of idiosyncratic individuals as both artists and managers inevitably results in the type of business structure and relationships that are not easily mapped or profiled using more traditional forms of management studies. In this sense, Johnny Rogan's claim that 'although all managers perform a range of similar functions, their individual strategies are often miles apart' (Rogan, 1988, p. 12) remains pertinent, though his attempt to list 13 different types of manager, less so. He described these as: the autocratic manager; the concerned parent; the indulgent manager; the neophyte (looked and acted like the star themselves); poachers and inheritors; the neutered lackey; the dilettante manager; the fatalistic manager; the over-reachers; the scapegoat manager; the dual role; co-management and team management; and the record company manager (Rogan, 1988, pp. 11–14); and while these characteristics may still be visible in many cases, the boundaries are porous and approaches stem from a combination of their background, education and personality and how these interact with the artists they work with.

If anything, in the nearly 40 intervening years since Rogan's book was published, some of the recurring myths of legacy artist management as it was both practised and journalled have been debunked. As Mike Jones noted, accounts like Rogan's 'deflect attention away from the lived reality of managerial practice to reposition the actions of successful managers as an outcome of some kind of supernatural ability that the success of their clients seems to suggest that they possess' (Jones, 2012, p. 93). Similarly, Chapple and Garofalo's 1970s characterization of artist managers as 'a sleazy bunch of businessmen out to bilk their often black, R&B clients for a few quick bucks, with little respect for artists as musicians or their rights in law' (Chapple and Garofalo, 1977, p. 131) retains little currency.

More recent accounts focus on the importance of 'managing vulnerability, health and wellbeing of artists' over more traditional management tasks surrounding 'legal and contractual negotiation' and 'accounting and financial planning' (Bonham et al., 2024, p. 12) alongside other hardy perennials like marketing and tour management. This type of description may make the job of the artist manager seem less dynamic and exciting than the one portrayed by Rogan in the last century, but it highlights the professionalisation of the role; the radical reorganization of the music industries; and wider societal, technological and economic changes in society and the economy in the meantime. And if none of this represents the pithiest of conclusions, then perhaps what this history of artist management shows is that these external factors, coupled with the individual traits of managers, mean that the only historic continuity comes from the certainty of further change and disruption, and the wheeling out of some old as well as new solutions, all of which will be further evidenced in studying the lived reality of managers across the following chapters.

References

Allen, P. (2022) *Artist Management for the Music Business*, 5th edn. Routledge, London and New York.
Bagehot, R. and Kanaar, N. (1998) *Music Business Agreements*. Sweet & Maxwell, London.
Berman, T. (2019) Architect of stardom: Irving Mills and Duke Ellington. Available at: leasekillme.com/irving-mills-duke-ellington/ (accessed 26 May 2024).
Blackwell, C. (2022) *The Islander: My Life in Music and Beyond*. Nine eight, London.
Bonham, P., Coldrick, A. and Webb, A. (2024) *Managing Expectations: Workforce Edition*. MMF, London.
Bullock, D. (2021) *The Velvety Mafia: The Gay Men Who ran the Swinging Sixties*. Omnibus, London.
Chapple, S. and Garofalo, R. (1977) *Rock'n'Roll is Here to Pay: The History and Politics of the Music Industry*. Nelson-Hall, Chicago, Illinois.
Coleman, R. (1990) *Brian Epstein: The Man who Made the Beatles*. Penguin, London.
Easlea, D. (2016) The managers that built prog: Gail Colson – the woman behind Peter Gabriel. *Prog Magazine*. Available at: www.loudersound.com/features/the-managers-that-built-prog-gail-colson-the-woman-behind-peter-gabriel (accessed 17 June 2024).
Forde, E. (2024) *1999: The Year the Record Industry Lost Control*. Omnibus, London.
Frith, S. (1978) *The Sociology of Rock*. Constable, London.
Frith, S. (1983) *Sound Effects: Youth, Leisure and the Politics of Rock'n'Roll*. Constable, London.
Glanville, J. (1984) In the business. In: Tennant, N. (ed.) *Smash Hits Yearbook 1985*. EMAP, London.
Goodman, F. (2010) *Fortune's Fool: Edgar Bronfman Jr., Warner Music, and an Industry in Crisis*. Simon & Schuster, New York.
Goodman, F. (2015) *Allen Klein: The Man Who Bailed Out the Beatles, Made the Stones and Transformed Rock & Roll*. Houghton Mifflin Harcourt, London.
Gunn, C. (2024) Built to last. *Music Week* February, 23–29.
Guralnick, P. (1995) *Last Train to Memphis: The Rise of Elvis Presley*. Abacus, London.
Guralnick, P. (2000) *Careless Love: The Unmaking of Elvis Presley*. Abacus, London.
Hammill, P. (2011) Gail leaves the building. Sofasound. Available at: sofasound.wordpress.com/2011/12/31/gail-leaves-the-building/ (accessed 17 June 2024).
Hilburn, R. (1989) Elvis's millions were disappearing when Priscilla Presley took charge and rebuilt the king's fortune. 11 June, *Los Angeles Times*.
Jones, M. (2012) *The Music Industries*. Palgrave MacMillan, Basingstoke, UK.
Jones, R. (2024) Raye's story brings an opportunity to set a precedent for female artists to be respected, listened-to and celebrated from the start. In: *Music Business UK*. Available at: https://issuu.com/musicbizworldwide/docs/mbuk_issue_26_digital (accessed 21 August 2025).
Judd, D. (2008) My mentor: Lulu recalls the manager who kept her singing career on the rails. *The Guardian*. Available at: www.theguardian.com/money/2008/aug/02/workandcareers1 (accessed 26 May 2024).
Kaplan, J. (2016) *Sinatra: The Chairman*. Anchor, New York.
Lash, S. and Urry, J. (1994) *Economies of Signs and Space*. Sage, London.

Live Nation (2024) *Annual Report*. Live Nation, Los Angeles.

Lulu (1985) *My Autobiography*. HarperCollins, London.

Marshall, L. (2013) The 360 deal and the 'new' music industry. *European Journal of Cultural Studies* 16(1), 77–99.

McDonald, G. (2023) *Elvis and the Colonel: An Insider's Look at the Most Legendary Partnership in Show Business*. St. Martin's Griffin, New York.

Morrow, G. (2024) *Artist Management: Agility in the Creative and Cultural Industries (Discovering the Creative Industries)*. Routledge, New York.

Negus, K. (1992) *Producing Pop*. Edward Arnold, London.

Oldham, A. (2000) *Stoned*. Vintage, London.

Oldham, A. (2003) *2 Stoned*. Vintage, London.

Oldham, A. (2012) *Stone Free*. Escargot Books.

Paine, A. (2023) Red alert: How red light's expanding UK operation is taking over the charts. *Music Week*. Available at: www.musicweek.com/interviews/read/red-alert-how-red-light-s-expanding-uk-operation-is-taking-over-the-charts/088053 (accessed 14 July 2024).

Paine, A. (2024) Tara Richardson launches T-time management. *Music Week*. Available at: www.musicweek.com/management/read/tara-richardson-launches-t-time-management/090026 (accessed 14 July 2024).

Peterson, R. (1990) Why 1955? Explaining the advent of rock music. *Popular Music* 9(1), 97–115.

Richardson, T. (2024) What i wish i'd known. Music Business UK 26–29. Available at: https://issuu.com/musicbizworldwide/docs/mbuk_issue_26_digital (accessed 21 August 2025).

Rogan, J. (1988) *Star Makers and Svengalis*. Transatlantic Publications, London.

Savage, J. (2008) Foreword. In: Gretton, R. (ed.) *1 Top Class Manager*. Anti-Archivists, Manchester, UK.

Stokes, G. (1977) *Star Making Machinery: Inside the Business of Rock'n'Roll*. Random House, New York.

Summers, J. (2013) *Big Life*. Quartet Books, London.

Sutherland, M. (2016) Under new management. *Music Week* 27 March.

Watkins, T. (2017) *Let's Make Lots of Money: My Life as the Biggest Man in Pop*. Ebury, London.

Webb, A., Bonham, P., Harmon, A., Coldrick, A. and Dethekar, M. (2022) *Essentials of Music Management*. Music Managers Forum, London.

Wikström, P. (2019) *The Music Industry: Music in the Cloud*. Polity Press.

Williamson, J. and Cloonan, M. (2007) Rethinking the music industry. *Popular Music* 26(2), 305–322.

Witt, S. (2015) *How Music Got Free: The End of an Industry, the Turn of the Century and the Patient Zero of Piracy*. Viking, New York.

3 Organizing Music Managers

Allan Dumbreck

Introduction

This chapter considers the emergence of management organizations and analyses how they have grown globally over the last three decades in comparison to the more historically developed representation in other theatres of the music industries (notably recorded music, music publishing). It then examines their impact by considering their stated objectives in comparison to the activities they undertake, and investigates their progress in the representation of artist management. It closes by envisaging future possibilities for these organizations, considering their own intentioned direction and the opportunities for artist representation within the broader sphere of the music and creative industries.

IMF/MMF

Manchester, 1992. The first 'In the city' music conference is set up by entrepreneur Tony Wilson and welcomes around 1000 industry professionals and emerging artists to three days of presentations, debates and live performances. ITC, as it was known, ran for 18 years through the 1990s/2000s across different locations including Dublin and Glasgow, and saw key early performances from acts such as Coldplay, Oasis and the Stereophonics before they became successful. Wilson (founder of Factory Records, home to New Order and previously Joy Division) had invited, amongst others, record executives, music publishers, emerging artists and, crucially, music managers to the event (Morley, 2007, 2022).

Bruce Findlay, former manager of Simple Minds was invited by Wilson and Elliot Rashman to chair a panel on artist management which attracted a considerable audience of industry personnel. Afterwards, elsewhere in the Midland Hotel, they agreed they should set up the first representative organization for music managers. As Findlay says:

> I chaired the first meeting in a packed room... about 200 or 300 people. On the panel were Gail Colson (former manager of Peter Gabriel), Ed Bicknell (then manager of Dire Straits/Mark Knopfler), Elliot Rashman (then manager of Simply Red), Peter Grant (former manager of Led Zeppelin) and others. It was so successful we immediately organized ourselves into a loose association and I again chaired a hastily put together press conference announcing a new managers organisation...the IMF (International Managers Forum) later the MMF... without Elliot and Tony Wilson the MMF wouldn't have happened...
>
> (Findlay, 2024)

MMF UK (based in London) has now existed for over 30 years, and under the most recent CEO, Annabella Coldrick, has grown in membership to over 1500 managers with a global network (through links to other national MMF organizations) of over 3000 (MMF, n.d.). Music management representative organizations have been formed in many other nations and territories in the intervening period, notably in North America, the Antipodes and Europe, with EMMA (the European Music Managers Association) having over 500 members excluding those based in the UK (EMMA, 2024).

However, as indicated in Chapter 1, these music management organizations don't exist in a vacuum; they join a broad range of other music industries representative bodies which have evolved over the last 175 years. It is therefore vital to examine the evolution of these organizations to correctly place the MMF network within that timeframe. Given also that all these organizations have, at different times, to interact with each other, to present a unified music industry 'front' in negotiations and agree/progress the issues they collectively or individually feel are critical, it is important to see where the MMF organizations sit within this landscape and to have some idea of the history of the development of representative bodies more generally, and the range of music industries sectors they represent. Equally, it is important to remember that managers will have to work with many of these organizations directly and so there is intrinsic value in examining who they are and what they do.

A Short History of Music Industries Representation

There exists an extensive and growing network of music representative organizations operating at national and global levels. Collectively, these bodies now speak on behalf of almost all music industry sectors although there are still some gaps. In the first part of this chapter, we examine the emergence and development of these bodies within each of the key music industries sectors.

Music composition/publishing

The first representative organizations in the music industries were the performing rights organisations or PROs (previously categorized as royalty collection societies although that is only one of their activities), specifically those for music composition, which were established to protect the copyright of composers who sought remuneration for the performance of their works, initially in theatres and later through recorded reproduction and radio play.

In 1847, concerned that their work was regularly being performed without any financial benefit to themselves, three French composers and lyricists secured payment for the live public performance of their compositions, with the French legal system recognizing these rights. Following this, the first representative organization within music, SACEM (France), was established by them in 1851 to protect the rights of librettists, composers and music authors, as well as their publishers. Initially having a membership of around 350, today SACEM represents over 240,000 members and their creative output, and has an annual gross revenue (in 2023) of almost €1.6 billion (SACEM, 2025; Dalugdug, 2025). As with all PROs, SACEM issues licences for public use and monitors venues, broadcasters, cinemas and other users throughout France, deriving income and ensuring fair distribution of that income (known as royalties) to the rights holders after deduction of operational expenses.

Around 50 years later, a further PRO came formed, again in Europe. The law concerning authors' and composers' rights, which came into effect in Germany in 1902, led the German composers' consortium to form AFMA (the equivalent organization to the French SACEM and predecessor of GEMA) in 1903. GEMA now has over 98,000 members and a gross income of over €1.33 billion (GEMA, 2025). In the UK, the Performing Right Society (PRS) was formed for the same purposes in 1914 (180,000 members; revenue of £1.15 billion in 2024; PRS for Music, 2025). ASCAP (US) was founded in the same year (1 million + members; over $1.835 billion revenue in 2024; ASCAP, n.d.). Many nations have only one PRO for each type of royalty. One exception to this is the USA where Broadcast Music Incorporated (BMI) (1.4 million members in 2024; almost $1.5 billion revenue in 2021/2021; BMI, 2024a, b) was set up in 1940 by broadcasters concerned by rising licensing costs being charged by ASCAP. PROs are predominantly non-profit-making, taking only their own running costs from the income they collect before passing all remaining revenue to their composer and publisher members.

These organizations were primarily intended to protect the copyright inherent in the composition of original work within live performance. By the 1920s and 1930s, music was moving towards jazz, big bands and solo performers, as examined in the previous chapter, when early managers such as Mills and Sanicola were emerging. With the advent of the recorded music market around the same time, composers and songwriters found that they also needed to monitor the mechanical reproduction and distribution of their work by record companies. Established in the UK in 1910, the MCPS (Mechanical Copyright Protection Society) was set up to protect the rights of composers and lyricists whose intellectual property had been recorded and mechanically mass-produced (composers do not always perform on the recordings of their works and might not even be aware that a musician or musicians have recorded them) (MCPS, n.d.). This particular aspect of royalty collection for composers/songwriters is normally included in the work of the performance and broadcast royalty collection societies outside of the UK (e.g. SACEM and GEMA).

Further equivalent non-profit PROs were set up in many nations and by the early 20th century an organization to collectively represent PROs globally in the music publishing sector was thought necessary. CISAC, the body which oversees all PROs collecting for composition was created in 1926. Initially representing 18 European countries, by 2025 CISAC comprises 227 member societies in 116 countries globally and reports on a worldwide music composition royalty collection revenue in excess of €13 billion annually (CISAC, n.d.).

CISAC also produces an annual collections report with statistics on the key global markets for music composition and royalty return (CISAC, 2024). This allows us to compare nations/territories to understand the scale of each marketplace. This information, for example, allows a manager to decide which territories to prioritize to give their artist/creator the best chance of growing their audience and revenue streams (however, only in the case where they are composing music or lyrics). Table 3.1 maps the ten highest grossing nations for composition royalty return as tracked by CISAC in 2022.

We can see that, although the USA is the largest single nation overall (24.2%), the collective European market is significantly greater (around 50%). Publishing collection began in Europe and is most developed there. Additionally, CISAC is based in Europe. For these reasons publishing royalties are tracked in euros.

In the UK, the Music Publishers Association (MPA) was set up in 1881 to collectively represent the music publishing companies. The MPA

Table 3.1. CISAC global collections report 2024. This shows the level of royalty collection in different nations. As such, it evidences public consumption/use of copyright material rather than source.

Nation	€m equiv. gross	% of market
USA	2616	24.2
France	1325	12.2
UK	1011	9.3
Germany	903	8.3
Japan	848	7.8
Italy	448	4.1
Australia	345	3.2
Canada	337	3.1
Spain	274	2.5
South Korea	247	2.3

now represents over 200 of these companies and other relevant parties in the UK. Their website demonstrates considerable transparency, hosting their articles of association and the equality and diversity policy (MPA, n.d.). An equivalent organization with the same title was set up in the USA in 1895.

While these organizations all protect the rights of, and collect the income streams due to, songwriters and composers, the actual craft of music creation remains a separate issue. Therefore, separate organizations were required for this purpose. The Songwriters Guild of America originated in the Songwriters Protective Association formed in 1931 to represent composers, lyricists and songwriters (Songwriters Guild of America, n.d.). Similarly, the British Association of Songwriters, Composers and Authors (BASCA), tracing their roots back to 1944 and collectively representing these same groups in the UK, became the Ivors Academy in 2019. UK creators of original musical works have been recognizing their most successful members with the annual Ivors awards, named after the founder, Ivor Novello, since 1955 (Ivors Academy, n.d.).

Music publishing royalties can constitute a significant part of an artist's income if they are a songwriter/composer (Allen, 2022; Anderton et al., 2022). As MMF UK states in *Essentials of Music Management* (Webb et al., 2022): 'It is crucial that [your original compositions] are registered with your PRO'. Hence, this sector is of significant importance to artist managers.

Recorded music

The invention of the phonograph and gramophone (Edison/Berliner) in the late 19th century and the mass-produced gramophone player brought a second intellectual property asset – that of the master recording – into being (Gronow and Saunio, 1999). Distinct from the rights associated with the composition (which composers and music publishers are primarily concerned with), the need now arose for the protection of rights associated with the ownership of each audio recording. In many countries the already existing society for the protection of composition rights (e.g. SACEM/GEMA) took responsibility for this; however, in the UK, a new organization, Phonographic Performance Limited (PPL), was created in 1934 to protect and administer rights and royalties for the performers and record companies who were now able to benefit from the new development. PPL now represents almost 150,000 performers and recording rights holders and has over 20 million recordings in its repertoire database, generating £283.5 million of revenue in 2023. It is also run on a non-profit basis (Paine, 2024b; PPL, n.d.).

Over time, the commercial record companies realized that they, too, needed a collective voice. In the mid-20th century, the focus of the recorded music industries was the USA, where record sales grew significantly after the Second World War (Gronow and Saunio, 1999), and this time America led the way with the RIAA (Recording Industry Association of America), forming in 1952 (RIAA, n.d.). The UK followed suit with the BPI (British Phonographic Industry) in 1973 (BPI, n.d.). Given the strength of the independent record companies in the UK (often having between 20% and 30% of the annual market share) and the feeling that the BPI better represented the major labels, the creation of the Association of Independent Music (AIM) in the UK in 1998 helped promote their interests (AIM (Association of Independent Music – UK), n.d.). AIM is part of the Worldwide Independent Network (WIN) of music trade

Table 3.2. IFPI chart of highest grossing territories for recorded music sales in 2023 (public consumption).

1	USA
2	Japan
3	UK
4	Germany
5	China
6	France
7	South Korea
8	Canada
9	Brazil
10	Australia

associates, which now has 37 members across 43 countries (WIN, n.d.).

As with the PROs within the music publishing sector, other nations set up their own recorded music collective representation in due course. Reflecting the formation of CISAC for music composition and publishing, the International Federation of Phonographic Industries (IFPI) was established to represent global recorded music, although in this case it began operation in 1933 before any of the national organizations. A collective international representative organization for all national recorded music industries, it now tracks global revenues of $28.6 billion annually across 70 nations (IFPI, n.d.).

Similar to the global collection of composition royalties (CISAC), available IFPI data allows us to examine the nations with the highest revenue (public consumption of recorded music) but also the most successful artists and their country of origin.

The first chart (Table 3.2) informs us of the principal markets for recorded music sales. It features, as we might expect, many western or developed countries (North America, Europe, Japan, Australia), but we can now see emerging markets in developing countries (Asia and South America) appearing in key positions on the chart (China, South Korea, Brazil), countries where the populace is increasingly buying or streaming music. Perhaps of greater interest, however, is the second chart (Table 3.3), which shows the nations from which the most successful global

Table 3.3. IFPI global chart of the most successful recording artists in 2023 and their country of origin.

Taylor Swift	USA
Seventeen	Indonesia
Stray kids	South Korea
Drake	Canada
The Weeknd	Canada
Morgan Wallen	USA
Tomorrow X Together	South Korea
New Jeans	South Korea
Bad Bunny	Puerto Rico
Lana Del Ray	USA

artists originate. North America (historically home to many high-achieving performers) is still represented but there is an increasing number of Asian artists who are challenging the established source nations with their own successful acts (Lindvall, 2011; Adams, 2022).

The critical difference here is that while Table 3.2 tells us which nations are consuming the most recorded music (purchase of physical product such as CDs and vinyl plus streaming of digital product), Table 3.3 tells us which nations the most successful artists come from. Therefore, while the nations identified in Table 3.2 are primary targets for managers working with artists regardless of which nation they originate from, those appearing in Table 3.3 are where some of the particularly successful artists and managers originate (research indicates that most of these artists have a manager who is based in, or comes from, the same country, e.g. Stray Kids, JYP Entertainment – South Korea; Bad Bunny, Noah Assad – Puerto Rico; Morgan Wallen, Austin Neal – USA). Although this is a limited snapshot, we can see that the USA and South Korea are each home to 30% of the most successful global artists (and their management companies). This represents a significant shift in the geographical balance of artists and management away from the western-centric (North America and Europe) model which we were familiar with in the late 20th century. Overall, we can see here that, in 2023, what were once developing nations have now grown their own domestic consumer market where the population buys significant volumes of music and many of those nations now also have indigenous artists who are successful on a global stage.

This significantly changes the global artist management landscape and marketplace in terms of both the territories that consume music and those that produce it. This may also change the way business is done as the emerging nations may operate a different business culture. While some work has been done in this area (Hwang, 2024), this could be a further line of future possible research.

To return to our original focus, however, and to summarize, all PRO organizations (music publishing and recorded music), whether overseeing composition or master recording rights and royalties, are representative but also administrative, collecting royalties from copyright users (e.g. concert promoters, venue owners, broadcasters on radio and later television) which they then pass on to the copyright holders (e.g. music publishers and songwriters/composers). They negotiate on behalf of their members (rights and rates) and also manage the distribution of collected royalties to the music publishers, composers, lyricists and master recording owners who have signed up as members and have identified themselves and their works. Additionally, they also represent the rights of music composers and lyricists (or performers in the case of master recording PROs) to their respective national governments and negotiate on their behalf in business conflicts and internationally (Lindvall, 2015). Many also run support initiatives to help nurture emerging talent in their sector (ASCAP, n.d.).

Chronologically, the second major sector of music to develop, recorded music, has grown to become a key source of artist income globally. As such, it is of significant relevance to managers and to our research (see chapter 5).

Live events/performance

The Concert Promoters Association (CPA), initially formed in the UK in 1986 to represent those setting up and managing live events as a reaction against the then proposal from PRS to raise their live events royalty collection rate (Cloonan, 2012). The CPA have been involved in industry-wide campaigns including the recent 'Let the music play' action which sought support for live music when almost all events were shut down during the COVID crisis (CPA, n.d.). Additionally, a second UK representative body for live music exists. Set up during lockdown in 2021 to counter the closure of venues and the issues facing touring acts due to Brexit, LIVE (Live music: Industry, Venues and Entertainment), represents the broader live music sector in the UK. The organization brings together 16 key music associations with direct interest in live music events (including the CPA, the MU and the MMF). Over 3000 businesses and over 4000 artists are represented (LIVE, n.d.). LIVE has given a collective voice to a sector which lost around 85% of its revenue during COVID (LIVE, 2024; Paine, 2024d).

Other representative organizations for events exist such as Live DMA within Europe, with 20 members from a series of continental EU nations representing the live music industries across the continent. Their objectives include developing a fairer, greener, more inclusive European live events industry. They run a series of working groups examining issues affecting live events including the disparity in sound regulations in different nations across the continent, fair practice for event bookers, the value of music venues to local authorities (Live DMA, 2024), and the significant increase in the market share of conglomerates AEG and Live Nation within the live music industry, which has been recognized and has raised some concerns (Sweney, 2013; Hanley, 2018b).

Where statistics on the scale of recorded music and music publishing mostly come from those sectors within the music industries, those on the global live music industries can come from sources outside music. They are, however, aligned in identifying the significant scale and ongoing growth of that marketplace (Goldman Sachs, 2024 as reported by Paine, 2024e; Sweney, 2024; Tencer, 2025). Figures can vary, and it is important to distinguish between those estimates which include merchandising or sponsorship revenue and those which are ticket sales only, for example. We should also remember that live events were particularly detrimentally affected by the COVID pandemic and have only seen recovery over the last few years. However, most researchers accept that the global live music sector generates a greater gross income then recorded music. MMF UK agree, stating: 'live music is the most important revenue stream for the majority of artists, generating on average 80% of earnings' (Webb et al., 2022), making it a key theatre of interest for managers and therefore again a focus for our research (see Chapter 5).

Musicians/performers

As with composers, the musicians of the 19th century, seeing the benefits of union activity in other trades, recognized the advantages of collective organization; and so, beginning in Manchester in 1893, theatre musicians formed themselves into unions to establish a stronger negotiating position for their wages and working conditions (Musicians' Union, n.d.; University of Stirling archive, n.d.). These grew and combined over time to become the Musicians' Union (UK). As with other sectors, similar organizations swiftly sprang up across Europe and North America. The MU in the UK now has over 30,000 members.

The American Federation of Musicians (representing the USA and Canada) was founded in 1896 and now has over 70,000 members (AFM, n.d.). Broadly offering similar support and representation as their UK counterpart, the AFM works with musicians from all genres and backgrounds, negotiating with broadcasters on remuneration rates and raising financial assistance in emergencies, for example.

Many nations have similar organizations. The International Federation of Musicians (FIM) based in France lists 55 in total (31 in Europe and North America, 11 in Africa, 9 in South and Central America, 4 in Asia and the Pacific). They do not give clear figures for membership but globally there are over 100,000 members of musicians' representative organizations merely taking the MU (UK) and AFM (US) figures combined. The number of musicians signed to representative organizations who are working professionally or with managers is not easy to define. It is not necessarily the case that every MU member in the UK is working professionally, for example.

In the UK at the start of the new century, it was felt necessary to create an organization representing the named artists identified and featured live and on records distinct from the other (backing) musicians who played alongside them. These artists had always benefitted from being paid a royalty by record companies on each record sold and a percentage of the ticket income from an event at which they performed. This would normally be a considerably higher level of income compared to the backing musicians who were usually paid a performance fee or a wage commensurate with the level of success of the featured artist. The Featured Artists Coalition (FAC) was formed in 2009 to give this group collective representation. Membership in 2023 was over 4000 and the organization continues to strengthen and grow (Martin, 2023).

More recently the organizations that represent songwriters and performers formed the Council of Music Makers in 2018 (CMM). This is a body which represents the artists/creators, managers, composers and other relevant organizations, effectively building a combined front for all the organizations working with creative talent to give them a stronger, united voice (CMM, n.d.). This was necessary, according to Annabella Coldrick at MMF UK, as she told us during one of our interviews:

> 'The reason we [worked towards setting up the Council of Music Makers] is because we're all part of the umbrella organization UK Music, which represents the whole music industry – from songwriters and musicians, producers, artists and managers to major labels/indie labels to collection societies to big publishing companies, all of which are rights holders. We found that those representing the interests of music makers were badly co-ordinated and we really struggled [to make our voice heard]. We would turn up at UK Music board meetings and find that all the policy positions ended up being those of the rights holders because we could not co-ordinate ourselves to properly advocate for the music makers.'
>
> (Coldrick, 2020)

There are, therefore, a significant number of organisations representing musicians and music makers within different working environments for different reasons across a series of territories.

Music production

Originating in 1985, the British Record Producers Guild was formed to take forward issues affecting studio producers, including broadcast rights, A&R development, producer royalties, digital distribution and recording technology. Becoming the Music Producers Guild in 2000 (MPG, n.d.). It has begun one of the first music industry education accreditation mechanisms via JAMES (Joint Audio Media Education Support) (JAMES, n.d.), 'an alliance of music, entertainment and media industry organisations collaborating in the support of education and promotion of excellence' (MPG). Alongside almost all the UK organisations addressed in this chapter, the MPG is a member of UK Music (see below). In the USA, the Association of Music Producers (AMP) was formed in 1998. Similar to the MPG in the UK, AMP raises issues affecting producers and gives them a collective voice. They run awards, panel events, field trips and conferences. In line with recent developments and other representative organizations they also have a diversity, equality and inclusion committee (AMP (Association of Music Producers – US), n.d.).

Cross-industry representation

In the early 21st century, most of the British organizations identified here came together to create the umbrella trade body for all sectors of the UK music industries to speak as one voice, notably on trade and representation at a national level, and in 2008, UK Music was born. Reporting on the overall status of the combined British music industries (now worth £6.7 billion GVA; UK Music, 2022) and negotiating directly with government, the cross-industry representative organization has developed significantly creating a collective platform for the key theatres of the modern music industries in Britain.

UK Music was instrumental in representing the music industries in parliament, including during the COVID crisis when the live music sector was so badly affected (Sweney, 2021). UK Music also undertakes research into the development and scale of the music industries as well as supporting diversity and education. Together with the MPG (through their JAMES initiative), UK Music funds the Music Education Directory (MED) which tracks all university and college music courses across the UK as well as the more prominent training programmes (MED, 2024).

Artist management

As we have seen, apart from early short-lived efforts to unite the music management community such as Larry Parnes' British Impresarios' Guild in the 1960s, artist management as a profession has only recently benefitted from collective representation, starting with the formation of the MMF in the UK and the USA in the early 1990s. Our research has identified at least a further 10 MMF organizations worldwide which are well established and currently active. These are listed below (Table 3.4) with their date of formation and approximate membership numbers (where this could be determined). All the European MMFs listed in the following chart (and the Australian and New Zealand MMFs) are members of EMMA, the pan-European collective for most of the MMFs operating across the continent. It can be seen from the following chart that our research indicates the global membership of MMF organizations is now in excess of 3800.

MMF UK appears to have the greatest number of members of any single-nation MMF. This is a well-developed organization judging by the level of online activity and through their social media profile. Unsurprisingly, given the UK has significant recorded music markets and considerable numbers of successful native artists, France and Germany also have active MMFs. More broadly within continental Europe, the Scandinavian countries have been particularly proactive in artist/creator management representation with the Swedish, Norwegian and Finnish MMFs driving initiatives. Per Kviman, for example (Chair of MMF Sweden), is also Chair of EMMA (Paine, 2023).

Given the smaller scale of the individual EU nations in comparison to the North American marketplace, the formation of pan-European EMMA was valuable in giving a united voice to managers across the continent. This is particularly important in terms of engaging with the European Union to address legislation affecting all nations in the bloc. Collectively, public consumption of music in the European market and the North American market represents almost 70% of global recorded music revenue (IFPI) and almost 80% of the global music publishing market (CISAC), hence they are highly active marketplaces where it would be expected that artist managers would be operating. However, as we have seen, we have to be careful to distinguish between where the vibrant sales markets are and the nations from which internationally successful artists (and their managers) originate. These territorial groupings are not always the same.

Table 3.4. List of researched MMF organizations.

Organization	Est.	Members	Website/link
MMF UK	1992	1500+	themmf.net
MMF US	1993	600+	mmfus.com
EMMA (EU)	2018	500+	@emma.community
MMF Canada	2000	300+	mmfcanada.ca
AAM Australia	2007	300+	www.aam.org.au
MMF New Zealand	N/A	400+	mmf.co.nz
AMA France	2014	40+	ama-france.com
IMUC Germany	N/A	80+	www.imuc.de
MMF Sweden	2008	66	mmfsweden.com
NEMAA Norway	N/A	72	nemaa.no
MMF Finland	2000	60	mmffinland.com
IMMF	N/A	N/A	immf.com/

Beyond Europe, MMF US and MMF Canada, in North America, and AAM Australia and MMF New Zealand, in the southern hemisphere, also have high membership numbers and a significantly developed online presence with evidence of continuous ongoing activity, recent news items and regular events. Unsurprisingly perhaps, given the scale of the US music markets, MMF US appears to have the second highest membership of any single-nation MMF, with Australia, Canada and New Zealand close behind. These organizations are addressing issues specific to their own territory, but all have common concerns (e.g. rate of return from DSPs, ticket pricing etc.). There is also a reasonable concensus on the objectives which most managerial representation bodies are pursuing, with education, advocacy and networking being identified as key.

Historically, the largest percentage of globally successful artists in the late 20th century originated from the USA and UK along with other English-speaking nations (Canada, Australia). Several European countries (Sweden, for example) have also brought forward international breakthrough acts (Johansson, 2010). These nations all have their own active MMF organizations. However, as we have seen, artists from Asian nations have recently been appearing on the IFPI global charts (notably South Korea). Some of these nations have not yet seen the establishment of their own MMF organizations.

The music industries in some of these nations operate entirely differently to US or EU models (Fuhr, 2015), where, for example, South Korean artists sign exclusively to a talent agency (e.g. JYP Entertainment, Hybe or SB Entertainment) rather than working with a music manager. This means that the traditional role of artist manager does not exist in the way we know it in other territories. However, given that the artists are still managed, albeit in a different way, it is not inconceivable that a management representation organization of some kind might be set up in the future.

To take another not dissimilar example, in Japan the Federation of Music Producers is the organization which the IMMF (International Music Managers Forum) recognizes as the national representation for managers. FMP (Japan) represents those involved in 'production' of an act or artist where management is part of that job description; however, the role is broader than that of the recognized manager in EU/US terms and can include activities such as studio producer and live agent. It therefore appears that different nations have different approaches to the management and development of artists with different roles and job descriptions associated with the required tasks. Hence, a more fluid interpretation of the role of the manager is perhaps required when considering how to group and represent music management in other territories.

As we have already seen with other sectors, international representation can have certain key benefits (IFPI/CISAC). The IMMF, set up to represent managers globally, has now been in existence for over 15 years. Many national MMFs are members (around 50 in total). However, until recently, their online and media presence was somewhat limited with only a handful of recent news items listed, for example (it should be noted that the IMMF is currently run by members of national MMFs who work voluntarily). As of July 2024, however, incoming IMMF President Neeta Ragoowansi (also President of MMF US) has stated that she is committed to developing the organization and its media and online visibility to better reflect the work it carries out. This could perhaps be a significant step forward for artist management in terms of role recognition and contribution to national and international economies.

One final point for consideration before we start to examine the individual MMF organisations is criteria for membership. Some MMF organizations only accept managers who are distinct from the performers in the managed act (non-players) as members. When we spoke with MMF UK, for example, they stated that they did not accept self-managing artists as members, although they were happy to offer artists looking for managers the opportunity to approach them for assistance in locating representation. The IMMF and other national MMF organizations on the other hand *are* accepting self-managing artists as members. This is often explained as relating to the way different music cultures operate in different territories and is an issue we will examine later in this chapter.

What Do the MMFs Do and Why Is It Important?

Generally, all music management organizations have broadly similar objectives. They are established as non-profit making membership representative organizations with a series of stated aims. Here we will examine and compare some of the leading organizations and their objectives (as explained in interviews with ourselves and presented within their online and media presence). It should be noted that the available information on each national MMF varies considerably. It is not always possible to confirm certain data (e.g. availability of a code of conduct for members). We have endeavoured to present as much data as possible on each but cannot always give a like-for-like comparison. Some issues which require broader examination and consideration will be addressed in more detail elsewhere in this book, notably EDI (equality, diversity and inclusion; Chapter 8) and health issues (Chapter 9).

MMF UK

As the original and longest-established music managers' representative organization, the key priorities of the MMF UK are examined first. These are defined on the MMF UK's extensive and supportive website (MMF UK, n.d.) as:

> **Educate** – the Music Managers Forum UK supports managers' continuous professional development within an evolving music industry.
> **Innovate** – to create and highlight opportunities to develop and grow management and artist businesses.
> **Advocate** – to provide a collective voice to affect change for a transparent and fairer music industry for artists and their fans.

These objectives address both internal regulation (e.g. the published code of practice for managers) and outward-looking issues (e.g. engagement with government and proposed legislation). Taking each of these items individually we can examine what the MMF UK has done to progress these initiatives.

Educate

There is a significant series of documents and publications on the MMF website or available through it, allowing members access to key information. There is a code of practice outlining what managers should and should not do in representing their artists/creators. This is obviously important for establishing standards of service which artists and managers can expect from each other. It should be noted that within the scope of our research, although other representative organizations in music address key issues in the workplace (e.g. equality, diversity, inclusion), almost no other representative organization in music (apart from other MMFs) had a code of practice presented in full on their websites. There is also a series of manager profiles giving practical examples of manager activity and advice for emerging professionals. Further, there are many MMF publications listed from documents on digital income to their most recent book, *Essentials of Music Management*, which has been necessary reading for all those involved in writing this book.

Additionally, there are notifications for the training courses run each year for members (e.g. digital marketing, essentials and mechanics of music management) as well as the Accelerator programme which annually supports more than 20 emerging managers including the possibility of 12-month grants. The website states that the Accelerator programme has resulted in at least £9.4 million of generated turnover for the artists represented by managers involved in programme participation. Accelerator participants have worked on eight UK top 40 singles and 13 UK top 40 albums, including a number 1. Addressing equality and diversity within this initiative is also key. Forty-two per cent of Accelerator participants to date have been female, while 43% are from Black, Asian or ethnic backgrounds. Over 50% of participants are based outside of London (Webb et al., 2022).

There is also a range of resources available for anyone (not just MMF members) to access on the MMF website, which is obviously valuable to those generally interested in the management of music creators; however, access to its events, network and more extensive resources are via the members' portal.

Innovate

While the Accelerator programme is an educative initiative, it is also innovative. Funding has been secured from YouTube Music, Arts Council England, Creative Scotland and the Scottish Music Industry Association (accessed 6/7/25). The MMF in the UK has also been instrumental in helping to set up several other representative organizations where this has been thought necessary. They were closely involved with the establishment of EMMA, for example, which brought the European MMF organizations together to generate a stronger, singular voice within the EU. Additionally, as we have seen, in 2018 the MMF was instrumental in setting up the Council of Music Makers (CMM) establishing a collective voice for all those working with performers/creators (Hanley, 2018a). Recent CMM activity includes raising issues with the UK government over the limited engagement offered to creators in AI cross-industry discussions (Dredge, 2023a). In this instance, the MMF recognizes the strength in a united front for all creators and their representation when trying to represent their members' interests and has taken action to address this.

Advocate

Beyond the above, the MMF has worked with many of the musician/creator organizations (e.g. MU, FAC, Ivors Academy) to address developments such as the EU Copyright Directive (European Commission, 2019). MMF research has been utilized in parliamentary investigations such as the low royalty return rate to creators from streaming (UK Govt, 2021) and the problems associated with Brexit. The MMF were part of the Fan Fair Alliance campaign to combat online ticket touting, producing their own guide for managers and artists on the subject. They were also a key part of the 'Let the Music Play' movement fronted by UK Music, which lobbied the UK government for crucial financial support during the COVID lockdown (UK Music, 2022). Their website also hosts statements and publications on topics as diverse as AI (interim guide), childcare for music professionals (working with PiPA - Parents and Carers in Performing Arts (PIPA, n.d.) and mental health issues for artists and managers.

MMF UK has a management team of nine persons in different roles and a board of 15 professional artist managers who are all MMF members. They charge a fixed membership fee on a monthly or annual basis and offer a reduced rate for the under-30s. As already identified, they do not currently accept self-managing artists as members.

EMMA

The European Music Managers Alliance, founded in 2018, currently comprises the MMF organizations from 13 European nations (UK, Ireland, France, Spain, Germany, Poland, Denmark, Belgium, The Netherlands, Norway, Sweden, Finland and Estonia). This effectively gives many of the key European music markets a collective voice on artist/creator management within Europe and a platform from which to address EU legislation. The EMMA website also lists three key objectives – licensing and fair remuneration; public policy; and education and research (EMMA, n.d.).

Licensing and fair remuneration

Working alongside other organizations, EMMA has been involved in campaigns to spotlight the limited remuneration for creators from streaming services (EMMA, 2020). One example here is the statement made by EMMA, reported by MMF UK, which addresses European governments and requests the full implementation of the EU copyright directive in an effort to redress the balance of payments in favour of the artists and therefore also the managers (MMF UK, 2020). Additionally, creating partnerships with organizations involved in developing technologies such as that with BeatBread opens potential new income streams for managers (Paine, 2024c)

Public policy

EMMA is pursuing a new European vision on touring to address, amongst other things, the visa, tax and carnet issues which make cross-border touring unnecessarily complex. Additionally, EMMA is among the partners in the Keychange gender-equality initiative which has been working across all sectors of the music industries since 2018 (Keychange, n.d.; Music Week, 2024). Keychange is examined further in Chapter 8.

Education and research

There are several indicators of the work which EMMA is undertaking in these areas. The EMMpower initiative supported by a three-year grant from Creative Europe, aims to provide new market research, mentoring, networking, professional development and advanced training opportunities (Dredge, 2023b). As an example of the work being conducted as part of this drive, the *Music Management in Europe* report (Calkins et al., 2023) gives a detailed analysis of music managers operating in the EU and some of the issues they are facing (this mirrors work already published by MMF UK). Additionally, EMMA has a YouTube channel with a series of masterclasses, genre market studies and territorial market spotlights, which are publicly available for viewing.

Per Kviman, Chair of EMMA, echoed MMF UK's Annabella Coldrick's comment on the formation of the CMM when he stated one of their key aims in our interview with him: 'We believe it's very important that management and the artist have a strong voice within the industry. We don't want it to be that label organizations or publisher organizations are talking for the artists when they really are not connected to the artist in the same way we are' (Kviman, 2022).

Additional information is available on the EMMA websites and social media platforms including those of the individual EU MMFs.

MMF US

Formed in 1993, MMF US has a central administrative hub (based in New York) and a series of further regional subgroups (known as chapters) in Los Angeles, Miami and Chicago, with new chapters opening in Nashville, Atlanta, Austin and Boston. Contacts for the New York, Los Angeles and Chicago chapters are listed on the MMF US website (MMF US, n.d.). MMF US is a member of the IMMF with Neeta Ragoowansi becoming President of the US organization in January 2020 (and now also President of the IMMF, since July 2024). It is the leading trade association for professional artist managers and self-managed artists in the USA and is a registered not-for-profit organization. It has similar objectives to MMF UK and EMMA. Its website lists four key fundamentals. These are: advocacy & representation; diversity; education; and inclusion and safety. Again, examining these in relation to their activities we find the following:

Advocacy and representation

To further the interests of managers and their artists in all fields of the music industry, including live performance, recording and music publishing matters providing a collective voice to lobby and affect policy change for a fairer and more transparent music industry

(MMF US, n.d.)

MMF US actively advocates on many key issues facing managers and the music industries in North America. These include (but are not limited to) AI, ticketing, digital and tech companies, radio, tax regulation and freedom of expression. The organization has an established advocacy committee. Under 'news and advocacy' on the website there is a series of articles on issues affecting artists/creators and managers which the organization is taking forward. Included here are items on the MMF US support of proposed legislation which is currently making its way through the American government. This include the Fans First Act, which 'aims to ban the sale of fake tickets, make deceptive marketing illegal, require transparent ticket pricing, and establish clear penalties for violations' (MMF US). Also highlighted is the MMF US support for the American Music Fairness Act, which addresses the issue that 'the U.S. is the only democratic nation in the world that doesn't compensate artists when their music is played on AM/FM radio'. There are further articles on other policies which MMF US is engaged in and is attempting to lever into legislation, demonstrating recent political activity.

Diversity

'To provide a diverse forum to discuss the issues and problems facing the music industry manager'

(MMF US, n.d.)

There is evidence on the MMF US website to support this stated initiative. The website lists a series of online seminars and masterclasses, many of which address diversity topics including, for example, 'Navigating neurodivergence and disability in music management'. (See also Perspectives as part of 'Inclusion and safety' below.)

Education

'To educate and disseminate information regarding areas of interest to managers – creating continuous professional development within an ever-evolving music industry'

(MMF US, n.d.)

Again, similar to the MMF in the UK, the US organization hosts (or links to) an extensive series of seminars on key issues in areas such as publishing, record labels, marketing, royalty, distribution, technology and other subjects. They have a designated YouTube channel for this and also work with Music Ally to provide music marketing analysis. A series of publications are also listed. Where the MMF in the UK often commissions and prints its own research/documents, MMF US appears to focus more on already existing documents (e.g. Donald Passman's standard industry text, *All You Need to Know about the Music Business*). While a code of conduct might appear in the section of the site restricted for members, it does not appear to be in the public access information.

Inclusion and safety

'To promote an inclusive and safe environment for artist managers to connect and grow their careers – facilitating both in person and virtual events where our community has the opportunity to learn, share and connect with one another'

(MMF US, n.d.)

MMF US hosts a webinar series called 'Perspectives', bringing voices and ideas from a variety of genres, races, ethnicities, backgrounds and identities, from all aspects of the music industry, ranging from managers and self-managed artists to professionals. It also provides a series of online seminars and masterclasses including MMF US Presents: Navigating the Emotional Landscape of the Music Industry: A Guide to Thriving.

The organisation also hosts summit events (US national) as well as regional summits and networking events for face-to-face group meetings in the key locations where each chapter is based, consisting of keynotes, panels, presentations and networking opportunities. Beyond this there is also a range of resources and member benefits including a dedicated member portal with access to benefits, event information, a member directory and additional resources.

MMF Canada

The website for MMF Canada states five goals of education, networking (Doole, 2024), lobbying on behalf of members, developing their managers' businesses, and building the association and its value to members. They hold award shows (Bliss, 2019) and, similar to MMF US and UK, they have an extensive set of online panels, masterclasses and information sessions, sometimes working together with MMF US but equally with MMF organisations elsewhere (MMF Canada, n.d.).

Similar to MMF UK, they have a published a code of conduct for managers on their website. MMF Canada, additionally, have a statement on 'expected competences and occupational standards', which outlines the knowledge, abilities and expertise they identify as vital for artist managers. Unlike MMF UK, but in line with MMF US, the Canadian organization states that it does work with self-managing artists.

There is also evidence that MMF Canada is addressing EDI issues. It has an anti-racism and equality committee and in its mission statement it acknowledges that 'there is a historical lack of representation of black, indigenous and people of colour within the sector and our team works diligently to bridge those gaps in a non-performative way'. There is also a significant list of anti-racism resources which they draw attention to.

They run mentorship programmes not dissimilar to MMF UK. The 2022 mentor/mentee information lists ten of each with clear evidence of diversity and gender balance given the profiles of those selected. As with MMF US, it also has an advocacy committee.

Music management as a business across the world is usually conducted by SMEs (small to medium enterprises). These are companies often with less than five employees. MMF Canada recognises that artist management in their territory is no different to this with over 80% of its members operating as small companies with one to four employees

Interestingly, it publishes a list of 62 nations with MMF organizations. The list has links to those which have active websites – 15 in total. These closely match the sites which our research also found to be the most active.

One point perhaps worth mentioning here (although it is not directly connected to the work of MMF Canada) is that, similar to a broadcasting regulation in France, the Canadian government has ruled that a certain percentage of music broadcast on domestic radio and television should be of Canadian origin. This may help to create media opportunities for Canadian performers and songwriters and may therefore be of advantage to Canadian managers and the domestic music market in comparison to other nations where this is not the case (Govt of Canada, 2022). MMF Canada informed us that this may not have so significant an impact on its members, but it is part of the national music landscape.

AAM Australia

Similarly to other MMFs, the Australian organization lists advocacy, professional development, networking, and health and well-being amongst its stated aims (AAM, n.d.). Its objectives further discuss protecting, promoting and developing artist managers. Its 14-person board demonstrates gender balance. MMF Australia are trying to protect and support its own artists with 'Michael's Rule' being a key part of its strategy (founding member Michael McMartin suggested that every international artist touring or playing concerts in Australia should feature an Australian artist among their opening acts). Interestingly, this perhaps can be seen to 'mirror' within the live sphere the ruling in Canada and France (in national broadcasting) that certain percentages of the music played on radio and TV should be of domestic origin.

Alongside MMF UK and EMMA, the Australian MMF is engaged in research – for example, having commissioned the University of Melbourne to survey their members. Published in 2022 and available on its website, some of the key findings of the survey include 62% of respondents having university degrees, 60% being male, 38% being female and 2% gender-variant/non-conforming. Seventy-five per cent were working outside music to supplement their incomes. These statistics broadly replicate those established by research elsewhere in the MMF network (Calkins et al., 2023; MMF UK, 2020, 2021). We will further examine these data in the subsequent chapters (4–6).

One of the more striking outcomes, however, is that a significant number of Australian managers reported health issues relating to the pressures of the role (University of Melbourne/AAM, 2022), an issue which is examined in Chapter 9 of this book. A further research paper on its site examines the potential social return on investment for artist managers.

AAM has an extensive list of conferences, support meetings and awards ceremonies which it hosts and/or participates in. These include panels addressing managers' health issues. There is also evidence of engagement in government policy-making.

AAM also 'acknowledges the traditional Aboriginal and Torres Strait Islander owners of the country throughout Australia and pay our respects to them, their culture and their Elders past and present', demonstrating diversity awareness.

MMF Aotearoa (New Zealand)

Taking its name from the indigenous language word for their country, the MMF in New Zealand is engaged in many similar activities to other MMFs elsewhere. Apart from its bespoke website, it also has Facebook and Instagram pages showing considerable recent and historic activity. As with MMF organizations in the UK and Australia, it has a stated code of conduct. Its main website carries news bulletins, information on workshops and panels (NZMC, 2024). There is clear evidence of engagement with, and inclusion of, indigenous culture with many of the speakers, panel members and the executive committee coming from an indigenous background.

Their mentorship programme appears to have 24 industry mentors, again demonstrating diversity in terms of gender and cultural origin. They appear to interact with other music bodies in the country including the New Zealand Music Commission, musicians' organizations and government.

AMA France

AMA (l'Alliance des Managers d'Artistes) in France lists 42 member companies on its home website (AMA, n.d.). The management team (president, treasurer and secretary) are all female, supporting the AMA's diversity statement on its 'Our values' pages, claiming that it 'fights against all forms of discrimination, and advocates and claims diversity and difference as the basis of a wealth essential to the development of creativity. We defend diversity through practices and different approaches to our profession.' It further states that it has engaged in negotiation with the French government to defend the rights of managers, notably with the Ministry of Culture.

Regarding education, they offer training courses in conjunction with SACEM. It also offers a form of mentorship – one-hour meetings to discuss a particular project or issue which is then taken forward by a designated AMA member with relevant experience. There is also a series of conversations (currently 14) with key industry figures which can be found on YouTube but this can only be accessed by members. An application form is given for artists seeking managers which they can complete and await responses from AMA members.

AMA also work closely with PAM, a representative organization for all music activity in south-east France and Corsica (PAM, 2024).

Similar to Canada, French government legislation rules that 40% of music broadcast on radio must be in the French language (BBC, 2015). Introduced in 1996, this is seen to give French artists a promotional advantage within their own territory, a law which may be viewed as being of benefit to French managers operating inside France.

IMUC Germany

IMUC is the German organization for artist managers. It lists its three key objectives as to educate, promote and represent. This is expanded upon in ten goals detailed elsewhere. These include representation of its members' interests; education of the public, as well as their own members; provision of example contracts; and the development of international relations (IMUC, n.d.).

It has a published *gütesiegel* (effectively a code of conduct) for its members. This includes one item which indicates 25% as a commission rate – slightly above the 20% taken as standard in the UK. In relation to EDI issues (at least in terms of the balance of gender representation), the board of seven has three female members. Eighty-one members are listed on the website of which 20 are female.

The website lists news items, conferences, workshops and events (IMUC and EMMA). Similar to AMA, it has an arbitration service for members to help resolve disputes. Where some MMFs set their membership fee as a percentage of their members' turnover, the membership fee for IMUC appears to be €300 for all members.

MMF Sweden

The website for MMF Sweden states that it is active in lobbying government at national and European levels. Similar to many EU MMFs, it carries a code of conduct. The website lists 66 members. The website states the organization's statutes or terms of business, one of which appears to indicate a standard membership fee (rather than a percentage of business turnover).

The organization appears to be funded by its members and by partnerships with other music businesses in Sweden. The board of ten shows evidence of gender diversity with 40% female membership.

A series of seminars and information sessions is listed. Many of these are online and are run centrally by EMMA.

NEMAA Norway

Rather than an MMF, Norway has NEMAA – an organization for artist managers and booking agents. Non-profit-making, its stated aims are education, networking and advocacy. Its website is not so extensive but states that the organization has over 80 member companies and lists 69 of these. Membership fees appear to be based on a percentage of business turnover. Students on relevant courses can join (apparently at a reduced rate). The Facebook page carries information on (mostly online) events run by EMMA (of which NEMAA is a member) and there are also notifications for events in Norway.

MMF Finland

Information available on the website for MMF Finland includes the names of the seven members of its 'government' (board). Forty-four member companies are named and the figure for total membership is given as 60 (MMF Finland, n.d.). Originally Finnish managers were predominantly overseeing incoming international artists but in the last ten years or so there have been increasing numbers of domestic acts managed by members (Immonen, 2020).

As we will see in Chapter 5, our interview with Virpi Immonen, Chair of MMF Finland, further confirmed that the Finnish organization was part of a Europe-wide mentoring scheme to support emerging management talent. She also mentioned the significant level of government support for culture in Finland adding, 'I think Scandinavian countries are ahead of other European countries regarding the government support and also how they are supporting all the export work'.

IMMF (International Music Managers Forum)

The potential importance of a globally inclusive organization to represent national MMFs and artist management generally is reasonably clear if one examines the contributions which IFPI (recorded music) and CISAC (music publishing) have already made within their own sectors, even if we only consider their work in quantifying the scale and value of their respective sectors internationally. The IMMF has been aiming to support artist management on a world stage over the last 15 years as new president Neeta Ragoowansi states:

> The International Music Managers Forum (IMMF) is a global umbrella network comprising approximately 50 national and regional associations for artist managers and self-managed artists. Rooted in the principles of fairness, transparency, and access to opportunity, IMMF has historically supported artist manager associations through advocacy, education, and promotion of cross-border collaboration, while also helping to inspire and nurture emerging organizations.
> (Ragoowansi, 2025)

To be clear, while certain national MMFs have staff working full-time for their organization, the IMMF is primarily run by those who already work for one of those national MMFs and are therefore effectively managing the global network on a largely voluntary basis collectively. Despite these structural limitations, the IMMF has stated its intention to 'continue to evolve and adapt'. As of July 2024, under the leadership of Ragoowansi as its incoming president, the organization has focused on the objectives of 'renewing its commitment to supporting and serving its members, enhancing and updating communication of its activities to the wider industry, and strengthening internal capacity that reflects its expanding impact' (Ragoowansi, 2025). During our interview with her, Ragoowansi then went into greater detail:

> Building on the foundation of my predecessors, IMMF is now expanding its strategic focus to include improved digital engagement – including highlighting the approaches, challenges, and insights of artist managers and self-managed artists from around the world, reflecting diverse market perspectives – as a way to share practical strategies, surface innovative ideas, and foster enhanced peer-to-peer learning. This sits alongside increased access to learning resources and connections with an emphasis on practical training tools and services, and stronger engagement with policymakers and industry stakeholders – efforts aimed at better supporting the evolving role of artist managers and the artist business in a global music economy.
> (Ragoowansi, 2025)

The IMMF mission statements are listed on its website as:

- Support PLURALITY & DIVERSITY in the cultural and entertainment industries
- Deliver EDUCATION & TRAINING for lifelong learning, and the nurturing of future generations, in order to improve and consolidate the professionalism and expertise of artist businesses (SMEs)
- Foster FAIRNESS & TRANSPARENCY
- Nurture opportunities to raise artists ACCESS TO FINANCE

These reasonably replicate the three common key objectives which many national MMFs identify (education, advocacy and networking) although perhaps with more of a focus on EDI issues. Ragoowansi agrees:

> Our role is to support our national and regional manager associations across the globe and to foster connections between them so that they can share knowledge, strengthen their communities, and learn from one another. Whether formally articulated or not, many of these forums are grounded in the same three core pillars: education, networking, and advocacy.
> (Ragoowansi, 2025)

As we discussed previously in this chapter, many of the IMMF member organizations have broadened their definition to serve not only artist managers but also self-managed artists. The IMMF itself supports this:

> This shift reflects a practical reality: there simply aren't enough managers for the number of artists out there. Increasingly, artists are managing their own careers and running their own businesses, and many are doing it successfully. Given that, we thought it made sense that as we build educational modules and provide networking opportunities, we [should] make it accessible to the self-managed artists as well. It's important for those artists to have a forum where they can access professionalised business resources and connect with peers.
> (Ragoowansi, 2025)

On the topic of the number of MMF organizations involved, there is apparently a move towards expansion, with the IMMF 'helping to build new MMFs in places where there are not [currently] MMFs' (Ragoowansi, 2025).

The IMMF, therefore, is in a position of change and development. This could result in an organization which is better prepared and positioned to take forward the voice of the manager and artist on a global stage. If that happens, it could perhaps (similarly to IFPI/CISAC) create a different perspective of artist management and potentially raise awareness of the issues faced internationally.

Analysis of the MMFs' Collective Successes and Ongoing Objectives

Geographical representation

Our research indicates that music management representative organizations in different territories have evolved in slightly different ways and each has its own priorities, concerns and identity. Although broadly similar in direction, each must operate within its own specific geographical, political, economic and social framework. Equally, although they work collectively with other MMFs, they must act to represent the differing requirements of their boards and memberships. Some are more developed than others, appearing to update their online profile more frequently or holding more regular events.

We contacted as many of the MMF organizations as we could locate. We did not always get a response. Around 60 MMFs are named or identified online across relevant websites relating to artist management representation. Within these we found clear evidence of the existence of 42 national and international MMF organizations in total; 18 of those have bespoke, functioning websites, a further six are operating through social media or professional networking platforms (Facebook, Instagram, Linkedin), but the remaining 18 do not appear to have an active online presence. Some of those sites we did locate had not been updated for some time. While this cannot be interpreted as meaning the organizations in question are inactive, it does make cross-checking quite complex. In total, we were able to speak directly with 12 MMF organizations (listed in Table 3.4), mostly operating in key music territories. These conversations proved to be very helpful and informative. Further information was located through the media, journals and our own interviews with individual managers.

It may be that the somewhat limited scale of MMFs with active online visibility is simply a timescale/development issue. These organizations are only around 30 years old. CISAC (116 nations represented) and the IFPI (70 nations represented), which each have almost a century of existence behind them in representing music publishing and recorded music, respectively, do not have complete global representation or statistics for many nations across the world.

In total, what our research found does appear to represent a reasonably comprehensive package of advocacy, support and guidance for MMF members and the wider group of those interested in artist management across the nations where these organisations are visible and active. Additionally, as we shall see in the next few chapters, those managers we were able to interview generally felt the MMF organizations offered a valuable range of benefits and support. However, the most active MMFs are mostly operating in Europe and English-speaking nations. Broader international representation is still emerging both in the individual nations and globally in different shapes and forms.

MMF objectives

The national and international management organizations have broadly similar stated primary objectives (education, sector representation, business development). Having examined these in this chapter, we can see, firstly, that many of the more developed MMFs have significant provision of online support and education sources as well as regular events and training programmes to update their members' awareness and skills (notable examples include MMF UK, MMF US, EMMA, AAM Aus). Secondly, there is also clear evidence of advocacy – representation at national and international levels in negotiation with government and with partner organizations to progress national objectives (e.g. MMF UK, EMMA, AAM, MMF US). Thirdly, we have seen evidence of MMFs assisting development of their members' businesses. Examining mentorship schemes, for example, we have found many organizations which have established these to the significant benefit of emerging managers (e.g. MMF NZ, MMF Canada, EMMA, MMF UK).

Broader initiatives (EDI, codes of conduct, mental health) vary considerably between nations. Certain MMFs emphasize these issues. A code of conduct has been published by the MMF in the UK, Canada, New Zealand, Germany and Sweden, amongst others. To take another example, the Canadian, Australian and New Zealand MMF websites carry statements recognizing minorities and specifically the indigenous population of their countries. While each national organization might have different priorities, the opportunity to further align their objectives (if this is advantageous) exists, although having a single overarching well-developed representative global body might be of assistance here.

Again, we should stress that these visible activities, often evidenced by those we spoke with directly, are predominantly happening within the more developed, western nations. We are not able to confirm MMF organizations developing these types of initiatives in the South American, Asian or African nations, for example. In conversation with the IMMF, however, activity from MMF representatives in Zimbabwe, Mexico and Saudi Arabia was mentioned, so it is possible that, over time, we will see further growth in visible MMF activity in other territories.

Conclusions

Scale

The primary strength here may simply be in numbers. Having grown global membership to a total of over 3800 managers gives the collective MMF organizations reasonable legitimacy in representing artist and creator management worldwide. A significant number of the key recorded music, live events and music publishing markets have a national and active MMF; hence, combined, they represent artists and creators in the same commercially important territories as the major concert promoters, record and publishing companies. That representation is generally present and engaged, notably in the established European, North American and Antipodean markets.

This growth has allowed the MMFs to become more vocal in their support for creators and managers. As we have seen in this chapter, recent campaigns at European regional, national and continental level, for example, have seen the MMFs taking action on behalf of managers and artists, gaining media attention and getting the voice and message of the creators across the table (Paine, 2021; UK Gov, 2024; IMPALA, 2024).

However, MMFs in some of the recently developing marketplaces (e.g. South Korea, Japan) either do not yet exist or are constituted quite differently, reflecting the local music environment. Of the ten highest grossing publishing royalty nations in the CISAC chart, one does not yet have an MMF-type representative organization (South Korea). Three out of ten do no appear to have an artist management representative organisation when we consider the IFPI chart for recorded music revenue (China, South Korea, Brazil). As discussed earlier in this chapter, this possibly relates partly to the way that artists are developed in these nations and this could change over time.

Global representation

The IMMF was initially created as an umbrella organization bringing together the MMF organizations across the world. As can be seen from its website, while this organization could perhaps have been more historically active, this may be about to change. EMMA, initially created to collectively represent the individual European national MMFs, has grown to include organizations outside of the geographical boundaries of Europe (notably the Australian and New Zealand MMFs, which are now members) but does not include all of the most significant organizations (e.g. MMF US). Hence, at time of going to print, collective MMF representation at an international level might be considered to be incomplete or could yet be more developed.

However, given that other major sectors *do* have a single organization for global representation (CISAC for music publishing, IFPI for recorded music), it could be of value for artist managers to have that single collective voice which could speak on their behalf at an international level.

To take one emerging issue, where concert promoter organizations are growing to become multinational (e.g. AEG, Live Nation) and live events have been identified as one of the more polluting music activities at a time of global ecological challenge (Corner, 2021; Paine, 2024a), there could be considerable purpose for such an organization in artist and manager representation.

Equally, where performers previously may only have had representation from Musicians' Union organizations in governmental debate and policy-making, the advent of an alliance of managers (often regarded as the toughest negotiators in the music industries because they have to negotiate with every other sector) with a unified international position might be regarded as a significant step forward.

Data

Tracking the scale of the sector (metrics) is complex. The total number of managers operating professionally in music globally is difficult to approximate as many have not yet joined the representative organizations in their respective nations. Those organizations do not always publish their member numbers and there are nations where successful artists are being managed but where no MMF body currently exists. No figure appears to exist for the total income for the sector (global manager income), although it could be argued that since the manager is responsible for every aspect of an artist's income, the combined total of global recorded music income, music publishing income, live events income and merchandise would give an approximation.

References

AAM (Association of Artist Managers Australia) (n.d.). Available at: www.aam.org.au/ (accessed 26 November 2024).

Adams, T. (2022) K-everything, the rise and rise of Korean culture. *The Guardian*. Available at: www.theguardian.com/world/2022/sep/04/korea-culture-k-pop-music-film-tv-hallyu-v-and-a (accessed 7 July 2025).

AFM (American Federation of Musicians) (n.d.) Our Musicians: Symphonic. Available at: www.afm.org/ (accessed 26 November 2024).

AIM (Association of Independent Music – UK) (n.d.). Available at: www.aim.org.uk/ (accessed 26 November 2024).

Allen, P. (2022) *Artist Management for the Music Business: Manage Your Career in Music: Manage the Music Careers of Others*, 5th edn. Focal Press, New York and London.

AMA (Alliance des Managers D'Artistes, MMF France) (n.d.) Alliance des managers d'artistes. Available at: www.ama-france.com/ (accessed 26 November 2024).

AMP (Association of Music Producers – US) (n.d.). Available at: www.associationofmusicproducers.org/ (accessed 7 July 2025).

Anderton, C., Hannam, J. and Hopkins, J. (2022) *Music Management*. Marketing & PR. Sage, London.

ASCAP (American Society of Composers, Authors and Publishers, US) (n.d.) *Annual Report 2024*. Available at: www.ascap.com/~/media/site-pages/annual-report/2023/2023-ascap-annual-report.pdf (accessed 13 June 2025).

BBC (2015) French rebel over music language quotas. Available at: www.bbc.co.uk/news/world-europe-34422307 (accessed 26 November 2024).

Bliss, K. (2019) Canada's Music Managers Forum, CIMA announce honorees for 2019 awards shows. Billboard. Available at: www.billboard.com/music/music-news/canada-music-managers-forum-indie-music-assn-set-awards-shows-8508479/ (accessed 17 November 2024).

BMI (Broadcast Music Inc., US) (2024a) Annual Report 2023. Available at: www.bmi.com/pdfs/publications/2023/bmi-annual-report-2023.pdf (accessed 29 September 2024).

BMI (Broadcast Music Inc., US) (2024b) BMI announces record-breaking revenue and royalty distributions. Available at: www.bmi.com/news/entry/bmi-announces-record-breaking-revenue-and-royaltydistributions#:~:text=In%20addition%2C%20BMI%20once%20again,rights%20organization%20in%20the%20world (accessed 28 September 2024).

BPI (British Phonographic Industry, UK) (n.d.). Available at: www.bpi.co.uk (accessed 22 September 2024).

Calkins, T.III., Berkers, P., Wijngaarden, Y. and Kimenai, F. (2023) *Music Management in Europe*. EMMA (European Music Managers Association). Available at: emma.community/wp-content/uploads/2024/01/EMMA_Music-Management-in-Europe-Report.pdf/ (accessed 26 September 2024).

CISAC (Confederation of Societies of Authors and Composers, Global) (2024) *Annual Report 2024*. Available at: www.cisac.org/Newsroom/annual-reports/2024-annual-report (accessed 26 September 2024).

CISAC (Confederation of Societies of Authors and Composers, Global) (n.d.) *Global Collections Report 2024*. Available at: www.cisac.org/services/reports-and-research/cisac-annual-report (accessed 13 June 2025).

Cloonan, M. (2012) Selling the experience: The world-views of British concert promoters. *Creative Industries Journal* 5, 1&2. DOI: 10.1386/cij.5.1-2.151_1?needAccess=true. (accessed 5 May 2025).

CMM (Council of Music Makers) (n.d.) Association of Music Producers. Available at: councilmusicmakers.org/ (accessed 26 November 2024).

Coldrick, A. (2020) Questions on artist management. Interview by Allan Dumbreck [Zoom], 7 April.

Corner, A. (2021) Time to shake things up: Music industry confronts climate crisis as gigs resume. *The Guardian*. Available at: www.theguardian.com/music/2021/apr/27/music-industry-confronts-climate-crisis-gigs-resume (accessed 1 December 2024).

CPA (Concert Promoters Association) (n.d.) Concert Promoters Association. Available at: concertpromotersassociation.co.uk/ (accessed 26 September 2024).

Dalugdug, M. (2025) SACEM's payouts to composers and publishers rose 12% to nearly $1.5 bn in 2024. *Music Business Worldwide*. Available at: www.musicbusinessworldwide.com/sacems-payouts-to-composers-and-publishers-rose-12-to-nearly-1-5bn-in-2024-on-strong-collections-outside-france/ (accessed 7 July 2025).

Doole, K. (2024) Billboard Canada. Available at: ca.billboard.com/music-news-digest-zoon-music-pei-awards-musicounts-more (accessed 7 July 2025).

Dredge, S. (2023a) Music creators' body criticises UK government over AI roundtable. Music:)ally. Available at: musically.com/2023/11/21/music-creators-body-criticises-uk-government-over-ai-roundtable/ (accessed 7 July 2025).

Dredge, S. (2023b) Management body EMMA launches EMMpower initiative in Europe. Music:)ally. Available at: musically.com/2023/03/03/management-body-emma-launches-emmpower-initiative-in-europe/ (accessed 7 July 2025).

EMMA (2020) Request to EU governments regarding EU copyright directive. Available at: www.themmf.net/news/european-music-managers-alliance-issues-new-statement-calling-for-streaming-reforms/ (accessed 12 October 2024).

EMMA (2024) YouTube channel. Available at: www.youtube.com/channel/UCMLbgrYuxD6lKEpz1wpmDzw/videos (accessed 16 October 2024).

EMMA (European Music Managers Alliance) (n.d.) The European Music Managers Alliance (EMMA). Available at: @emma. community/ (accessed 7 July 2025).

European Commission (2019) EU copyright directive. Available at: digital-strategy.ec.europa.eu/en/policies/copyright-legislation (accessed 26 September 2024).

Findlay, B. (2024) Personal interview.

Fuhr, M. (2015) *Globalization and Popular Music in South Korea: Sounding Out K-Pop*. Routledge, New York. DOI: 10.4324/9781315733081.

GEMA (Gesellschaft für musikalische Aufführungs) (2025) *Annual Report 2024*. Available at: https://www.gema.de/en/w/annual-report-2024-press-release (accessed 8 October 2024).

Govt of Canada (2022) CRTC maintains support for Canadian artists on commercial radio. Available at: www.canada.ca/en/radio-television-telecommunications/news/2022/12/crtc-maintains-support-for-canadian-artists-on-commercial-radio.html (accessed 5 July 2025).

Gronow, P. and Saunio, I. (1999) *An International History of the Recording Industry*. Cassell, London & New York.

Hanley, J. (2018a) The current model is failing future talent: New coalition to fight for music makers' rights. *Music Week*. Available at: www.musicweek.com/talent/read/the-current-model-is-failing-future-talent-new-coalition-to-fight-for-music-makers-rights/073828 (accessed 5 July 2025).

Hanley, J. (2018b) AIF renews call for investigation into Live Nation's festival 'dominance. *Music Week*. Available at: www.musicweek.com/live/read/aif-renews-call-for-investigation-into-live-nation-s-festival-dominance/073614 (accessed 5 May 2025).

Hwang, A. (2024) K-pop management innovation changes global music industry. Available at: www.korea.net/NewsFocus/Opinion/view?articleId=254952 (accessed 5 May 2025).

IFPI (International Federation of Phonographic Industries) (n.d.) IFPI making music thrive. Available at: www.ifpi.org (accessed 5 May 2025).

Immonen, V. (2020) Questions on artist management. Interview by Allan Dumbreck [Zoom], 6 May.

IMPALA (2024) Call for changes to withholding tax reduce barriers for touring Artists. Available at: https://impalamusic.org/call-for-changes-to-witholding-tax-to-reduce-barriers-for-touring-artists/ (accessed 5 July 2025).

IMUC (MMF Germany) (n.d.) IMUC. Available at: www.ivorsacademy.com (accessed 5 July 2025).

Ivors Academy (UK) (n.d.) We are The Ivors Academy, champions of songwriters and composers. Available at: www.ivorsacademy.com

JAMES (Joint Audio Media Education Support) (n.d.) JAMES - The Industry Seal of Approval. Available at: www.jamesonline.org.uk/ (accessed 5 July 2025).

Johansson, O. (2010) Beyond ABBA: The globalization of Swedish popular music. Available at: onlinelibrary.wiley.com/doi/abs/10.1111/j.1949-8535.2010.00016.x (accessed 21 April 2025).

Keychange (n.d.) The manifesto. Available at: www.keychange.eu/themanifesto (accessed 5 July 2025).

Kviman, P. (2022) Questions on artist management. Interview by Allan Dumbreck [Zoom], 16 May.

Lindvall, H. (2011) K-pop: How South Korea turned around its music scene. *The Guardian*. Available at: www.theguardian.com/media/organgrinder/2011/apr/20/k-pop-south-korea-music-market (accessed 5 July 2025).

Lindvall, H. (2015) PRS for Music takes legal action against SoundCloud streaming Service. *The Guardian*. Available at: www.theguardian.com/technology/2015/aug/27/prs-for-music-takes-legal-action-against-soundcloud (accessed 1 December 2024).

LIVE (2024) DCMS takes on grassroots music venues investigation. Available at: livemusic.biz/dcms-takes-on-grassroots-music-venues-investigation (accessed 18 November 2024).

LIVE (LIVE music Industry Venues and Entertainment, UK) (n.d.) LIVE is the voice of the UK's contemporary LIVE music sector. Available at: livemusic.biz (accessed 5 July 2025).

Live DMA (2024) Calling for mentees for our newest start programme! Available at: live-dma.eu/ (accessed 8 October 2024).

Martin, D. (2023) Questions on artist management. Interview by Allan Dumbreck [Zoom], 22 December.

MCPS (Mechanical Copyright Protection Society, UK) (n.d.) PRS for music. Available at: www.prsformusic.com/help/help-with-joining-as-a-member/what-is-mcps (accessed 5 July 2025).

MED (Music Education Directory) (2024). Available at: www.jamesonline.org.uk/jamesresources/med_2024/ (accessed 8 October 2024).

MMF Canada (Music Managers Forum, Canada) (n.d.) The collective voice for Canadian Music Managers and Self-Managed Artists. Available at: mmfcanada.ca/ (accessed 8 October 2024).

MMF Finland (Music Managers Forum, Finland) (n.d.) Music Managers Forum Finland. Available at: mmffinland.com/ (accessed 5 July 2025).

MMF UK (2020) European Music Managers Alliance issues new statement calling for streaming reforms. Available at: themmf.net/news/european-music-managers-alliance-issues-new-statement-calling-for-streaming-reforms/ (accessed 14 August 2025).

MMF UK (2021) Managing Expectations. Available at: themmf.net/wp-content/uploads/2023/10/MMF-Managing-Expectations-Report-2021.pdf (accessed 22 October 2024).

MMF UK (Music Managers Forum website, UK) (n.d.) MMF UK. Available at: www.themmf.net (accessed 8 October 2024).

MMF US (Music Managers Forum, USA) (n.d.) MMF - US. Available at: www.mmfus.com/ (accessed 5 July 2025).

Morley, P. (2007) Obituary: Tony Wilson. *The Guardian*, 13 August 2007. Available at: www.theguardian.com/news/2007/aug/13/guardianobituaries.media (accessed 5 July 2025).

Morley, P. (2022) *From Manchester with Love: The Life and Opinions of Tony Wilson*. Faber & Faber, London.

MPA (Music Publishers Association, UK) (n.d.) MPA Music Publishers Association. Available at: www.mpaonline.org.uk (accessed 5 July 2025).

MPG (Music Producers Guild) (n.d.) MPG. Available at: mvpg.org.uk/ (accessed 5 July 2025).

Musicians' Union (n.d.) History of the MU. Available at: musiciansunion.org.uk/about-the-mu/history-of-the-mu (accessed 5 May 2025).

Music Week (2024) Keychange issues 5-year progress report & updated manifesto for 'equitable and sustainable industry. Available at: www.musicweek.com/talent/read/keychange-issues-5-year-progress-report-updated-manifesto-for-equitable-and-sustainable-industry/089498 (accessed 23 October 2024).

NZMC (New Zealand Music Commission) (2024) MMF back to basics seminar is back for 2024! Available at: nzmusic.org.nz/music-commission-news/mmf-back-to-basics-seminar-is-back-for-2024/ (accessed 21 October 2024).

Paine, A. (2021) MMF's Annabella Coldrick calls on music industry to tackle streaming 'inequalities & dysfunctions. *Music Week*. Available at: www.musicweek.com/management/read/mmf-s-annabella-coldrick-calls-on-music-industry-to-tackle-streaming-inequalities-dysfunctions/082879 (accessed 6 May 2025).

Paine, A. (2023) European Music Managers Alliance names Keychange's Jess Partridge as executive director. *Music Week*. Available at: www.musicweek.com/management/read/european-music-managers-alliance-names-keychange-s-jess-partridge-as-executive-director/088644 (accessed 21 October 2024).
Paine, A. (2024a) Warner Music, Live Nation and Coldplay fund MIT study of live sector's carbon footprint. *Music Week*. Available at: www.musicweek.com/live/read/warner-music-live-nation-and-coldplay-fund-mit-study-of-live-sector-s-carbon-footprint/089178 (accessed 1 December 2024).
Paine, A. (2024b) PPL revenue up 4% as international income dips in 2023. *Music Week*. Available at: www.musicweek.com/labels/read/ppl-revenue-up-4-as-international-income-dips-in-2023/089572 (accessed 29 October 2024).
Paine, A. (2024c) European Music Managers Alliance teams with BeatBread on advances for members. *Music Week*. Available at: www.musicweek.com/management/read/european-music-managers-alliance-teams-with-beatbread-on-advances-for-members/089847 (accessed 23 October 2024).
Paine, A. (2024d) Amid the Covid crisis and Brexit, a major new industry body emerges to represent the live sector. *Music Week*. Available at: www.musicweek.com/live/read/amid-the-covid-crisis-and-brexit-a-major-new-industry-body-emerges-to-represent-the-live-sector/082642 (accessed 23 October 2024).
Paine, A. (2024e) Music in the air 2024: Live, publishing and superfans boost Goldman Sachs' global growth forecast. *Music Week*. Available at: www.musicweek.com/labels/read/music-in-the-air-2024-live-publishing-and-superfans-boost-goldman-sachs-global-growth-forecast/089723 (accessed 5 May 2025).
PAM (2024) Le PAM. Available at: www.le-pam.fr/Le-PAM (accessed 7 July 2025).
PIPA (Parents & carers in Performing Arts) (n.d.) Building foundations for a flexible, future-proofed workforce inclusive of parents and carers. Available at: ipacampaign.org/ (accessed 22 November 2024).
PPL (Phonographic Performance Ltd, UK) (n.d.) Championing music rights. Available at: www.ppluk.com (accessed 7 July 2025).
PRS for Music (Performing Right Society, UK (2025) *Annual Report*. Available at: www.prsformusic.com/-/media/files/prs-for-music/corporate/financials/2024/prs-accounts-2024.pdf (accessed 13 June 2025).
Ragoowansi, N. (2025) Questions on artist management. Interview by Allan Dumbreck [Zoom]. 7 January.
RIAA (Recording Industry Association of America, US) (n.d.) RIAA. Available at: www.riaa.com (accessed 7 July 2025).
SACEM (Société des Auteurs, Compositeurs et Éditeurs de Musique) (2025) *Annual Report 2024*. Available at: rapportannuel2024.sacem.fr/ (accessed 13 June 2025).
Songwriters Guild of America (n.d.) Protection Songwriters Since 1931. Available at: www.songwritersguild.com/ (accessed 7 July 2025).
Sweney, M. (2013) AEG bid to run Wembley Arena sent to the Competition Commission. *The Guardian* Available at. Available at: www.theguardian.com/media/2013/mar/22/aeg-wembley-arena-competition-commission (accessed 5 May 2025).
Sweney, M. (2021) UK music festivals face cancellation without government support. *The Guardian*. Available at: www.theguardian.com/music/2021/jan/05/uk-music-festivals-face-cancellation-without-government-support-insurance-coronavirus (accessed 23 October 2024).
Sweney, M. (2024) Economic impact of UK live music industry hits record £6.1 bn. *The Guardian* Available at. Available at: www.theguardian.com/business/article/2024/sep/04/economic-impact-of-uk-live-music-industry-hits-record (accessed 5 May 2025).
Tencer, D. (2025) Live Nation posts Q1 revenue decline, but says 2025 will be historic year for live music. Music Business Worldwide. Available at: www.musicbusinessworldwide.com/live-nation-posts-q1-revenue-decline-but-says-2025-will-be-historic-year-for-live-music/ (accessed 5 May 2025).
UK Govt (2021) Economics of music streaming inquiry. UK Parliament, London. Available at: committees.parliament.uk/work/646/economics-of-music-streaming/ (accessed 11 October 2024).
UK Govt (2024) UK Voluntary Code of Good Practice on Transparency in Music Streaming. Available at: www.gov.uk/guidance/uk-voluntary-code-of-good-practice-on-transparency-in-music-streaming (accessed 6 May 2025).
UK Music (2022) Policy: Let the music play. Available at: www.ukmusic.org/policy-campaigns/policy-archive/let-the-music-play/ (accessed 18 October 2024).
University of Melbourne/AAM (2022) Association of Artist Managers. Available at: drive.google.com/file/d/1SwtDvdRAM9j3peYHggRanYtf7cvk5U3g/view (accessed 16 October 2024).

University of Stirling archive (n.d.) Archives and Special Collections: Musicians' Union. Available at: libguides.stir.ac.uk/c.php?g=530467&p=3628559 (accessed 5 May 2025).

Webb, A., Bonham, P., Harmon, A., Coldrick, A. and Dethekar, M. (2022) *Essentials of Music Management*. Music Managers Forum, London.

WIN (Worldwide Independent Network) (n.d.) Connecting the global independent music community. Available at: winformusic.org/ (accessed 7 July 2025).

4 Getting Started

Allan Dumbreck

In the first part of this book, we examined why artist management matters, the history of management, representative bodies and the key supporting organizations. Collectively, these comprise the theoretical and operational framework of artist management. The following three chapters will investigate some of the practicalities of existing managers' experience as drawn from the interviews we undertook with current artist/creator managers and relevant industry professionals. They are intended to present our findings on the emergence of managers, the growth and development of the artist and their management company, environmental factors, and the difficulties and issues which both artists and managers face in the longer term. We will examine these themes using examples and opinions given by the respondents.

This chapter will begin that narrative arc by examining where music managers come from, their early development, and how they establish themselves. Considering the responses we received from interviews with current artist managers and some of those working in relevant representative organizations, we will consider the origins of music managers and the earliest stages of their work.

> Why does someone decide to become a music manager?
> How do they define their role?
> Which key skills / abilities do they require?
> Do they need qualifications or experience?
> What should they be looking for in an artist?
> What are the main business models?
> How do they generate income?

These key questions were central to our research and are addressed in this chapter.

Short biographies of all interviewees can be found in the preliminary page of the book.

How Do Artist Managers Get Started?

What is the initial motivation? Why does someone decide to become an artist/creator manager? Academic, author and manager Guy Morrow at the University of Melbourne gives this explanation, which echoed by many voices in the sector:

> I am driven to manage artists because I am chasing the 'five minutes of magic', it may take the form of a song in a studio, a performance or video, then hopefully many other people will find [it] to be amazing.
>
> (Morrow, 2018)

This is supported by many of our respondents. Scottish manager Lyle Scougall, for example, identified the experience of hearing his first client sing as the point where he made the decision to become a manager, as we shall see. The emotional impact of the music itself does therefore appear to be one significant driver. But where do managers come from? What is their background?

The UK Music Managers Forum, in their publication *Essentials of Music Management*, identify the two principal routes into artist management which most of their membership have taken as either from gaining experience inside the industry and transferring to management or being effectively self-taught and coming in from outside the music business (Webb et al., 2022).

Identifying journalism, record labels and live events as sectors where managers often start out, the MMF also recognizes the significant number who were previously artists/creators themselves (around half). Taking a broader geographical perspective, the 2023 survey *Music Management in Europe*, which questioned EMMA members, gives considerably more detail, identifying 37% as having a background in live/touring, 32% having worked with record labels, 29% with previous marketing experience, 27% having been artists themselves, 16% coming from (non-music) businesses and 4% from a legal background (Calkins et al., 2023). While this indicates a lower number starting as performers than we found elsewhere, this research still identifies other positions in music and related industries as key sources.

Taking examples from our interviews, the same range of backgrounds is evident. Some begin as musicians, performers and band members themselves, often starting by organizing shows and recordings before moving to management when they perceive the need for the business side to be handled more effectively (Guy Morrow is one example). Chas Chandler, Jimi Hendrix's manager, was the bass player for the 60s band The Animals; Scott Kirkwood, Lewis Capaldi's first manager, also played with his own band prior to entering artist management, as well as working for a record label. A considerable number of those we spoke with also had previous experience, working with record companies (Ellie Giles, Chris Chadwick), live events or retail sales (Bruce Findlay, original manager of Simple Minds and founder member of MMF UK, previously ran his own chain of record stores).

Lawyers, brought in to review contractual offers and able to demystify legal terminology for musicians, often get asked to take on managerial roles. One example of this is Queen's long-term manager Jim Beach, who was originally a lawyer, although Paul Allen counters this, having been told by a lawyer that perhaps they are not the best choice due to their 'conservative nature' in conducting business (Allen, 2022). One further source is immediate family. Beyonce was originally managed by her father, Mathew. Glasvegas are managed by a close relative, Denise Allan, also interviewed in our research (Allan, 2023).

It should be noted that wherever managers come from, most of the above sources have one common skill – good communication and social interaction skills. As Anderton et al. (2022) indicate, 'Managers may be regarded as occupying the centre of a network of relationships'. Michael Jones (2012) point that artist management is the 'only position in the music industry which interacts with all other areas of activity' only serves to reinforce this.

Previous performers

Starting with those who initially came into music as creators/performers, the realization that they might be better suited to the business side appears to have shifted their focus. Ross Patel, founder of Whole Entertainment and board member for MMF UK, explains his own personal progression from artist to manager:

> I was in a band when I was 15, 16 and realized I was really bad, and that I was surrounded by people with talent, and that it was probably better that I let them do the creative bit and I'll try and stay involved somehow helping that process along. So, from that point I was involved – that's kind of where the journey started for me and it evolved over time.
> (Patel, 2024)

Karl Nielsen, former manager of Goldie, current manager of William Orbit, had a similar experience:

> It was an artist that asked me. I was in a band many years ago and I realized as an artist I wasn't getting my royalties because I didn't know how and why and what [needed to be done]. I wanted to learn about business and I built some individual businesses and they did quite well and one of the artists we [were]

working with, Goldie, asked me, 'Would you run my management?', and I said 'I don't really know what management's all about, I know about business', but as I had kids it was like babysitting really. Babysitting with business on top.

(Nielsen, 2024)

Lyle Scougall, manager of emerging artist Joesef, had been a musician. He was studying music at college when he met a fellow student:

I went back to college and [while there] I just see this big, tall guy in the corner; big, loud, proud, east end of Glasgow voice; he's got a Fred Perry T-shirt, he's got his Doc Martens, and I'm [thinking], "this guy is cool". His name was Joseph. We went to an open mic night, and he gets up and he sings "California Dreaming", Mamas and Papas, and I've never heard a man sing like that before and I [thought], "I'm going to be a manager".

(Scougall, 2023)

MMF UK (Webb et al., 2022) believes that perhaps 50% of managers start as performers, stating 'there are . . . artists, songwriters and other music makers who make the move from creator to manager. MMF research suggests that around half are in this position.' Having previous experience of the music industries (as per the examples above) has the advantage of the proto-manager being aware of the music environment and many of the potential pitfalls their artists might encounter. However, this also applies to those who are already working elsewhere in music.

breakthrough moment occurred while working in that role:

I was scouting for free for Zomba, now part of Concord, and they didn't have the budget to employ me, but I found a band without a manager that my boss there wanted to sign so I left the scouting job and became their manager and signed them to a six-figure deal after four shows.

(Braines, 2023)

Dutch manager and EMMA board member Steijn Koeijvoets had also previously worked for a record company when an opportunity came up:

I got involved in artist management through my previous job which was working at a record label [where] I met up with a lot of artists and managers, and I never intended to become a manager but I just clicked with an artist of mine who also happened to be a manager, and when I decided to work for myself he asked me to join his company as a partner, and then, What's that now? I think 13 years ago? So, we've been working together on the management side of things for 13 years and, you know, I still [use] my label skills and that knowledge.

(Koeijvoets, 2023)

We can see here that abilities and opportunities which arose in a previous role, particularly when it was more business-orientated, can lead to the career switch to artist management. This is also recognised by MMF UK (Webb et al., 2022): 'Many MMF members were initially working in an entirely different part of the music industry'.

Previous music industry role

As previously noted, some of our interviewees came to management from other music industry sectors. Chris Chadwick (Famous Friends management), for example:

I was at university and working with promoters in the live sector in Liverpool. Then, subsequently, worked at labels.

(Chadwick, 2023)

Steven Braines, founder of HE.SHE. THEY events and record label, was gaining experience scouting for a record company. The

Family

Denise Allan, manager of Glasvegas, is related to members of the band. She became an artist manager after being asked to help:

There was a band that was created that consisted of my brother, who is the chief songwriter, and my cousin Robert Allan, who is the lead guitarist, and I could see them really try their best at being a band but that failed dismally just because their organizational skills are absolutely zilch. They couldn't get themselves to a gig on time, get themselves organized, understand their equipment. It was actually

Robert that said to me, 'Can you just help us out a bit with this?' and the fatal words, 'How hard can it be?' 'How hard can be?' because it means you're starting to embark on a path that you never really anticipated would be overtaking your life and something you would feel really passionate about.

Allan (2023)

This last category is also identified by MMF UK (Webb et al., 2022) as a possible way into management: 'individuals who might be a friend, fan or relation of the artist, or even one of their parents'.

It would appear then that there is no single route into artist/creator management but perhaps proximity to the music industries or musical creativity for those who discover a desire to be involved but do not feel that they themselves could realistically be the creator/performer might act as a catalyst. The opportunity to engage in management in a situation where there is little to lose and possibly much to gain could be a further factor. Whatever the reason, many of those interviewed had transitioned into artist/creator management from other roles and sectors rather than having made an initial decision to start there.

Defining the role of the manager

How do artist / creator managers define their work? More than half of those interviewed stated that the range of activities undertaken by the manager depends on the nature of each artist-manager relationship, specifically, "who does what?". Some artist / creators have a clear vision of the business side and take a significant role in deciding the steps of their own career trajectory and development, effectively directing the manager, while others wish to focus on the artform and leave all the business decisions to management.

In most responses the role was variously defined as "*business manager*" (Chris Chadwick, Ross Patel), as "*project management*" (Steven Braines) and "*business developer*" (Ellie Giles). Mark Melton divided the role into three parts, "*one third adviser, one third protector and one third enabler*", which clearly brings the pastoral / semi-parental elements to the fore. Similarly, Virpi Immonen (EMMA & MMF Finland) described the artist-manager relationship as a "*business marriage*". Polly Comber used the slightly more distant term "*caretaker*", while Chris Chadwick preferred "*facilitator*", stating -

> Effectively as an artist manager you're running a business, so you have to have a grasp of marketing, live booking, accountancy and the business side of things
>
> (Chadwick, 2023)

Karl Nielsen's response "*supreme juggler! - you become the de facto CEO, running the artist's business*", highlights the considerable range and volume of tasks which can be involved. Steven Braines went into further detail regarding his own approach to the position, describing his work as -

> To be able to shield the artists from the rest of the industry, trying to give artists informed consent as to what the positives and the negatives of any outcome can be and then the artist can decide (for) themselves... making what seems impossible possible.
>
> (Braines, 2023)

In the earliest stages of development, the manager often takes on almost every role as indicated by Scott Kirkwood –

> The manager needs to really do a bit of everything in those first stages - be the booking agent, be the record label, be the publishing, be the promoter, be the PR, the radio plugger. As the manager you have to speak to everyone.
>
> (Kirkwood, 2023)

We can see that different managers interpret their role in different ways. Hence, as discussed in earlier chapters and as we were frequently told, the actual role of the manager depends on a series of factors which defy a singular definition.

Key skills: the manager

Looking beyond a potential job description, we also wanted to investigate which key skills managers felt were the most valuable for their sector. The most frequently identified by those we interviewed were –

Honesty / trust / openness (10 responses)
General business skills (8)

Knowledge / experience and a network of contacts within music (6)

Creativity (in a business management sense - 5)

Drive / determination (4)

To understand why these factors are so important we need to consider how our interviewees explained them.

Honesty, trust and openness between the creator and the manager were highlighted in many interviews focusing on the importance of integrity in this core relationship. In particular, managers identified having a clear mutual vision and a joint understanding as being cornerstone to building careers. As Annabella Coldrick (MMF UK) explains :

> It's building a trust but maintaining a professional relationship and being able to have boundaries that are professional (which) the relationship requires.
> *(Coldrick, 2023)*

Kirkwood re-enforces this message –

> (It is) important just to make sure that ... you're (as) open as you can (be) with your artist on everything.)
> *Kirkwood, 2023)*

Immonen further clarifies –

> You need to have complete trust to each other. Somebody is giving his/her career (in)to your hands and she needs to be trusted 100% and the same goes the other way around.
> *(immonen, 2020)*

While not every interviewee referred to this issue it should be notes that no-one contradicted it.

a. General business skills were unsurprisingly identified as critical given that the manager is essentially the artist / creator's business representative.

Braines describes the required business skills as follows –

> Project management. The role involves .. pitching actively, ... and deciding what is good and what isn't good. I enjoy the challenge of that having an entrepreneurial spirit.
> *(Braines, 2023)*

Chadwick appears to agree, stating :

> I would describe my role as an artist manager as primarily helping artists run the business side of their operation, (as) I see my role, it's like a facilitator, and maybe CEO / COO of the artists' business.
> *(Chadwick, 2023)*

Many more referred to specific individual business skills (negotiation, planning, financial management or having an understanding of the legal side). Again, no interviewee stated an opposing view.

b. Knowledge, experience and network were the next most important skill set identified by the research. Depth of understanding of, and engagement with the music and related industries was highly rated by our interviewees. Hardin, based in Los Angeles gives a US perspective -

> The knowledge of the industry, the rolodex (network connections), just having the ability to guide, that comes from experience and from putting in the time.
> *(Hardin, 2020)*

The picture is similar on this side of the Atlantic, Horace Trubridge (then with the MU) told us –

> Experience and knowledge are really important but also being able to demonstrate that they've got good, open relationships with key people within the industry.
> *(Trubridge, 2020)*

Moon succinctly agrees –

> Network and experience.
> *(Moon, 2020)*

These responses highlight the critical level of connection between the manager and the music environment. Further responses also recognised the importance of "what AND who you know".

a. **Creativity in a business sense** (identifying new routes to market, problem solving) came next in the skills list. A manager needs to think their way into a market and out of difficulties. David Martin at FAC has seen this many times :

> The ability to evolve and adapt and the ability to be, I don't want to say entrepreneurial , but sort of creative in their thinking as well as creative in their output if that makes sense. .. they're the enduring characteristics .. of managers that I still see working and managers that I still see being successful.
> *(Martin, 2023)*

Melton agreed, explaining –

> Creativity, an entrepreneurial nature, somebody who is like a dog with a bone really (not letting go).
> (Melton, 2020)

Given the range of difficulties and challenges which a manager can face it is highly valuable for them to be able to generate creative solutions and opportunities.

b. Drive / determination also featured highly in our responses with four subjects stating this clearly and others implying it's importance. Giles was adamant about this in her first interview -

> And then drive, on the manager side that's important.
> (Giles, 2022)

Mills-McLaughlin also believes that both partners require this –

> Having the drive to push your own career (the artist) as well as the manager, not fully expecting your manager to be the only one pushing you and getting your name out there, it's important.
> (Mills-McLaughlin, 2020)

Beyond these key skills / attributes the following were also identified in a number of our reponses. Neilsen, Patel and Coldrick all identified **resilience** at the start of their response to this question without further explanation. **Communication skills**, which have been identified as a primary ability by previous studies across all theatres of the music industries (e.g. *Sounding out the Future*, Dumbreck et al., 2006), were also stated by three interviewees (Koeijvoets, Giles & Patel).

Required management skills - parallels with existing literature.

The results of the research we have conducted map well with current publications on many points. Key documents in this field include the MMF's wealth of materials as well as other artist management guides (eg : *Artist Management for the Music Business* – 5th edition by Paul Allen, Routledge, 2022 and *Music Management, Marketing and PR*, Anderton et al., Sage, 2022)

The primary response we discovered to Q1, for example, on the key qualities within the role of the manager (honesty, trust, openness) is echoed by Steven Taverner (East City Management) quoted in the latest MMF guide "Essentials of Music Management" (Webb et al., 2022) when he states "trust is essential in any manager relationship" and cites the value of "solid, truthful advice". This is further underpinned by the MMF's own Code of Practice on their website, item 2 of which states that managers should "**be committed** (and duty bound) to **absolute transparency** in all contractual and financial business dealings that concern their client".

The second and third responses (importance of general business skills and knowledge / experience including a network of contacts within music) is referenced on page 4 of "Essentials", "There will be important administration and paperwork to take care of . . (including) contracts, campaigns, strategies and schedules" (Webb et al., 2022). This is reinforced in Paul Allen's book as early as page 3 when he states that "the artist manager must develop an understanding of team-building, marketing, budgeting and sales as they apply to the income streams available to the artist".(Allen, 2022).

The second chapter of "Essentials" is entitled "Creative development" which was our fourth required skill for managers (creativity in a business sense).

Generally then, we can see agreement across a series of sources including our own primary research in identifying the key series skills and abilities required for this sector.

The Value of Education/Qualifications

The MMF UK survey of its membership, *Managing Expectations*, published in 2019 and available on the MMF website, indicates that 54% have achieved a bachelor's degree, with a further 18% educated to master's level. However, 73% report not having had any formal music management or music business [specific] education (MMF UK, 2019). This does indicate that many future music professionals are transferring to the music industries after studying other subject areas, at least in the UK.

This pattern is replicated elsewhere. More recently, EMMA's 2023 survey of their membership, *Music Management in Europe* (Calkins *et al.*, 2023), indicates a similar level of higher education overall but with a significantly greater number achieving master's. The report identifies 68.1% of respondents having a bachelor's degree or higher-level qualification. This breaks down as 36% at bachelor's level, 31% with master's and 1.1% with PhD or doctorate certification. The research found that while over 50% had studied subjects directly related to their music careers (business, marketing, communication, economics, music management, law), over 70% of all respondents stated that they did not gain the skills they use in music management from degree programmes which aligns with the MMF UK data. This is a similar outcome to the MMF UK data.

The statistics above are slightly lower than the group of managers we interviewed, of which 10 out of 14 (71%) had studied at higher-education level (university) before becoming managers. If you include those returning to education later in life while still actively working as an artist manager, this rises to 79%. Amongst those who had studied at this level, 60% had studied for a music-specific qualification and 60% had studied subjects which were business-orientated. This cannot be taken as anything more than a rough indication, however, as the sample group involved in our research was intended for qualitative analysis and the number of interviewees is low. However, it does appear that a university-level education might have a value if you wish to work in this theatre as these statistics are significantly higher than national averages for the UK populus (although 51% have studied at HE level, only 33.8% have a bachelor's degree or higher in the UK compared with 50% studying at degree level and 37.7% with a bachelors degree in the US (Statista, 2022, 2024/ONS, 2023).

The value of higher education (university-/degree-level qualifications) was acknowledged by many of our interviewees. Scott Kirkwood, for example, notes the advantages of connecting to a professional network:

> I think for me it was certainly more important in the earlier stages because the relationships that I made within the time I was at [university] were really really important, and it's what helped me get my first job with Sony.
> (Kirkwood, 2023)

Chris Hardin, founder of Hardin Bourke Entertainment, based in the USA, agrees, citing academic staff connections within industry as a key entry point to potential employment:

> I went to NYU for the Music Business programme. One of my first jobs in the industry was from a connection I made with one of our professors and that led to a two-and-a-half/three-year position [in industry]...that led to other things and springboarded me further on – a lot of those relationships started when I was in NYU, in grad school, in the music business department.
> (Hardin, 2020)

Although she initially studied an unrelated subject, UK manager Ellie Giles points to the value of the parallel track of studying the music industries while simultaneously gaining critical music business awareness by working in the sector:

> I [studied] pharmacology at university and then went [on] to (study) popular music [but] I kept doing a lot [in the music industries] outside of my degree to build the experience that I wanted – if you don't have the skillsets for business, the soft skills (e.g. communication, negotiation), then that's a real big issue.
> (Giles, 2022)

The response from those in representative organizations was similar. Virpi Immonen, for example (Chair of MMF Finland and EMMA member), stands with Giles on the benefits of the twin-track (education and experience) approach:

> There are some schools where you can study music management but it's only half of the job. You need to have the experience in the field, you need to have your networks, you need to know people, you need to know how business works.
> (Immonen, 2020)

Others took a slightly different view. Chris Chadwick, as one example, saw the value of learning but not specifically HE or FE qualifications. He was also among many who highlighted the value of MMF training and support:

> I don't necessarily think that a formal education is important to be a good manager. I do think that a willingness to learn is. Effectively, as an artist manager you're running a business, so you have to have a grasp of marketing, live

booking, accountancy and the business side of things. I've certainly really benefitted from some of the educational tools that places like the MMF have offered and also just from experience within the industry but I don't think formal education is essential if you have the bug for management and are willing to learn.
(Chadwick, 2023)

Polly Comber, former manager of Rag'n'Bone Man goes even further, although she still recognizes the need for learning in some shape or form:

I think they're completely irrelevant [qualifications]. I think if you are doing a music degree, that could be useful in terms of maybe understanding a bit about law or promoting or agents or the money side of things; I don't think there is a course out there that will teach someone how to manage an artist.
(Comber, 2022)

Additionally, she cites instinct and individual character traits as vital:

[The music environment] changes every day, you are going with your gut and your instincts all the time and I think if you haven't got that kind of brain where you can't just rely on your gut and your instincts, you're going to find it quite hard.
(Comber, 2022)

Across the board, all our manager interviewees pointed out the requirement to learn about the role and the business environment in some way (whether within formal education, being self-taught or by experience). Eleven supported a formal education while two felt it was less important.

Certain subject areas, beyond those which are music related, can be seen as advantageous to the role of artist/creative manager. Steven Braines, for example:

I have a first-class honours degree in psychology [and a] distinction at master's [level] in business psychology as an occupational psychologist, so I guess the psychology [ability to understand others] is good.
(Braines, 2023)

Taking a different angle, Mark Melton, originally (and still) a qualified and practising lawyer, reflects positively on his education when he was starting out in management and states:

[On a law course] you're teaching managers to think like lawyers as well as [thinking like] managers, and I think that's a good thing really.
(Melton, 2020)

Unsurprisingly courses in music (performance or business) were prevalent amongst the interviewees with seven of our 11 managers studying these subject areas. Ross Patel, CEO of Whole Entertainment, commenting on his music business course, states:

Courses are so much more developed now and they offer a really good route into the music industry with up-to-date, tangible case studies, guest speakers and best practices.
(Patel, 2024)

Brendan Moon, who discovered and managed Paolo Nutini and returned to formal music-specific education later in his career, concurs:

These days it's imperative. I've benefitted from the [music business] course[s] incredibly and as I've always said, my [professional] portfolio wouldn't exist if I wasn't a university graduate.
(Moon, 2020)

Other aspects of the education system which were highlighted included the internship or placements which a college or university can offer. This was illuminated by Cara Mills-McLaughlin, formerly a member of Scott Kirkwood's management team, who echoed Chris Hardin's point regarding connections between academia and industry:

[Staff on my course] put me up for the internship [with a major concert promoter] so through that course I got the job.
(Mills-McLaughlin, 2020)

Aside from the direct benefits of a formal education, many of our respondents identified inherent skills in studying and completing assessments as vital. The general rigour of simply completing a programme of education was also thought to be valuable. Steven Braines states:

> Those softer skills that you learn are really important like presenting, doing dissertations and theses, you have to finish something.
> (Braines, 2023)

Supporting education generally, David Martin (Featured Artists Coalition) sees the issue from a purely practical business-awareness perspective:

> I want artists to know enough of it to feel confident that they understand what's going on, on a day-to-day basis. So I think, in lots of different ways, education is important.
> (Martin, 2023)

Horace Trubridge, former general secretary of the Musicians Union in the UK, is also a strong advocate for learning, focusing on an essential understanding of the different aspects of management in day-to-day work:

> You need to know what distribution means, what sub-licensing means, how the collecting societies operate and whether or not you should sign to one or go through an agent etc. Learn and learn and learn as much as you possibly can, because only if you've learned all that stuff, will you make the right decisions about your career. It's very tempting to just think 'I'll sign all these contracts', but if you go down that road, you will be ripped off, you will come unstuck.
> (Trubridge, 2020)

Examining this issue within existing literature, Paul Allen, for example, in his book *Artist Management for the Music Business*, emphasizes the importance of undertaking ongoing learning within artist management. This can be done in many ways, however:

> The smartest managers realize that for genuine growth a career requires continuous education. Attend an occasional seminar or take an online course, read relevant blogs and bookmark websites and podcasts that keep you current in the music business.
> (Allen, 2022)

More specifically, he then makes the case for university-level qualifications, identifying the types of higher education programme which might be of greatest value to those seeking a career in artist/creator management:

> Earning a degree in business is very useful – especially one that emphasises marketing, brand management and salesmanship. Earning a degree with an emphasis in the recording industry can give a graduate a very broad, contemporary look at the business that many active players in the industry do not have. A degree in law is helpful as is a master's in business administration.
> (Allen, 2022)

It is no real surprise then that our respondents did appear to take education and business knowledge within the music industries seriously. The representative organizations also took a similar stance. Individually and collectively, they have taken a proactive approach to educating their members over the last few decades, investing significant time and effort in developing resources to support artist managers (MMF), featured artists (FAC) and musicians (MU). The MMF website (MMF UK, 2021), for example, offers free access to reports and publications which address the key issues in artist/creator management (e.g. 'Managing expectations'; 'Dissecting the digital dollar') as well as interviews with existing members and advice on mental health. Regular training programmes for members alongside the Code of Practice for managers and the recently published *Essentials of Music Management* give clear guidance on the responsibilities and expectations of a professional music manager. Similarly, the MU has advice on rates of pay, health and well-being, legal support, and training and development opportunities. The FAC offers a range of relevant publications along with news of upcoming events and supporting initiatives.

Both (MMF UK, n.d) and (MMF US, n.d), as two key examples, cite education as one of their three key pillars. MMF UK also identifies a music-specific education as a recognized route into artist management emphasizing the practical experience elements: 'Study a music business course at university or college, many of which encourage participants to find new talent' (Webb et al., 2022).

Previous research (1996–2024) into the scale and scope of the developing music education provision at college and university level (*Music Education Directory*) shows near continual growth in numbers of programmes and students, at least in the UK with the latest edition showing over 2000 courses (Dumbreck, 2024). However, music industry employers have in the past occasionally been wary in accepting these as an access route (Bennett, 2015). While this *might* be becoming a more recognized pathway over time (Homewood, 2019), there still appears to be no accepted specific education pathway which leads directly to employment in professional music (including artist management) which other professions such as law, health and teaching have had for some time.

Having said this, in summary, the research we have undertaken appears to indicate that there is a clear value in gaining an education at university level and possibly also in music or business-specific subjects. The majority of those responding to the MMF survey (2019), the EMMA survey (Calkins et al., 2023) and our requests for interviews have studied at degree level, and many have completed programmes in areas which are related to their current position. While it might appear, given these data, that the music industries, at least in the artist/creator management sector, are becoming more professional via an increase in the number of those working there having qualifications, without further more detailed research we cannot assert this conclusion.

The Value of Previous Music Industry Experience

Do those who have previous music industries experience have an advantage over those who don't when getting started in artist/creator management? Our interviewees seemed to believe they do. We asked them about the work they had done previously in music and related areas as part of the interview. Almost all of them identified the value of experience and, more specifically, transferable skills (e.g. communication, negotiation, logistics and finance management).

Steijn Koeijvoets, based in The Netherlands, discussed the ten years of work in other sectors he built up prior to moving into artist management:

> I've been working in the music industry for over two decades, started as an A&R/marketing manager for an independent label. After a while, I went on to the publishing branch to act as general manager for the Benelux [region]. and after that, which was a total of ten years, I wanted to do something for myself. Then I started a management company called Three Years Music Management, in 2010.
> (Koeijvoets, 2023)

Ross Patel values the considerable experience he gained, first as a performer and, secondly, the success he encountered in a varied role involving promoting live events, record releases and management:

> So by the time I'd left university, I set up my first company [during my second year], which was a record label, events company and a management company. Amongst others, I worked with an artist called Flux Pavillion who later became a global electronic DJ producer. We worked together in his first years of university. I was his driver and the promoter for a lot of those early drum & bass and dubstep shows. At the time that sound was taking off.
> (Patel, 2024)

Ellie Giles, with a record company background, also agrees that experience brings benefits, remembering her own first steps in management, although she has encountered recent arrivals who have impressed her:

> You meet some young managers who are just super smart, you know, and just have those skills from the off and really have good questioning skills to be able to instinctively just know, because they might have been an artist themselves or have been in a creative part in the industry before and have moved over to the business side. I know numerous people like that who I admire. But I do think that the more you do something, the better you become and the more knowledgeable you become. So as time goes by, as a manager, I wasn't as confident – when I first started, I wasn't as confident about situations, whereas now, I know what I want to fight for and what's important for my client. So yeah, I think experience [is important].
> (Giles, 2022)

Specifically citing the advantages of her time working in recorded music, Ellie told us: 'But as a younger manager I was very fortunate because I worked at a label for a certain amount of time, so instinctively I knew certain things.'

Scott Kirkwood, originally a band member, equally recognizes the advantages of working in other roles (again, specifically record label work) prior to artist management:

'[Business] relationships, in general I think, [are] pretty much what [brought] me success with most of my clients, particularly the higher-profile artists. It's something that I started building when I was only [just] out of uni. I graduated when I was 19. The first thing I did there was working with David Bates and his Sony A&R Academy, which was going at the time and through that I got the job with Columbia Records (part of Sony) where I was for a year. I didn't really do anything when I was there apart from meet people. I think that was my real access point to London, where I started meeting all the scouts, A&Rs, publishers, agents etc. Even though I didn't have anything, I didn't have an artist to be pushing to them or whatever; being able to create personal relationships with them – that's really what sort of made the whole thing for me.'

As already noted, the MMF has identified that its members often come from a different sector of music and have benefitted from what they have learned in those previous roles prior to managing an act:

> Many MMF members were initially working in an entirely different part of the music industries, or continue to combine management with other roles in music. For instance, they might have been a journalist or worked at a record label or live agency before stepping into management and utilizing their experience and connections.
> (Webb et al., 2022)

It would therefore appear that having previous experience of working in another sector of music breeds a certain awareness and understanding as well as bringing a raft of network connections which can assist the emerging manager as they develop.

The combined value of education and experience is significant according to author Paul Allen who states:

> Experience coupled with education can move an artist or manager through the early years of the entrepreneurial experience more quickly and with greater prospects of success.
> (Allen, 2022)

Further to this, he adds that mentoring is also advised (supported by the MMF amongst others):

> Another way to gain experience is through the experience of others...find a mentor or counsellor with whom you can have continuing conversations about... developing as an artist manager.
> (Allen, 2022)

Again, similar to the question regarding education, it is not particularly surprising to hear that artist/creator managers benefitted from experience in other related roles prior to taking on their current position. We did find several respondents who had previously worked for record labels, but others had come through the events management route, for example. Working in a parallel field allows the proto-manager to see the pitfalls and springboards associated with that role and decide whether they wish to get involved. It should be remembered that many other roles have limited or fixed incomes/turnovers where managers (often on a percentage of the turnover they generate) have the potential to earn more (although they may often earn very little to start with, as we shall see). Is this an incentive to jump ship and become a manager? Again, this question will have to be more fully addressed by future research, but it does suggest another possible reason why many switch to artist management as their career progresses.

Previous experience as an advantage is backed by data from further afield. The 2023 survey into European artist managers, commissioned as part of EMMA's EMMpower project (accessed 9/7/25) also addresses some of the points made above. Results from the survey show that although most music managers have ten years or less experience in artist management (particularly women), many have worked elsewhere in music before coming to that role (68%), often having worked in live/touring, record labels, marketing and communication, and as an artist/musician/creator (Calkins et al., 2023). As we have seen, this broadly aligns with our findings.

Selection of Artists

The selection of artists by managers can happen via any number of routes. The qualities which a manager is seeking can also vary, but there were some themes which evolved during our research. Starting by tapping into recent published research, Anderton *et al.* (2022), for example, identify that 'Managers discover artists in a variety of ways. At live shows, online through social media platforms such as Soundcloud, YouTube, Instagram and TikTok or through personal introductions through friends, acquaintances, other musicians and music industry contacts at both the local and national level'.

Key skills - the artist / creator Having questioned our interviewees on the required skills for the manager we felt it equally important to research key abilities for the artist. Perhaps unsurprisingly we found that these replicate those expected of the manager in many ways. Interestingly the number five skill for a manager is apparently the most important trait required in an artist as far as our interviewees were concerned.

Drive / determination is the key quality an artist / creator needs according to our interviewees. Kirkwood speaks from experience -

> I've worked with artists in the past and the music's great, the looks (are) great and then it's just the drive and the attitude isn't there and you can try as hard as you want with something like that, but at the end of the day if they're not willing to work hard for it there's no hope.
> *(Kirkwood, 2023)*

Hardin is also looking for a high level of commitment –

> they've got to work at least as hard as us (the managers).
> *(Hardin, 2020)*

Giles is more adamant still –

> Drive?...that's important but equal drives, you've both got to be reading from the same page. I've parted ways with artists where they're lazy, there is no value for me to carry on dragging someone along
> *(Giles, 2022)*

None of our interviewees disagreed. Notably another of the primary artist / creator traits identified across all interviews is also critical for a manager.

a. **Honesty, trust and openness** between both parties are equally important for the artist as for the manager (5 responses). The clear direction, the shared vision and a common understanding of what they are collectively trying to achieve is vitally important. Mills-McLaughlin summarises this -

> you have to trust your manager, because they're essentially, taking your life into their hands to make it work for you.
> *(Mills-McLaughlin, 2020)*

Martin also agrees that creator and manager need to be on the same page –

> (In) good partnerships in management and between managers and artists, you can see their shared recognition of the goal or their understanding of each other.
> *(Martin, 2023)*

b. Creativity, talent, vision – perhaps unsurprisingly most of those working in artist development cited creative talent as key (4 responses).

Chris Hardin simply states –

> It's got to be great, it's got to be unique.
> *(Hardin, 2020)*

c. **Lack of ego / awareness of the contribution of others.** The need for artists to have a strong character and a personal belief can spill over into the way they interact with those around them. Many of our industry professionals identified the ability to switch between the on-stage persona and the everyday team-player as being particularly valuable.

Patel candidly states what his company is looking for –

> a far reduced amount of ego .. the narcissism and delusion that comes with, you know, someone needing to be a global superstar. That is just not something that we've enjoyed working with in the past.
> *(Patel, 2024)*

Braines frames this slightly differently -

> one of the biggest things is .. a willingness to not self-sabotage. So many careers I've seen, artists are their own worst enemy (they can

have) a psychological phenomenon called the actor-observer bias where a lot of (artists), if (they're) doing good, they've done well (all by themselves), if (they're) doing badly, they blame it on the team.

(Braines, 2023)

Other abilities of value in an artist which were identified by a number of respondents included **depth / breadth of experience and networking skills**. Some managers identified a necessary duality in the artist's character requiring resilience balanced with a vulnerability. They felt that the artist / creator had to develop a thicker skin to counter setbacks and negativity along the way but also a softer side to have the necessary empathy to write songs which resonate with their audience. This could of course create pressure on the artist / creator where they have to decide which side of their character to play in any particular situation. We will return to this when examining mental health issues.

Beyond essential artist skills, what else might a manager be looking for? In some cases, our interviewees felt it was more relevant to reverse the question and define what they were *not* looking for. Polly Comber, for example:

> I've met artists that are literally wanting just to go out and make loads of money, and I've turned it down. I've said, "No, I'm not the right manager for you. I'm not the 'let's go and make s***loads of money, and whatever happens happens" kind of manager. That's not the school of thought that I come from.
>
> *(Comber, 2022)*

Other managers had a clear direction in mind, sometimes as a reaction to their perception and experience of problems within the existing environment. Denise Allan, for example:

> I really really wanted to move from quite a macho indie world managing Glasvegas to developing young females, so from that point I searched high and low, searched everywhere to try and find some artists that had a lot of potential that were still quite young and that were female, so I have a young band called Plasticine, I have a hip-hop artist called Lamaya and I have another artist – she's kind of indie-soul – called Cherry.
>
> *(Allan, 2023)*

Gender issues will be addressed more fully in Chapter 8, but it is notable that they appear here as a driver for the manager as a selection criterion for the artists.

Considering other sources, the Musicians' Union (UK) offer a considerable level of advice to artists on finding a manager (Musicians' Union, n.d) including supplying an example artist-manager contract. Many of the MMF organizations, notably the UK operation, offer artists the chance to submit 'seeking management' requests, which they then circulate to their membership. In terms of what an artist can do to raise their profile, academic Paul Allen (2022) cites 'commercial potential' as the key criterion in attracting a manager (ability to sell concert tickets and generate streaming stats). The Musicians' Union agrees, adding that this will demonstrate the motivation and drive that our interviewees mentioned.

The managers we spoke with rarely identified specific characteristics as clearly as Chris Hardin or Denise Allan. They tended to indicate that they were seeking an undefinable quality which they believed they could recognize in artists. Drive (as in ambition) and a uniqueness in their sound/look were as far as most would go in defining what they were looking for. Determination on the artist's behalf, perhaps unsurprisingly, was the factor that arose most frequently in our conversations and seemed to be the most important.

Business Models – Company Structures

The EMMA survey (Calkins *et al.*, 2023), looking into the business arrangements of European artist managers, shows that most either own their own company (36%) or work as freelancers (22%). Those we interviewed corresponded well to this pattern, operating a series of different business models but operating independently (i.e. not directly employed by someone else). The structure of their company was dependent upon a number of factors. These included whether they worked alone or with others, how long they had been established, which type of artist/genre they worked with, how many acts they managed and the nature of the work they had agreed to undertake on their clients' behalf.

To examine the nature of their clients as one defining factor, we can see from the MMF (UK) 2019 survey, *Managing Expectations*, that those who responded represent music-makers in the broadest sense. Whilst 73% manage featured artists, 42% represent songwriters, 33% represent producers and 17% represent DJs. Most manage one or two clients. However, 14% juggle four to nine clients, often at different stages of career development (MMF UK, 2019)

How many artists can one manager realistically manage? As John Williamson identified in Chapter 2, the approximate 1:3 ratio of managers to artists within a management company appears to be reasonably accurate (Chosen Music with four managers and 11 artists; Q-Prime with nine managers and 30 artists). This aligns well with the EMMA survey of 354 European managers, which also established the median number of artists managed by their respondents as three (Calkins *et al*., 2023).

Taken collectively, these data resonate with the point made in the first chapters of this book that there is no single template for artist management, a maxim which apparently extends to the business models and the types of creator they are working with. When speaking with those managers we interviewed, we discovered a series of different business models which reflected the diversity of the data given above.

Solo Manager/Smaller Number of Acts

Many of our interviewees operate as sole traders – one-person companies – where they handle all the tasks themselves, perhaps outsourcing some of work but essentially overseeing everything. As the MMF explain in *Essentials of Music Management*, even if an individual takes no active steps to set up a formal business, if they are operating by themselves they will be categorized as a sole trader for tax and legal purposes (Webb *et al*., 2022).

Ellie Giles, for example, runs a one-person company looking after four clients ranging from a band to producers:

> I manage a guy called Erland Cooper. He is a composer as well as being an artist, and has a strong visual world. He has many different income streams. And then I've got Bill Ryder-Jones who is an artist, producer, writer and can write for people as well because he's a very, very good writer; same with Erland as well, actually. Warmduscher are an incredible live band. And then I've got a producer, Adam Noble. So yeah, I kind of have consciously built up a roster that is a little bit more, kind of, diverse than normal.
> (Giles, 2022)

Chris Chadwick works a similar model with a larger roster of artists. However, he started out with just two who were experiencing different levels of success:

> At the moment I manage, I want to say, four artists. In truth, probably two of my producers would say they're artists as well so maybe it's more like six. But, you know, four predominantly are artist clients, and then I have two songwriter/producer clients, and two kind of mixer clients, and who are mainly focused in the mixing world doing other bits as well. But when I started famous friends in late 2016/early 2017, I basically had two clients who were Puma Blue, who at the time was like an emerging artist, and then the other person was Guy Sigsworth who is a producer and songwriter with an incredible history in the music industry of over 30 years of writing for people like Bjork, Madonna, Imogen Heap, Britney Spears. He's had a very, very long career.
> (Chadwick, 2023)

Chris then went on to explain the value of a diverse roster in terms of levels of achievement and the advantages that can therefore be leveraged:

> Guy was a client I brought with me from a management company I was working with before. That was quite a conscious decision, actually. Having an established writer-producer on my roster gave me a legitimate excuse to go and talk to everyone. I never really had to go in any direction to pitch Puma Blue. I went in there to talk about Guy Sigsworth and the stuff he was writing. It really helped my education as a kind of newly independent manager and helped me to build my network. I'm now at a point where Puma Blue is more established; he's not necessarily a household name but he

has a sustainable artist business, and he makes records that he can tour and he's in demand to write and produce with other artists.

(Chadwick, 2023)

This is a valuable point. Having one developed client who allows you to operate at a higher level in terms of contacts and finance means you can introduce your emerging clients to business contacts at a more advanced position in the industry than might otherwise be possible. Chris then went on to discuss his overall business philosophy towards growing his company:

> I'm looking to grow a management company and it's really difficult, unless you have something that is instantly breakthrough, and reaches a much higher level very quickly. That's not what I'm trying to do with the artists that I work with; I'm trying to find ways to help the people I work with stay credible and stay true to what they want to do but to create sustainable businesses. Some of those artists, they're not six-figure-a-year businesses, and so as a manager, when you're taking a percentage of that smaller artist turnover, it's about working out what volume [of acts] you need. If I can create two or three artists' businesses that are on the kind of levels that Puma Blue is at, then I would be able to grow my own business and bring in more people to continue that growth.
>
> (Chadwick, 2023)

This gives us an indication of one way that a small-management business model might be developed over time. This approach indicates that some solo managers would prefer to remain so rather than joining a larger company as their career progresses.

Management Teams

Other managers we spoke with operate within a company structure where many managers are working together to develop the careers of a greater number of artists/creators. In the UK, this is often categorized as a partnership (normally where each partner is entitled to an equal share of the income and responsibility), as a financial and fiscal designation. To avoid personal responsibility for debts incurred, mature businesses may establish themselves as a Public Limited Company (PLC) or a Limited Liability Company (LLC) as outlined in *Managing Expectations* (MMF UK, 2021).

Steijn Koeijvoets, for example, is part of a much larger team. The company functions in a way which might be familiar to those who are aware of the structure of larger record labels where a series of departments handle each stage of the process. As he explained himself:

> Our company is divided, [on one side there's] a live division. [On the other side,] I'm heading, because of my background, the label and marketing division. Then we also have a social media and data division. So if you're signed to us, then you get a team instead of one dedicated manager. My role in the whole process is obviously to sign acts to the management company and then develop them musically; [to] make sure we find the right label partners to find the right publishing partners, [and] work together with the right brands and partners. That sums it up. If you're a lone working manager and you get sick, then there's no one [to work with your artists]; with our company, people can take over some work and so the process continues. That's what differentiates us.
>
> (Koeijvoets, 2023)

When we interviewed Scott Kirkwood he explained his current model for his company (Kingdom Management), which involved bringing in managers working directly with their own group of artists. In this way the company worked almost as a managers' collective. This is quite a different model from that which Stein works within, but it is still successful. Initially, Scott worked alone but after the success of Lewis Capaldi he was able to grow the company:

> For an independent artist, [if the manager aims] to earn a £20,000 salary, you need to make your artist £100,000 in that year. That's almost unheard of. So, for younger managers, [they are] generally having to work other jobs to be able to balance it; that's a really big thing. We're bringing a few different managers with their own rosters and that's how Kingdom operates. We've got salaried staff and, basically, 100% of their income goes in towards recouping their

salary and once it's recouped it can go to a split. So it's similar to the way that the bigger management companies work but we work on much more reasonable flips [split percentages].
(Kirkwood, 2023)

Brendan Moon also has a team but is not working with other managers. He has younger assistants who are experienced in audio production and in working with digital platforms and social media:

I'm lucky, I've got two members of staff, [from] the [younger] digital generation and [a studio producer] as well who helps, and these are smart kids, who live and breathe this kind of stuff. So what I'm bringing is the traditional method of how we're reaching out to fans, and what they're bringing to the table is the fans' perspective and just how to reach out to people [online]. It's reaching out [to the fan base] that a lot of people [managers] are not doing... Google analytics are there, but [they] just look at them and [they] don't know what to do].
(Moon, 2020)

We will examine the need for social media content and the value of online analytics in Chapter 5.

These models (and others) have been examined by other researchers including Anderton et al. (2022) who set out four models/levels of management company beginning with the artist acting as their own manager, then individual managers working alone and finally small and large management companies. Our interviewees fell broadly into the second and third categories here, but some operated models which were outside this categorization (e.g. Kirkwood). There are clear advantages and disadvantages associated with each type/model, but key elements to consider include the workload for the manager and the level of attention an artist gets depending on the scale of operation and on the number of artists managed.

Clearly, there is no single operating model for managers. Some work alone with a small group of artists/creators, others work in teams or partnerships to manage larger numbers of artists or to engage with new media. However, even here there are different operational models.

Finance

Early funding of an artist

As already identified by Scott Kirkwood, when an artist starts their career, it is very likely that they will not be generating sufficient income from music alone to keep them financially afloat. When the manager initially becomes involved with an emerging artist, they might equally not be able to do so for themselves, *or* for the artist (MMF UK, 2019). The period between the point where the artist and manager begin to work together and the point where the relationship becomes financially self-sustaining may be several years. During that time the artist and/or the manager will most likely have part-time jobs outside music which support them. This raises the issue of who should fund the artist (and possibly also the manager) while they are becoming established.

On this particular point, most managers and the MMF organizations agree that however the development of the artist is funded, it should preferably not be by the manager themselves (although this does happen). This does not stop certain individuals from other sectors within music advising that this is exactly what should be done. Ellie Giles found herself in the position of having to defend herself and her artist against the suggestion of a record company that they financially support themselves on tour:

[Sometimes] labels will take advantage of you; [that] certainly was the case when I first started managing. One tried to get me to get the artist to take a bank loan out, which I was horrified by, to go touring. I thought it was just rude and immoral – trying to get the band into bank debt.
(Giles, 2022)

The MMF UK (2019) position largely agrees with this, firstly advising members 'to ensure their own finances are sustainable'. They then further state:

If you are investing your own finances in a specific project...then you should also be discussing how your investment will be compensated. A smart manager will often look for and exhaust potential sources of (external) investment before spending their own money, or at the very least ensure that boundaries and structures are established.

(MMF UK, 2019)

A range of funding sources can be examined by the manager including Arts Council grants, support from other (larger) management companies and, of course, gaining advances on contracts with record or publishing companies. The artist and manager should, however, decide on remuneration for the manager at the outset of their relationship. Once the artist has become a little more established and is generating income, there should be a clear, previously agreed mechanism which ensures the manager is being appropriately rewarded for her/his/their work. This brings us to the subject of commission, which is widely accepted within the music industries as the principal form of payment for managers.

Commission rate – why 20%?

The standard accepted form of remuneration for managers is the commission rate. This dictates that a manager is entitled to a fixed percentage (gross, before deductions) of any income which she/he/they generate on behalf of the artist(s)/creator(s) they represent. As we saw in Chapter 2, historically, this rate was considerably higher than it is today. Typically, 50% in the USA (Mills, Sanicola, Parker, 1920s–1940s) and still 40% in the UK in the 1950s (Parnes, Kennedy). By the 1980s, the manager was on a reduced percentage of 20–25% (Frith, 1983) and a decade later the range was broader but lower again (15–25%) (Negus, 1992). In the last few decades, in the UK, this has settled at an almost universal 20%. Many have theories on where this figure came from (average of four members in a band equally sharing the income with one manager?), but nobody has a definitive explanation of why it is exactly one-fifth of gross generated revenue. Some, notably within the artist management community, believe that it could, or should, be more. The USA appears to have more of a sliding scale ranging approximately between 15 and 25% depending on a number of factors. In the EU we have seen a similar range.

EMMA research has found that 60.6% of respondents were paid by commission (Calkins et al., 2023). MMF UK identifies 66% of their members relying on commission-based earnings with 75% of those (around 50% overall) operating on the 20% of gross earnings commission rate (Webb et al., 2022).

Anderton et al. (2022) give the following definition/clarification: 'Commission rates usually fall between 15 and 25%, with the industry standard being 20% of gross income (prior to other costs being deducted). Touring and live shows are usually commissioned as net income (after other costs are considered)'. Allen gives the US perspective, which is a little more flexible: 'The amount of commission paid by an artist to a manager may be in the range of 15 to 20% but can be as high as 25% for new artists and as low as 10% for established artists who have high incomes' (Allen, 2022).

What is a fair return for the risk, investment, time and effort a manager commits to an artist/creator? MMF CEO Annabella Coldrick identifies the problem from the manager's perspective:

> In terms of the relationship with the whole industry, you will see from our *Managing Expectations* [report] that the industry has shifted an awful lot of responsibility for artist development to the manager. Partly because the industry, for probably the last ten years, withdrew in doing that early-stage talent development. So you would have managers potentially not only investing their own time but also their money. And time is money if you work for nothing for two or three years. Managers need to know more than ever before and become bigger risk takers. It can be quite heartbreaking. You'll find someone who works for three years on something and then the artist gives up and you're like, "Oh God! Nothing happened!".
>
> (Coldrick, 2020)

MMF UK's position therefore reflects other voices raising concerns regarding the level of manager remuneration:

> Our whole report shows how that has shifted and how the nature of the business models of management potentially need to shift as well. Just earning 20% with a relatively short sunset clause (post-contract income clause in the management contract), if you have spent three years earning nothing before the money starts to come in, means that the balance of risk and reward probably isn't quite right.
>
> (Coldrick, 2020)

Coldrick goes on to identify an additional problem:

> I think it is fair to say there is a shortage of professional managers at the moment. There's not a shortage of people wanting to be artists, so we would argue that there needs to be greater support and greater recognition from the industry.
> (Coldrick, 2020)

She does clarify, however, that some of the record labels are changing their approach to recognize this:

> Some of them do, like BMG for example, insist that when they sign artists there's a budget allocated to the manager as well. So not just necessarily commission, which can then inflate advances potentially beyond what they should be, but actually setting a [budget for] what they need to develop the artist and what they need to live off while we're working on the project together – so you're not giving crazy advances to an artist, so they're forever in debt, in order for the manager's commission to be enough to live off. It's clearly important to explore different ways of structuring deals to recognize the value that the manager brings.
> (Coldrick, 2020)

This indicates that in some situations, key players in the development of the artist (record labels and managers) are working together to reach agreement on budgets for artist development which are in the best interests of all involved which may be significantly different from the standard 20% commission rate.

Speaking on behalf of featured artists, David Martin at the FAC believes that the commission rate depends on the level of work the manager is undertaking for a particular artist:

> I think the answer to that is 'How long is a piece of string?' It depends on that relationship – manager A and manager B can be very different managers and business partners and very different parts of the team of an artist's business, and I think it's really hard to put a sort of generic answer to that, it depends on the circumstances on a co-relationship basis.
> (Martin, 2023)

Artist manager Ellie Giles expressed her concerns regarding the current 20% suggesting that managers should perhaps be rewarded at a higher level and warning that they should also consider how much work they are undertaking for the return they receive:

> The deal that we're on, which is the 20% commission deal, which is the reality at the moment, I still think that the artist should be driving a lot of that because they're getting 80% of their business. So, I think that, ultimately, until that changes . . . and maybe that goes into a 50/50 model. . . I think you've got to be conscious of what time you put into something. . . If you're only getting 20%.
> (Giles, 2022)

She goes on to address the issue of managers increasingly engaging with developing technologies, citing this as an additional workload which should be rewarded above and beyond the existing structure, possibly recognizing a new model operating within the digital/online side of the work:

> You are basically the facilitator, the business developer, but I also think there's a lot of new managers who are very digital-savvy and are really pushing things in the digital world and maybe should be getting more than 20% because they're actually flipping things on a business level (and a digital level too). So they may be coming up with really interesting ideas of how to take that artist to market. But where we're ultimately at, there's still the old-school management, which is that sense of business development and facilitating, but I do think that our jobs are changing from what they were 20 years ago and going more digital based.
> (Giles, 2022)

Ultimately, Ellie believes that the return to the manager will change over time and might eventually look more like the 360-degree deal which record companies introduced around 20 years ago to combat the digital revolution (Marsh, 2024). This could potentially entitle the manager to further income in perpetuity (beyond the sunset clause):

> I don't think 20% works and I think the value of the manager, as much as we've done a lot of work in the MMF, is still underrated. I think that ultimately managers are going to start asking for parts of the master [recording] and parts

of the publishing. I think they'll be asking for 5% or 10% of their artists' publishing or label monies, rather than saying "Well I'll get 20% and then when you sack me, what do I get?" [This would be] in perpetuity or for [perhaps] 30 years. If you're doing a lot more than 20% you need to be getting more than 20%.

(Giles, 2022)

During this research we have found that different models and different rates of commission exist in different territories. Based in The Netherlands, Steijn Koeijvoets has a different norm:

We do everything for 15%. Twenty per cent is all right but I think the commission should be based upon a certain level of income. So the more an artist earns,. the less a manager should take, I think. Then, you know, you should be pragmatic. If we have an artist which barely breaks even on a tour, we don't take commission. We see it as an investment, and hopefully [they'll] grow.

(Koeijvoets, 2023)

He is aware that the UK accepted standard of 20% is increasingly being adopted across Europe but points out that there should be room for manoeuvre:

I think 20% [gross] is becoming more the standard. What I do like about gross is that it's clear. You don't get discussions on "Why did you travel to the gig with a limo or a helicopter rather than the tour bus?". So that's transparent. [The correct figure should be] somewhere between 15 and 20 [%]. It also depends if you're just one manager doing one act who's doing well then you should be flexible; but for us, we work on a 15% commission base and we have six people working in the company.

(Koeijvoets, 2023)

To take a different approach altogether, a number of respondents suggested looking at the relationship a different way. Perhaps instead of a partnership, it should be looked at as a start-up business with the manager as the CEO of the artist's company. She/he then has equity for as long as there are assets under that artist's company – meaning that the manager will have some form of equity and therefore income in perpetuity.

This is quite a radical departure from the traditional commission model. It leans more towards the recording and publishing rights/royalties model which artists and composers enjoy, but perhaps it could be argued that this is more appropriate within the music industries generally and should include the manager's income stream.

There does therefore appear to be genuine debate over whether the standard UK 20% commission is justified, sufficient and/or acceptable to managers. Other rates exist in the international arena, depending on territory and the level of management activity being offered, but many of the UK-based managers we spoke with believed that the fixed percentage required some review, particularly in a changing environment where more is expected of the manager prior to the involvement of a record or publishing company (at which point additional funding is likely to become available).

Overall, artist / creator managers can expect a relatively low level of income, notably in the early stages of their artist's development. The EMMA survey of European managers in 2023 found 40% of those responding earned less than €10,000 per annum (approx £8500 p.a.), requiring them to undertake additional forms of employment, often in other sectors. A further 14% earned less than €20,000 (approx £17,000), meaning that more than half of all those surveyed earned considerably less than the average EU annual wage of just over €28,000 (European Commission, 2024).

In the UK, the MMF found that just over 64% of women and men working in artist management made less than £20,000 p.a., with 70% of the men and almost 78% of the women making less than £30,000K p.a. Given that the average wage in the UK is around £35,000 (Forbesat, 2024), almost four out of five artist managers in Britain are working considerably below the national income level.

One final point comes from the EMMA survey; 52% of women make less than €10,000, while only 27% of men are in this category (Paine, 2024a). The MMF, in their latest report, found that while only 43% of UK music managers were female, they could currently expect to earn less than men in the same sector (MMF UK, 2021). Issues relating to gender within artist/creator management will be addressed in Clare Duffin's research and analysis (Chapter 8) later in the book, but this is an early indicator of potential disparity between male and female managers' incomes.

Beyond the commission rate there is also a negotiation required to agree the expenses which the manager incurs whilst working for the artist/creator. This is often charged separately. However, many of the managers we spoke with carefully considered which expenses to charge and which to meet themselves, as artists can be sensitive to additional costs being levied against them which they consider to be unnecessary. As we shall see in Chapter 6, finance is a key factor in maintaining the artist–manager relationship.

There are certainly other models being developed for artist funding (and therefore manager payment). The announcement of a new partnership between EMMA (all European MMFs) and AI-driven funding platform BeatBread (Paine, 2024b) heralds an innovative financial model:

> Using an algorithm that uses billions of data points to forecast an artist's earnings potential, BeatBread provides a unique funding mechanism for creative talent, enabling them to retain full ownership of their rights. BeatBread offers advances on existing catalogue as well as new and unreleased music. Advances range from $1000 to more than $4.5 million, and artists repay their advance as a percentage of their revenue, over a period of time that the artists themselves can set.
> (Paine, 2024b)

As another example, the artist manager/label services FAN deal, being set up by experienced manager Kwame Kwaten, which promotes individual record releases from emerging acts, takes a percentage of the income from the master recording only (Paine, 2023). This is a shorter-term, one-release approach as opposed to the more usual longer-term artist career development most managers seek, but it could be an attractive new model for emerging managers seeking to grow longer-term opportunities from a series of short-term sources.

Overall, on the particular point of manager income, there does seem to be some room for discussion between artists and managers on the commission rate depending on the level of work being delivered by the management team. Currently, it is still the standard method of income generation for managers. As we have seen, the latest publication from the MMF (Webb et al., 2022) estimates that two-thirds of their members 'operate their business around commission-based earnings', so it is important to reach a solution that is equitable for managers and artists/creators alike. While a percentage of all gross income the manager generates for the artist has been recognized as a standard level of remuneration for some time, it does appear from our research that there are deviations and alternatives within artist–manager agreements and between labels and artists. This flexibility may, over time, develop towards a new norm (as Giles suggests), or perhaps a new framework (the equity model, as several interviewees suggested). Alternatively, it might become looser and more subject to variation depending on the exact nature of the work the manager undertakes in each individual situation, as David Martin (FAC) and Annabella Coldrick (MMF UK) indicate.

Conclusions

It seems, given the existing research by MMF organizations and other observers, that most of those working in artist/creator management arrive in that role from other related professions rather than making a conscious decision to begin their career in music as a manager. Experiencing the skills/knowledge gap in the absence of a manager (as an artist themselves) or identifying an opportunity while working in peripheral sectors (record company, live events) are often key triggers.

A university education (bachelor's degree or higher) can be advantageous; certainly most research indicates that this plus some form of ongoing learning/training to understand the environment and gain critical skills, is of significant value in a rapidly changing industry. Those having worked in related theatres of music benefit from an advanced knowledge of what a manager needs to do as well as a considerable network of existing contacts. Hence, previous experience does seem to offer an elevated starting point.

There was no consensus on the manager's criteria for the selection of artists. Broadly, unique or engaging elements of the artist's material, persona or stage act, and having personal drive or motivation, were the most frequently identified.

The working ratio of managers to artists appears to be approximately 1:3. In the earliest stages of a manager's career they are likely to work alone or with limited assistance in specific areas (e.g. online, studio production). As their business grows, they apparently develop in different ways, in partnerships, collectives, or by forming a larger company. There does not appear to be a singular or definitive route here as much depends on the individual circumstances and ambitions of each manager and the artists they represent.

The commission that managers charge has generally settled in the region of 20% of gross income with some variation across the more developed territories. Many charge directly related expenses above this but caution is advised in this area to avoid disapproval and potential conflict with clients. The majority of managers are working for a level of remuneration below the average level of employment income for their nation, particularly in the early part of their careers.

References

Allan, D. (2023) *Practicalities of Artist Management* [lecture] [University of the West of Scotland, 17 November].
Allen, P. (2022) *Artist Management for the Music Business: Manage Your Career in Music: Manage the Music Careers of Others*, 5th edn. Focal Press, New York and London.
Anderton, C., Hannam, J. and Hopkins, J. (2022) *Music Management. Marketing & PR*. Sage, London.
Bennett, T. (2015) *Learning the Music Business*. UK Music, London.
Braines, S. (2023) Questions on artist management. Interview by Allan Dumbreck [Zoom], 5 December.
Calkins, T., Berkers, P., Wijngaarden, Y. and Kimenai, F. (2023) Music management in Europe. EMMA (European Music Managers Association). Available at: emma.community/wp-content/uploads/2024/01/EMMA_Music-Management-in-Europe-Report.pdf (accessed 10 October 2024).
Chadwick, C. (2023) Questions on artist management. Interview by Allan Dumbreck [Zoom], 15 December.
Coldrick, A. (2020) Questions on artist management. Interview by Allan Dumbreck [Zoom], 7 April.
Comber, P. (2022) Questions on artist management. Interview by Allan Dumbreck [phone], 19 September.
Dumbreck, A., Hermanns, K. and McBain, K. (2006) *Sounding Out the Future*. University of Paisley (now UWS) / BPI publications, BPI, London.
Dumbreck, A. (2024) *Music Education Directory*. UK Music/JAMES. Available at: www.jamesonline.org.uk/jamesresources/med_2024/ (accessed 10 October 2024).
European Commission (2024) Wages and labour costs. Available at: ec.europa.eu/eurostat/statistics-explained/index.php?title=Wages_and_labour_costs (accessed 10 October 2024).
Forbesat (2024) Average UK salary by age in 2024. Available at: www.forbes.com/uk/advisor/business/average-uk-salary-by-age/ (accessed 10 October 2024).
Frith, S. (1983) *Sound Effects: Youth, Leisure and the Politics of Rock'n'Roll*. Constable, London.
Giles, E. (2022) Questions on artist management. Interview by Allan Dumbreck [Zoom], 29 March.
Hardin, C. (2020) Questions on artist management. Interview by Allan Dumbreck [Zoom], 29 April.
Homewood, B. (2019) Learn baby learn. In: *Music Week*. London. Available at: www.musicweek.com/analysis/read/learn-baby-learn-a-special-report-on-music-education/076058 (accessed 12 July 2025).
Immonen, V. (2020) Questions on artist management. Interview by Allan Dumbreck [Zoom], 6 May.
Jones, M. (2012) *The Music Industries: From Conception to Consumption*. Palgrave Macmillan, London.
Kirkwood, S. (2023) Questions on artist management. Interview by Allan Dumbreck [Zoom], 19 December.
Koeijvoets, S. (2023) Questions on artist management. Interview by Allan Dumbreck [Zoom], 7 December.
Marsh, D. (2024) 360 degree deals, a label perspective. Available at: creativelaw.eu/newsandblog/360-degree-deals-a-label-perspective (accessed 15 October 2024).
Martin, D. (2023) Questions on artist management. Interview by Allan Dumbreck [Zoom], 22 December.
Melton, M. (2020) Questions on artist management. Interview by Allan Dumbreck [Zoom], 1 May.

Mills-McLaughlin, C. (2020) Questions on artist management. Interview by Allan Dumbreck [Zoom], 19 May.
MMF UK (2019) Managing expectations. Available at: themmf.net/resources/knowledge/?subject=managing-expectations&material= (accessed 22 October 2024).
MMF UK (2021) Managing expectations. Available at: themmf.net/wp-content/uploads/2023/10/MMF-Managing-Expectations-Report-2021.pdf (accessed 22 October 2024).
MMF UK (n.d). Available at: www.themmf.net (accessed 16 November 2024).
MMF US (n.d). Available at: www.mmfus.com/ (accessed 16 November 2024).
Moon, B. (2020) Questions on artist management. Interview by Allan Dumbreck [Zoom], 19 March.
Morrow, G. (2018) *Artist Management: Agility in the Creative and Cultural Industries*. Routledge, London and New York.
Musicians' Union (n.d.) How to get a music manager. Available at: musiciansunion.org.uk/events-career-development/career-development/career-guides/working-relationships/how-to-get-a-music-manager (accessed 8 May 2025).
Negus, K. (1992) *Producing Pop*. Edward Arnold, London.
Nielson, K. (2024) Questions on artist management. Interview by Allan Dumbreck [Zoom], 25 January.
ONS (Office for National Statistics) (2023). Education, England and Wales: Census 2021. Available at: www.ons.gov.uk/peoplepopulationandcommunity/educationandchildcare/bulletins/educationenglandandwales/census2021#:~:text=More%20than%203%20in%2010,%25%2C%20or%2016.4%20million%20people (accessed 20 October 2024).
Paine, A. (2023) Music manager Kwame Kwaten on a new model to power campaigns for emerging artist. In: *Music Week*. Available at: www.musicweek.com/management/read/music-manager-kwame-kwaten-on-a-new-model-to-power-campaigns-for-emerging-artists/088866 (accessed 22 October 2024).
Paine, A. (2024a) European Music Managers Alliance: Women in management more likely to earn less than men. In: *Music Week*. London. Available at: www.musicweek.com/management/read/european-music-managers-alliance-women-in-management-more-likely-to-earn-less-than-men/089102 (accessed 21 October 2024).
Paine, A. (2024b) European Music Managers Alliance teams with BeatBread on advances for members. Available at: www.musicweek.com/management/read/european-music-managers-alliance-teams-with-beatbread-on-advances-for-members/089847 (accessed 22 October 2024).
Patel, R. (2024) Questions on artist management. Interview by Allan Dumbreck [Zoom], 25 January.
Scougall, L. (2023) Practicalities of artist management [lecture], University of the West of Scotland, 23 November.
Statista (2022) University degree attainment by country. Available at: www.statista.com/statistics/232951/university-degree-attainment-by-country/ (accessed 20 October 2024).
Statista (2024) Educational attainment in the US. Available at: www.statista.com/statistics/184260/educational-attainment-in-the-us/ (accessed 20 October 2024).
Trubridge, H. (2020) Questions on artist management. Interview by Allan Dumbreck [Zoom], 26 March.
Webb, A., Bonham, P., Harmon, A., Coldrick, A. and Dethekar, M. (2022) *Essentials of Music Management*. Music Managers Forum, London.

5 Growing the Business

Allan Dumbreck

Introduction

Having examined the responses from our interviewees in relation to the start-up and early development of a management company, this chapter analyses how they explained the key activities and issues which affect their longer-term operation. The ongoing requirement for social media content, the importance of live events, and the involvement of record companies and music publishers are all addressed. However, first we examine the value of networks and mentoring.

Networks/Mentoring

How important is your network of business contacts? Is who you know really more important than what you know? Developing good working relationships with key players in the profession, gaining knowledge of the practices of the music industries from working alongside those with more experience, and finding a mentor – all these mechanisms can be instrumental in the process of developing a professional career, but what difference do they make? MMF UK and EMMA list many networking opportunities, social events and meet-ups for different groups of managers on their websites (MMF US, n.d., EMMA, n.d.), while MMF US regularly hosts networking brunches and mixer events (MMF US, n.d). Many of the MMF organizations we examined have established mentoring schemes for their members (notably MMF UK, EMMA, MMF Canada and MMF Aotearoa in New Zealand, as we saw in Chapter 3). Other sectors of music also see the value; the 2024 BPI/MPA music synchronization trade mission to Los Angeles deemed networking important enough to include it as a key part of their annual schedule (Paine, 2024a).

Our interviewees were reasonably well aligned on this subject. Horace Trubridge, then General Secretary of the MU, believes that the manager's existing network of industry connections is critical:

> Experience and knowledge are really important but also being able to demonstrate that they've got good, open relationships with key people within the industry. So, you know, if you've got a problem with PRS, they can pick up the phone and speak [to someone they know] and get that problem sorted out, that's crucial. There's no point in taking on a manager who, once he's signed you, has to build those relationships. They have to be able to demonstrate they've got those relationships already.
> (Trubridge, 2020)

Chris Hardin, working in the USA, suggested the number of names in 'the rolodex' (your personal directory of professional contacts) as a key factor here. As we saw in the last chapter, he identified a series of early connections he made through his university and professionally as key to his career development:

> One of my first jobs in the industry was from a connection I made . . . that led to a two-and-a-half to three-year position where I learned a lot; you know, with someone that I would say is a mentor, that led to other things and springboarded me further on.
> (Hardin, 2020)

He also identified other key professionals who he had the opportunity to work alongside which helped his progression as a manager, effectively mentoring him as he learned the business:

> I've worked with Gary Kurfirst [who] was my first mentor, he was manager for the Ramones and founder of Radioactive records and [manager of] Talking Heads and has produced films and is just an icon in our industry and is someone I worked closely with for 8 years, so I just felt really blessed to have that mentor. I had, you know, other talented managers I've worked with as well, and, again, I subscribe ideally to always [gaining experience from] someone that knows more and [learning] as much as you can from them .
> (Hardin, 2020)

Scott Kirkwood agrees, as we saw in the previous chapter, citing the work experience he undertook at a major record label in London as instrumental in growing his own professional network and his later success developing the early career of Lewis Capaldi, amongst others:

> [Business] relationships in general, I think, is pretty much what [brought[me success with most of my clients, particularly the higher-profile artists. It's something that I started building when I was only [just] out of uni. I graduated when I was 19. The first thing I did there was working with David Bates and his Sony A&R Academy, which was going at the time, and through that I got the job with Columbia [Records – part of Sony] where I was for a year. I didn't really do anything when I was there apart from meet people. I think that was my real access point to London, where I started meeting all the scouts, A&Rs, publishers, agents etc. Even though I didn't have anything – I didn't have an artist to be pushing to them, or whatever – being able to create personal relationships with them – that's really what sort of made the whole thing for me.
> (Kirkwood, 2023)

Scott has also seen the difference that having success of your own makes, notably at a national and international level, to the growth of your business network and the ability to engage with promoted personnel:

> I think with every artist that I've managed, I've met more and more people, and as artists grow in popularity internationally, that network grows naturally. I spent probably three months last year in LA. I did a lot of . . . touring internationally and that again is another example [of the value of networking].
> (Kirkwood, 2023)

He also identifies some of the key personnel who have helped him develop but cites the MMF organizations as a key link, too:

> I've been very fortunate when I've been moving throughout my career. I've had figures like Gill Maxwell [Deacon Blue's first manager] or Ollie Hodge, who was at Columbia when I was there, who I've been able to go to for advice on these sorts of things, but I think that if you're a young independent manager and you don't have that, there are other great resources out there where you can just pick up the phone to get advice.
> (Kirkwood, 2023)

Virpi Immonen (EMMA/MMF Finland) also rates mentoring as a key development tool. EMMA, alongside many of the MMF organizations, has instigated a programme to allow emerging managers exactly that opportunity:

> In Finland we have just started our mentoring programme which Creative Europe has funded. We have this European-wide mentoring programme where we have quite established managers mentoring the newcomers into the business, which we will do now for this year and we are now thinking about how to continue with it because we got quite a lot of applications and I strongly believe that that's the only way to get into the business, that you need your mentor, you need to get into the company as a trainee or [meet] someone who can actually teach you.
> (Immonen 2020)

Existing literature on artist management generally agrees on the benefits of working with a mentor: 'finding and working with a mentor is considered one of the most important aspects of career development' (Anderton et al., 2022). 'Look for a mentor who can guide your development and be a sounding board for issues you face in management' (Allen, 2022).

Overall, our interviewees tended to agree that a broad network of industry connections was valuable and recommended working closely with those who already have experience to learn from them, effectively as a form of training. Many identified a particular contact, similar perhaps to a favourite teacher, who advised and supported their early development, introducing key personnel and explaining mechanisms. Clearly, as we were told in many interviews, industry organizations, notably the MMF networks, can also be vital in this role.

Social Media/Metrics

The importance of a social media presence as well as online data or metrics (plays, views, likes, followers, etc.) in the growth of an artist's fan base/success and the further development of their career only appears to be increasing. The requirement to maintain near-continuous contact with the fan base and the wealth of detail on that demographic available to everyone involved in the creative and promotional processes also seems to grow over time. These data can and are being used to make decisions on who gets selected for potentially elevating opportunities such as radio play, promotional priority and festival slots (Baym et al., 2021).

However, generating the online material to boost these figures can be taxing. The never-ending need for social media content as a form of promotion within the music industries can lead to pressure on artists to continually report on their working lives. Those in the management sector have taken different views on this, but they do recognize that regardless of who takes responsibility for online promotion, it is a necessary mechanism to promote the artist and develop the audience figures.

Karl Nielsen, a UK manager with over 30 years' experience in music sees both sides of the issue:

> Social media is a nasty thing. It's the biggest paradox isn't it, they [the artist] hate it, but they've got to have it. But some artists genuinely do it very well, and they're very aware to it and they've seen they actually can increase [their online statistics]. Funnily enough, I was talking to the guys from media research yesterday about the Coral [a UK band originally successful in the early 2000s] about a comeback and they reckon it's all down to social media and running the post at the right time and doing the whole thing [well]. I would doubt if [artists such as] Coldplay ever do a post [themselves]; I'm sure it's done by a team. So it's different scales of [online] management for different people. Some artists are running their own social media campaigns. They're that good at it because they're part of that generation.
>
> (Nielsen, 2024)

Chris Chadwick, also working as a manager in the UK, agrees, seeing the value in an online presence, but sounds a warning regarding artist health, and draws a clear distinction between social media metrics and income generation, which management have to be critically aware of:

> So, social media; it is really important. It's also quite dangerous and, in my opinion, you have to view it as a marketing tool, and that's all it is. Being successful on social media, having popularity on social media, does not make a successful music career; and, equally, the demands of the content needed to create popularity on social media can be really taxing for an artist, and there's no point managing an artist who's going to burn out in six months because they're doing three TikToks a day and four Instagram posts, and [only] sees that value held in likes and clicks and plays. Obviously, the virality of content on social media has the power to be really explosive for an artist project; but, ultimately, it's a marketing tool and it doesn't [necessarily] make a sustainable career. What makes a sustainable career are all the other things – releasing music, performing live, selling merchandise.
>
> (Chadwick, 2023)

He goes on to clarify this train of thought, drawing a clear distinction between the perceived success of online metrics and genuine income streams which will commercially benefit the artist. Chris was also one of the first interviewees to raise the issue of stress on artists due to the pressures of social media content generation, as we see above. He further developed that train of thought:

> If an artist starts to measure their success in likes and follows, that can be deceptive and doesn't represent genuine income for [their] business; it's very widely publicized the challenges that social media poses, not just in music but everyone, when it comes to mental health. As a manager I'm very conscious that there's no artist business if you have an artist who has a breakdown or is suffering a mental health crisis. It's really important to recognize that danger and help to steer an artist into

a healthy relationship with their marketing platforms.

(Chadwick, 2023)

Chris Hardin sees that it is possible that others could take on this task. A manager could identify someone appropriate to undertake the work but still the artist would be expected to be involved in the marketing in some respect:

> It doesn't mean they have to be as good at social [media content generation] as they are at performing. Ideally, their skillsets complement ours; I mean they're the artist we're not, so they have to be, ideally, good at promoting themselves.
>
> (Hardin, 2020)

Ellie Giles also believes that delivering online content is critical to artist's development and notes that those who have that ability are at an advantage:

> To break an artist, that's difficult unless you're a good [online] content creator; then yeah, you probably can and it's only if you're a good content creator you are going to succeed right now; which is a shame because content's .. .not songwriting; so, you know, you could be an incredible songwriter but you might not be a content maker. I also think that's probably a good skillset to teach our artists – all the skills like filming, photos, all the extra skills that come in now with the advent of [online] content [being] king and queen.
>
> (Giles, 2022)

She also sees the possibilities in using advertising opportunities online. However, she advocates caution in this field as there is the possibility of creating the wrong impression with your potential audience:

> At the beginning, then, I think there's a real value in using digital advertising to get your story out there and get your name out there, but, equally, I also think you've got to be careful because, depending on the artist, it actually might push people away; and, you know, if you do too much advertising, I think it can actually really make someone feel like there's a desperation there.
>
> (Giles, 2022)

Agreeing with Chadwick, Ross Patel warns against 'clicks' and 'likes' being interpreted as potential purchases. He does, however, have a process for finding out the difference:

> So, I know that we've got listeners there. Great. People in these places love this music, or maybe it's just 50 cafés that have the songs on repeat, because it works. Are they gonna buy a ticket? Don't know. Are they gonna buy merch? Don't know. Are they even gonna sign up to the newsletter? No idea. I had a client who set up TikTok and within four months went from zero to nearly 180,000 followers, over 10 million views across the video that were uploaded. Based on that alone, we would have no idea whether any of them are fans or not. So we went through a process to work out what the conversion rate of those followers are, how real they are and how engaged they are.
>
> (Patel, 2024)

He goes on to explain the steps being taken to establish the level of commitment of those who have expressed an interest in the artist online:

> So, the first thing that we did was record a live performance. [The venue] was about 150 capacity and we put that online, but before that, we teased the clips of the show to that audience and getting people to sign up, to register their interest in whether or not they would want to watch that show. So that would be the first step, because the content that she [currently] posts is not live performance. It's covers, home songs, short clips of original material, but it's not seeing the full show, which is obviously what we want people to buy into.
>
> (Patel, 2024)

Agreeing with Giles in advising caution when advertising, he then discusses how this will be taken forward avoiding what has previously been seen as an accepted route:

> Then once we know who those people are, we'll start targeting them with follow-up things like, "Will you pre-save the next song?", and see what that looks like. Signing up [for] some newsletters and starting a conversation with people outside of the existing platforms that really are quite restrictive in terms of how you can communicate with the fans. I'm pretty sick and tired of spending thousands of pounds on

Meta [Facebook and Instagram advertising], to be honest, [I'm] not really up to doing that anymore especially now that there are better alternatives.

(Patel, 2024)

One of our younger interviewees working in artist management, Cara Mills-McLaughlin, has grown up with social media as a fundamental part of her life. This might make it easier for her generation to better embrace and engage in this activity when working professionally:

Social media in my time has always been a big thing, but [now] I think [even] more so. Social media is how you drive a campaign. In the past, maybe, 2 years, I've been trying to learn as much as I can about social media and how to market from that perspective, because I think traditional avenues of marketing are getting less and less [useful] as the years go by. [Also,] how they [the platforms] all connect into each other has been probably the biggest change, obviously streaming [is a] really big thing. Playlisting on streaming [platforms], I would say, is becoming more and more important, and the placement itself on the playlist is really important; if you're in that number-one spot on new-music Friday on Spotify, then, chances are, the song's going to do incredibly [well].

(Mills-McLaughlin, 2020)

Another aspect of the online side of the business is tracking sales information and interest data geographically and demographically [metrics]. This can deliver some very accurate information on who your audience is and where they are, as Steijn Koeijvoets points out:

It's not social media alone, it's also data. One of the important tasks is by doing ad campaigns, you can easily reach out to new fans or have a good target audience and reach out to them and try to convert them from interested people into fans and loyal fans. But describing the target audience and really finding out who they are, making a marketing persona, that's difficult. We collect data from every source we have and that's becoming more and more important. Data – that's a key.

(Koeijvoets, 2023)

Ellie Giles agrees and has seen the value of this first-hand:

I think the more data you have, the more you know. You can make a good decision from this. It shows you when a playlist [happens], where the playlist is, what they're doing, which countries it's hitting, what radio plays you're getting, and so it does give you a story of, actually, "this is working in Germany" or "this is working in Japan"; and so, ultimately, yes, there is a value in having that resource, and knowing when something's connecting in a country is hugely vital because to make a decision whether you're going to go to that country and make an impact in that country, and also persuade the label to put money into that country, you know?

(Giles, 2022)

Steven Braines agrees that the data you gain from online analytics can give you a solid argument for approaching others to help develop your business in new territories, for example:

In terms of analytics, [it's] important ... If you go to Helsinki, they're the ninth biggest city in our streaming on Spotify, and that also correlates with Apple where they're twelfth, and it correlates with what we're seeing on YouTube and Instagram. Then we could use all that data and go to the [events] booker for all festivals in Finland and say, "Look! [there's a potential live events audience for this artist in Finland]". I use data to justify my rationale and also to not do stupid stuff like, "Shall we go and play in this arena?". It's simply, like, why? Just for vanity? Because nothing's going to be worse than you have that moment where you have an arena in Italy and only seven tickets got sold – that's vanity.

(Braines, 2023)

The takeaway messages from our interviewees on this subject therefore appear to be, first, the importance of developing the critical online presence. MMF UK notes that 'maintaining the [artist's] website is therefore important'. It can be one way of 'building your mailing list and collecting important data' (Webb et al., 2022). It is vital, however, that the artist doesn't overstretch themselves generating the social media content audiences expect. As our interviewees pointed out, it can feel pressurized and possibly appear somewhat artificial to the target audience. The artist themselves might not be skilled in content generation. Identifying someone else who could make a key difference here could make a significant difference.

Secondly, online statistics do not necessarily equate to fans/purchases/income. A post could exponentially grow in popularity for many reasons unrelated to engagement with the artist. Potential audience data can also be sourced from other locations. Paul Allen has noticed that managers can 'search sites for similar artists, capturing the contact information of [their] fans [to then promote their own artist]' (Allen, 2022). This is seen regularly on music distribution platforms that inform viewers, 'If you like this, you might also like these artists', as a marketing tool to broaden audience tastes.

Finally, the data you can access on your own audience should be investigated in detail to gain a clearer picture of your fan base in demographic and geographic terms. It can be used as lever when negotiating and helps in avoiding errors of judgement. Academic observers have noticed, 'data analytics has become an essential tool, it can be gleaned from a variety of sources'. These include YouTube, Spotify, events promoters and ticket agencies as well as the artists' own platforms (Anderton et al., 2022).

Live Performance

How important do artist/creator managers believe live performance is to artist development? Does it depend on genre/audience? Have COVID and online platforms changed the landscape and reduced the demand/need for touring? The events and festivals sector has, in recent years, potentially, become the single most lucrative source of income for many artists and managers as recognized by a number of researchers and data analysts (Ernst & Young, 2014; Naveed et al., 2017; Hitters and Winter, 2020) with festivals growing to become a key economic driver (Frith, 2007; Webster, 2014; Vliet, 2019). The growth of streaming, where a lower level of income returns to the artist, and resulting loss of revenue from reduced physical product sales (CDs, vinyl, cassettes) means that ticket sales and merchandise income can now represent the most significant financial element of an artist's turnover, although in the UK the withdrawal from the EU has caused issues.

Polly Comber clearly stated the case for live events, suggesting that being at a live performance is a fundamental point of contact between the fan, the artist and the songs:

> I personally think that it's the last thing that we cannot recreate [digitally]. You can go and watch as many streams and videos [as you like] – Abba holograms or whatever – but nothing beats being in the room, be it with ten people or 10,000, and you'll see the artist that you love and believe in. I could be wrong. There may be something round the corner that's going to blow everyone's minds, but I don't see how you get a person [an artist] who's a human being in a room and how you replicate that. I've done these big streaming things [online live events]. We did one with Rag'n'Bone Man and Spotify and it did well because we were in lockdown, so we didn't have a lot of choice. But . . . it seems like we've been [performing live] for millennia, people have been singing to people for hundreds and thousands of years; how do you change that [form of] entertainment?
>
> (Comber, 2022)

Ellie Giles agrees, picking up on the human interaction aspect between the audience and the artist which Comber raised: 'I do think that live is still valuable because they want that intimacy, they want that connection, we all do.'

For Comber, however, every artist/creator is different:

> You're talking to someone who broke their last two acts via the live route. So for me, again, it's a personal perspective. Does Megan Thee Stallion need to be performing live all the time? [Probably] no, because she she's got so many fans online. Do Coldplay need to still perform live? [Probably] yes. It depends on the artist.
>
> (Comber, 2022)

Karl Nielsen backs up the case-by-case approach which Comber proposed but again stresses how vital live performance can be to an act:

> I think that it really does, once again, depend on the artist; they have to want to play live but, yeah, absolutely, it's as important as making a song. People think that – and they say that for

a reason – "I wanna see what they look like". There used to be a lot of showcases back in those days and it was kind of, "OK, what does this band look like?". Now it's like, "What are the [online] numbers?". Oh, what? And they realize [later] they've got a turkey that couldn't sing, couldn't dance, so it was all [studio/technology]-generated? So I think it's really good to see them live; you have to know they can actually perform. It's as crucial as the art itself, I think it's a fundamental part of being an artist.

(Nielsen, 2024)

This point is not lost on Brendan Moon, who discovered Paolo Nutini at a live performance and managed him over the critical growth period of his career. Here he points out the anomaly of artists who have significant online and/or recording success but perhaps limited or zero live experience:

Some artists will aim for the live arena with next to no live experience and potentially an online hit. So that guy who's got the 775 million streams may not have done a gig ever, and all of a sudden he's got an audience – a global audience. He could go to New York and sell out a gig probably pretty easily, but most people who could make a good record have got the inner suss to pull out a concert from themselves, somewhere. But there's a lot of people who will be entering the live arena who would never have played, never even have played a pub, never even sang a song at a birthday party, or whatever, and then all of a sudden you put them in front of an audience.

(Moon, 2020)

If you *can* play live, it can be extremely lucrative with successful records driving concert fees and changing career trajectories, as Moon explains, delivering some key insights into the festivals circuit:

It's where a lot of the money is. If you get to a level where you're on the festival circuit, even if you're just in the mid-afternoon slot, you could be looking at 30, 40, 50, 60 thousand pounds [or dollars] a performance, and you could be doing that every weekend from May until the end of September; and then you could take the whole thing down to Australia [summer festival season is November to February in the southern hemisphere] and do the whole thing again. I'd have to be quite mercenary and say that the income is the bigger appeal, you know, because playing big festivals like maybe Byron Bay or Bluesfest in America or Australia, I'm not sure they'd get anything back from it [in terms of kudos or record sales] in the way that [the] exposure [of] doing, like, Fuji Rock [would achieve]. The exposure that I noticed for the artist is having a really good record, and that was the cutting edge in helping book all of these festivals, helping book all of these tours.

(Moon, 2020)

Other interviewees also see that live events can be a key lever in developing the international career of an artist/creator, as Steven Braines discussed:

It's about playing in front of people. I think it's really important but also it's about focusing the PR team and saying, 'this is our French show in Paris, so let's get the French down, the French press, and write about it – it has a benefit of that kind of focus in the industry and a lot of times as well now when you go and send the marketing drivers over to Spotify, [then] Spotify is going to support your record more if you've got a bit [of play/interest] in France, and then you've got French press around that, so [you] can't really take anything in isolation.

(Braines, 2023)

Another of the concerns raised related to the post-pandemic live events environment. Steijn Koeijvoets and Polly Comber identify further difficulties here. First, Koeijvoets's experience of staffing issues:

Obviously, dealing with the after-effects of COVID [were difficult]. For instance, finding crew when bands are now touring again, but finding crew is [now] very hard [thousands of skilled workers left the live events industry due to the closure of venues over nearly 2 years of lockdown – many have not returned]. You know, normally, we could pick [from] seven people for one job. Well now we have seven jobs for one person. So that's hard; but, you know, that's due to COVID.

(Koeijvoets, 2023)

Comber has experienced another, different issue arising post-pandemic:

I think it's been difficult for live, funnily enough, because everyone came back onto the marketplace all at the same time, be that playing King Tut's [Glasgow venue] or be that playing Wembley stadium; there's just been this flush of artists, and getting [support slots on] tours is really difficult at the moment because there's hundreds and hundreds of acts trying to do support tours. So that got really concentrated and quite difficult. I know I've struggled myself with my current client trying to get onto support tours; we've got one now but, yep, it was really hard.

(Comber, 2022)

Turning to the financial practicalities of touring, Ross Patel has seen the recent economic downturn negatively affect the events market:

Live – that is such a key component of our business and our client's business. For touring, festival events, outdoor events, [the] cost of procurement has gone up around 30%. That increases the ticket price to cover those costs. [The] cost of living crisis means less disposable income for the consumer, with harder choices being made by the consumer as to how many events they're going to. How many events they go to affects how many live shows, merchandise and records they buy at the end of all of that. Fees are going down because there are other costs [for the promoter] that also need to be offset. So the majority of artists' fees are lower. They're selling less merch. They're touring less because there are less events taking place. Events are still being pulled. Competition for the slots is fierce.

(Patel, 2024)

The impact of COVID-19 on the live music industry was significant with almost 80% of all income lost across Europe (Live-DMA, 2021). In the UK, 70,000 jobs and £2.7 billion disappeared, predominantly from the events side of music (Paine, 2021). Recovery has been relatively swift but there have been some issues in restarting venues and festivals. Post-pandemic, with a glut of artists wishing to perform again, but with audiences suffering the effects of the recent economic downturn, the events market has become more pressurized with as many as 100 major festivals in the UK alone susceptible to financial failure in 2024 according to the Association of Independent Festivals (AIF, quoted in Paine, 2024b). The same article highlights a rise in the number of high-earning artists setting up their own events, which also impacts on the festivals market.

As Ross Patel pointed out, there is also the additional factor of the cost-of-living crisis pushing up all the costs of playing live for the artist, manager and promoter, while reducing the disposable income that possible audiences have to spend on tickets and merchandise. This 'cost-of-touring crisis', as David Martin at FAC has christened it, has led to a situation where an artist has to be working at a reasonably advanced level of success to make money from live events (Wray, 2024). Despite all of this, most managers we spoke with welcomed the return to live performance (after the COVID restrictions were lifted in mid-2022).

To summarize, then, it would appear from our interviews and the published research that while COVID severed the events income stream, causing a significant revenue loss for artists and managers, the return to live performance has thrown up other difficulties including the shortage of experienced staff and a 'log jam' of so many acts trying to return to touring at once. The cost-of-living crisis has added to this, increasing touring costs while causing fan bases to become more selective about their spending. While a great live performance can be a career-transforming step, bringing the attention of record companies and the media, the need to play live does depend on the genre of music and the nature of the artist. Generally, live events are still an important form of connection with music and with the artist, from an audience perspective, and remains financially attractive to artists and managers as ticket sales and merchandise are highly significant revenue generators once you achieve a reasonable level of success.

Record Company

We asked those working in the management sector the intentionally provocative question, 'Do you think you still need a record company?' This drew a broad range of differing responses. The advent of file sharing, digital audio downloads and streaming have often been criticized for the negative impact on the financial returns for artists/creators (although the reality may be more debatable (Hesmondhalgh, 2020)). More recently, the emergence of label services, where an artist or a manager can locate or negotiate exactly which combination of services they wish the label to perform (A&R, marketing, distribution, promotion, etc.), continues to significantly alter the marketplace. Companies such as AWAL and Sentric (AWAL, n.d., Sentric, n.d.), offering different services, and crowd-funding platforms such as Kickstarter, have changed the concept of what a record label (Kickstarter, n.d) can be, creating flexible solutions with different levels of support for different returns (AWAL).

To briefly overview how label services work, a record company would generally perform a series of functions including: artist & repertoire (A&R – the role at the record label responsible for working with the artist to select the songs, produce, studio and assemble the recordings for release); marketing (to establish and communicate with key demographic audiences in geographical locations appropriate to the artist/genre); promotion, through online and traditional mechanisms; and distribution of physical and digital product (Homewood, 2023). Artists and their management teams often decide they would prefer to handle one or more of these activities themselves, thus saving costs. In a label services agreement, the artist/manager can select which of these functions they require the label to take on (e.g. marketing, promotion and distribution, but *not* A&R), and which they intend to undertake themselves.

First, we examine the views of those who took a clear 'yes' or 'no' stance to the question. Brendan Moon, for example, has worked with record labels throughout his career and has seen the value of their involvement:

> Yes, I do. Anyone who thinks that they don't has never really worked [with] a major label. If you're lucky enough to get [your artist] onto a major label, what they do have is boots on the ground. So say you are a new act signed to Warner's, or whatever, [the label] has got relationships with all the Spotify playlists locally, across the world. So all of a sudden, you'd be on the Fresh Music Malaysia playlist, which would be sorted out for you by your local rep in the territory. You cannot do this [by yourself or with an independent label], they don't have the individual relationships, and if you do, you probably find that your independent record label is owned by a major label, like Fuelled by Ramen or one of these other labels that have got, you know, roots into the majors where they use the marketing department, the online departments. If you're completely independent, you'll have some relationship with a major label, you know?; your music could be very well distributed by someone like Sony Red or Caroline or maybe Warner's – they've got a distribution thing. So a major label will be playing a small role in your project, even though you might not realize it.
>
> (Moon, 2020)

Ellie Giles takes a different view although she agrees that the capital investment of a label is valuable:

> I don't think you do. I think you need a structure, and I think you need a distributor, and I think you need a very, very smart manager who can build a strategy and build a team, and, ultimately, I don't think you need a label now. I think it depends [on the] artist, so if you're Dua Lipa, yes, you probably still need a major label and/or the trappings of a major label because of the money spent, but if you're self-motivated and, you know, create your own assets, create everything yourself, [then] no, I don't think you do. I mean look at Stormzy; he went through ADA [label services company] at the beginning because he was more than capable of building his own world.
>
> (Giles, 2022)

However, she does recognize the advantages in taking the major label approach:

> There's a lot more investment when you go to a major, certainly, so that's why you do it, you get the money, and if you need to take it to the next level internationally, then there's a value in it.
>
> (Giles, 2022)

As we saw previously, however, Ellie has had some negative experiences of working with record labels. To recap:

> [Sometimes] labels will take advantage of you; [that] certainly was the case when I first started managing. One tried to get me to get the artist to take a bank loan out, which I was horrified by, to go touring. I thought it was just both rude and immoral – trying to get the band into debt.
>
> (Giles, 2022)

Generally, Ross Patel appears to agree with Ellie but advises analysis of what is offered/required:

> You don't need a label; it just depends on what you want as an artist. It depends on where your expectations and ambitions are set. They should take what you are already doing very well and add a ten times multiplier to the returns over 5 years, but making that happen with the right team, [making sure you're] getting the right deal, you know, you're adding in a whole bunch of new variables into something that you already have a lot of control over.
>
> (Patel, 2024)

These responses can be seen to be quite polarized. However, taking a more nuanced approach, Steven Braines believes that similar to the live performance situation, a lot depends on the genre of music the artist performs:

> I would say it's genre-specific. I think that if you're a pop act and trying to get broken [breaking through to success], then it definitely helps if you've got Universal's big spend behind you. Labels, I feel, work best when you're a heritage act because you just need a bit of money to go to the machine and service it out. I think it's harder to break [new] acts that way.
>
> (Braines, 2023)

Giles agrees that genre needs to be taken into account:

> I think it still depends, because ultimately there's some artists that just stream very well; you know, if you're the grime artist or you're a dance artist, that's where your business is. You can do really, really smart EP deals that are like millions of pounds because you're streaming so well; you can pull a great deal and be in and be out of that deal within 5 minutes [retaining artistic freedom], and so, again, it comes back down to the genre. So I think, ultimately, that [for example] a grime artist probably doesn't earn that much from live but earns a lot more from streaming.
>
> (Giles, 2022)

Steven Braines gave some further insight on how streaming can work well in a label services agreement:

> I've found I use label services for DJs because within that community you can go on tour. It's so different to rock, pop and hip-hop. So my artists [for example], they don't need a hit record to have toured in 40 countries. But my biggest artist, she's played in 57 countries. So, her having label servicing, it's all about 2000 plays from here, 10,000 from there, 5000 from there; and then the sum of those parts in synergy means that you've actually got, like, millions; whereas a Universal or Sony or something wouldn't be able to get their head around that.

Braines continues, discussing his experiences with the newer label services model where the process may be different but the roots may be more traditional:

> I had that [same experience] when I first came to label services. They [said] "Oh, well, the record needs to break in the UK", and we'd [say] "Why?" "Because she's from the UK." [But] it doesn't matter. The minute that a record is out in Germany it's getting played somewhere in Peru, it's getting played somewhere, wherever the DJs have been, [perhaps] eight countries [in the last] month. So you're just going to miss your window. So I feel [when] I've been at Kobalt, BMG and a few other label services places, every time I've always had to kind of school them in it, because most people come from, as I say, the old label of rock, pop, hip-hop, [which] breaks its domestic territory [first] and does well from that. I also feel that [with] the label services and digital companies, they're all kind of morphing into a similar model. But even if you haven't got a record label, you just still need to hire good independent PR people and pluggers.
>
> (Braines, 2023)

Scott Kirkwood came through an A&R background himself, meaning he is able to take on some elements of that role when working with his artists as a manager (not dissimilar to the label services model). Notably, this was critical when putting together the number-one

Lewis Capaldi album *Divinely Uninspired to a Hellish Extent*:

> We A&R a lot of our artists ourselves. A&R is probably becoming less and less a key role within a traditional label structure because a lot of it is done before an artist will sign a deal; the artist that will generally go in towards that major label sort of world. Nine times out of ten the majority of those artists will go into writing sessions most days with a songwriter and a producer; for example, there are artists I have worked with who have had about 150 songs recorded, ready for that one record [which had 12 tracks on final release], all out of writing sessions we put together.
>
> (Kirkwood, 2023)

To follow up on this angle, Chris Chadwick is also supportive of label services companies but, again, noted that self-releasing can be successful. He also appears to disagree somewhat with Braines's 'all label services morphing into one model' theory. So, do you need a record label?:

> Sometimes, not always; you know, I think what's amazing about being an artist now is that you really have, like, a massive spectrum of opportunities and deal structures; there is no one right deal structure or record deal for an artist and there are a massive variety of hybrid deal structures.
>
> (Chadwick, 2023)

He then identifies specific reasons for working with a record label:

> I think that labels can be really incredible for helping to kickstart international growth. I think that if you're looking to add a sense of identity to a project, that could be another reason for working with a label. If you're looking to place an artist within a certain community then there are some incredible labels that have a reputation that can help build an artist. If you're looking to be the biggest artist in the world, if you're looking to be global and be a top-tier artist then, yeah, I think at a certain point having a label team behind you with the international pull can be really helpful but that's not every artist and I don't think it should be. So I don't think they're essential but I think they still have a huge role to play.
>
> (Chadwick, 2023)

Nielsen, having worked with independent labels and majors, essentially agrees with this view and echoes some of the thoughts presented by Brendan Moon:

> It really depends what you're talking about. If you want to sell lots and lots of records and work with the big people, you need a major record company. You cannot get on a big scale [without them]; it doesn't matter what you do; even Adele, they had to do a deal with Sony in America. There's no way around that and that's because they [major labels] have boots on the ground in 40, 80, 90 territories, and that's just like running a big business; Do you know what I mean? . . . You've got to have that scale in place to be able to do that and know those markets well.
>
> (Nielsen, 2024)

Like other managers (Moon and Kirkwood to take two examples), Polly Comber has experience of working with majors. This has advantages but she seems to favour working by yourself in the early stages, as the artist develops:

> A really good question. So I'd say it's between a yes and a no, I'm afraid. No because there's no reason why you can't do it yourself with your management, get a little team together – quite expensive though, even doing certain things – you're suddenly scratching your head going, "Oh, I've just dropped £500 there"; it just adds up. I think you can do that for so long; [so] the "no" part is very much [at] the beginning; I don't think you do [need a record label at that early stage], I think it's actually probably detrimental to get a deal too early. I think you could lose out quite badly if it doesn't do well and I think it could be quite disheartening for the artist.
>
> (Comber, 2022)

She then moves forward to explain when and why a major label can make a difference, echoing Chadwick's and Moon's thoughts:

> But my only defence of the majors is that when they come together globally, I mean doing a deal with a major worldwide and you get into that top five global priority list, which I've had twice now with two different majors, the way they sync up with each other is [amazing]. I don't

think there's any organization that does it better at that level because you know if Australia wants you and America wants you at the same time [and you're signed to one major label], they'll work it out. Whereas if you've got a deal in Australia, a different deal in America, you've got something going on in Korea [different deals], everyone argues with each other and it just gets very messy for the artist.

(Comber, 2022)

Beyond all of this, there is evidence to suggest that major labels have greater leverage in generating streaming volume with the digital distribution platforms (Spotify, etc.). Recent research gives a series of reasons (including direct ownership of certain platforms by major labels and owned and curated playlists) why an artist might gain higher streaming figures if signed to a major label as opposed to working with an independent (Mariuzzo and Ormosi, 2022). The scale of operation and sheer volume of catalogue which a major label has can give it a key bargaining position in negotiation with streaming services.

It is also important to be considered a 'priority' act within the different departments of the label; 'artist managers need "buy-in" (committed support) from the various teams . . . within a label, so must use the negotiation and social skills' (Anderton et al., 2022). The A&R department may have signed the artist, but marketing, promotion and international are also needed to get behind them to make them successful. One further consideration here is manager workload. MMF UK identifies that this might be reduced with a record deal as 'the label will assume the bulk of responsibilities for releasing and promoting the artist's music' (Webb et al., 2022). Hence, the manager may be able to better focus on other opportunities (tours, international markets, festivals, merchandise, etc.). However, signing the deal, they point out, could mean some loss of creative control so that balance needs to be assessed.

In summary, then, it would appear that a record label is not necessarily something which is needed at the start of the artist's career but is quite critical if and when you want to step up to international level. The value of their experience coupled with a global network of staff located in (and highly familiar with) the individual marketplaces can be of crucial importance. The availability of capital investment is also a key advantage, but many artists and managers are now choosing to work with label services rather than take on a full record label deal, at least initially, handling certain elements themselves while benefitting from a greater awareness of markets and a significantly larger team to help develop the act.

Music Publishing

The third key sector for potential revenue for a developing artist and their manager after live events and recorded music income is music publishing. This clearly depends on the artist also being a songwriter or composer (see Chapter 3). The turnover can be considerable if the songs they write are successful, notably if a song is picked up for synchronization (or 'sync') to a film soundtrack, TV programme or video game, as the music will generate income each time it gains airplay or listeners without the artist/songwriter having to do anything further. Royalty collection organizations (PRS for music in the UK, for example) then monitor use, collect income and distribute revenue to the composers several times each year. We therefore asked 'How important is music publishing to an artist/manager in comparison to other revenue streams?'. Steijn Koeijvoets places music publishing third in terms of overall value:

> Publishing can be very important as a revenue stream for artists and their managers. It obviously depends on the amount of success/ catalogue, especially if sync monies are involved. Building and exploiting the catalogue of one's artist is a valuable asset [and relates directly] to the income. However, it is still behind the income from live and music streaming/sales.
>
> (Koeijvoets, 2023)

Lyle Scougall explained the mechanism from the manager's perspective:

> I would say that music publishing is an extremely valuable asset, in the sense that once you have released the composition [and it is successful] it will pay you for ever [or for as long as you have the rights to collect money from it from a management perspective]. I suppose

that is how it differs from live performance fees or merchandise transactions where they are "one and done" transactions. Another positive of having your compositions exploited via music publishing is that it can be used to generate income across public broadcast, synchronizations, remixes and covers to name a few off the top of my head. This again differs from other [income] streams as it can be utilized in various ways. The quarterly PRS payments are a godsend for cashflow, and as I always say to my artists, "that is your pension". To summarize, music publishing differs in a sense that it can be exploited in numerous ways, and it will pay you for [the] life[time] of the copyright. A little bit of money a lot of the time can really make the difference to your P&L [profit-and-loss accounts].

(Scougall, 2023)

Denise Allan agrees, explaining further and giving an overview of her experience with one of the acts she manages, drawing further attention to the longer-term benefits:

> Music publishing is generated through the writing/composition of songs and can go on generating an income for a long period of time. For example, Glasvegas have sync placements on *The Vampire Diaries* with "Geraldine" and also "Finished Sympathy", both written by James Allan. When this TV series is replayed again in other parts of the world, royalties are generated every time, so there is a longevity in this passive income stream from the songwriting and composition rights. There can be performance royalties, mechanical royalties (from the use of original compositions on records), and sync licensing income sources, which are all unique to publishing. Song ownership is a very valuable asset with writers able to sell their back catalogues in lucrative deals. A publishing deal can be financially advantageous to an artist and manager over the long term.

(Allan, 2023)

Steven Braines discussed the issue in further detail, highlighting significant examples which demonstrate the potential for direct and peripheral income:

> It just depends on how prolific a songwriter they are. We've had an artist who made an underground track. The original never charted, but it's been sampled in two huge international charting tracks and had easily generated six-figure sums, so it can be a huge revenue stream. Also, publishers help create new works and get syncs, for example, which bring in new audiences. Sometimes an advert or a TV placement can break a song. Just look at [the] Kate Bush placement in *Stranger Things* [which] led to it being the most streamed Spotify track over a particular time period in most of the world. Her whole catalogue got a bounce [as a result]. New audiences can also buy gig tickets. So it's all part of the wider machine [linking to other revenue streams], but also helping make new works is good for an artist's creativity. You might also not want to tour, or the song [which the artist has written] isn't right for [them], but you can give the song to another artist to perform, which publishers push, and it can create a lot of passive income. See Prince, Dolly Parton and a ton more [for example].

(Braines, 2023)

Ross Patel gave his own insight into the changing internal workings of music publishing, seeing some parallels with the 'label services' model pioneered by record companies:

> Interestingly, publishing seems to be one of the most relatively unchanged aspects of the industry. The role and function of the publisher has remained consistent compared to the recorded music industry, for example. At its core, the collection of publishing royalties has been, and always will be, a vital and often overlooked aspect of an artist's business. Where there are now more "administration" deals [publishing companies handling the registration and management of songs more than the promotion], readily available for artists such as Sentric, the responsibility is still on the manager to do the manual data input to ensure gigs and broadcasts are logged to ensure correct payments.

(Patel, 2024)

Patel believes that finding the right publisher/deal is the key:

> Where "exclusive" publishing deals are concerned, you would hope to find a dedicated publishing A&R who has the ability to bring creative opportunities or a strong sync team that are motivated to place catalogue. This can be hard to find as, more so than ever, publishers bank and rely on large catalogues with roughly 10–20% of the music rights

paying the costs of the rest of the company, and allows for the risk on signing new catalogue/artists. Overall, I would say publishing remains an essential part of an artist/manager career. Finding the right publisher can be hard. There are no guarantees of big payouts beyond the bare essentials of accurate song registration and royalty collection [even that is somewhat of a mystery due to the lack of transparency within the collection societies], but with good catalogue that is "syncable" or artists that are open to collaboration, which a creative A&R can provide, it could be a huge aspect of an artist's career; especially, of course, for writers/producers.

(Patel, 2024)

Essentially, then, if you sign to a publishing company that is prepared to work to get your compositions placed in film, TV or video games the rewards can be considerable. The percentage which a songwriter receives from a publishing company (typically between 50 and 80%) is usually greater than that which, as an artist, they would receive from a record company (between 25 and 50% after deductions) and can continue over a longer time period (film and TV repeat broadcast fees) (Webb et al., 2022).

Steijn Koeijvoets can, however, see potential for tension in the artist–manager relationship in this area: 'One sensitive issue is if the manager gets a percentage of the income from copyrights. This sometimes feels a bit out of balance from an artist's perspective, as copyrights are tied to their personal/artistic capital.' In essence, while from an artist's perspective they might think that they wrote the songs, so they own them and should get 100% of the income from the composition, the manager's position is that perhaps the only way those songs made money is because they were taken to music publishers, radio stations, TV and film companies by the manager. Should this particular activity undertaken by the manager therefore be subject to the same standard commission rate? Steijn thinks it should, but within the limitations of the contract:

> Yes, I think that's justifiable, but [again] only for the copyrights that have been created under the management contract. There's one exception – if the manager arranges a sync or is involved in the sync of an older work, then that is shared together, but that's more for clarity's sake. There should be one percentage overall.

(Koeijvoets, 2023)

Finally, Steijn identifies one instance where the income from music publishing could potentially become the most important:

> ...if you manage a non-performing artist. I'm managing two top-line producers and their biggest income I think is from publishing because they get the biggest cut from a song [composition] and the income of the song, and a much smaller cut from the master income [recording rights], so in that case publishing is very important, but in most cases, if you have a normal performing artist, the biggest sum of money is from playing live, but it depends on the nature of the artist's career.

(Koeijvoets, 2023)

It should be noted that music publishing is a steadily growing marketplace. CISAC reported that global music royalty collection for creators rose by 7.6% to a new record high of €11.75 billion in 2023 (Paine, 2024c). In summary, as Paul Allen identifies 'clearly there is considerable potential income for the artist who also develops into a good songwriter' (Allen, 2022). The MMF in the UK reported in 2024, that 62% of their members manage songwriters (up from 42% in 2020), indicating a greater level of manager interest in this sector (MMF UK (Music Managers Forum UK), n.d). Publishing income from composition of original music therefore appears to have the potential to be a significant revenue source. It must be registered correctly, and the copyrights need to be monitored and promoted, but it can be part of a longer-term income strategy as repeated use on public media might generate royalties for perhaps years after the song was first written. Finding the right publisher is vital, but if correctly managed, the benefits can be significant and long-lasting.

Conclusions

Our research tallies with existing literature in that networking and mentoring are of considerable importance for the emerging music industry professional. Who you know is as valuable as what you know and, in fact, the two may be intrinsically related. Education and industry support, such as established FE and HE programmes and that provided by the MMF, are also vital parts of this mechanism.

Social media promotion, while essential, should not be allowed to become the sole focus for artist development. There is not necessarily a direct correlation between online popularity and financial income. Critically, it should not become a source of stress to artists trying to generate content. Metrics (online fan base data) can be of considerable value in understanding your market demographic and should be analysed to guide artist growth.

The post-COVID live music environment has had recovery issues, notably in the initial shortages of experienced staff and the bottleneck of many artists trying to return to the stage simultaneously. Events and festivals are once again a growth market and a prime source of income (including merchandise) for acts and managers. Rising costs have also impacted performers but the sense of 'connection' between artist and audience is significant and will most likely drive this sector forward.

The extent of their global network, experience in marketing and availability of financial investment make major labels quite fundamental for artists wishing to succeed internationally. Not necessarily required by every act, particularly with the advent and growth of label services, major labels still have a key role to offer once the artist reaches a certain level of development.

While live events now represent the largest single income source for most artists, with recorded music as a strong second, music publishing can be a key finance generator if your artist is a songwriter and if the compositions are managed well. Distinct from live performance and merchandise sales, but similar to recorded music income, publishing can also function beyond the immediate timeframe of a tour or a record release, providing longer-term income.

References

Allan, D. (2023) *Practicalities of Artist Management [lecture]*. University of the West of Scotland.
Allen, P. (2022) *Artist Management for the Music Business: Manage Your Career in Music: Manage the Music Careers of Others*. Focal Press, New York and London.
Anderton, C., Hannam, J. and Hopkins, J. (2022) *Music Management, Marketing & PR*. Sage London.
AWAL (n.d.). Available at: awal.com/how-it-works/ (accessed 8 December 2024).
Baym, N., Bergmann, R., Bhargava, R., Diaz, F., Gillespie, T. *et al*. (2021) Making sense of metrics in the music industries. *International Journal of Communication* 3418–3441.
Braines, S. (2023) Questions on artist management. Interview by Allan Dumbreck [Zoom].
Chadwick, C. (2023) Questions on artist management. Interview by Allan Dumbreck [Zoom].
Comber, P. (2022) Questions on artist management. Interview by Allan Dumbreck [phone].
EMMA (European Music Managers Alliance) (n.d.).
Ernst & Young (2014) Creating growth – measuring cultural and creative markets in the EU. Available at: www.ey.com/Publication/vwLUAssets/Measuring_cultural_and_creative_markets_in_the_EU/%24FILE/Creating-Growth.pdf (accessed 10 October 2024).
Frith, S. (2007) *Taking Popular Music Seriously: Selected Essays, Ashgate*. UK, Aldershot.
Giles, E. (2022) Questions on artist management. Interview by Allan Dumbreck [Zoom].
Hardin, C. (2020) Questions on artist management. Interview by Allan Dumbreck [Zoom].
Hesmondhalgh, D. (2020) Is music streaming bad for musicians? problems of evidence and argument. *SAGE* 23(12). Available at: journals.sagepub.com/doi/full/10.1177/1461444820953541#:~:text=This%20article%20identifies%20and%20discusses,and%20ownership%2C%20(c)%20tendencies (accessed 10 October 2024).
Hitters, E. and Winter, C. (2020) The festivalization of live music: Introduction. *International Journal of Music Business Research* 9(2).
Homewood (2023) Special report: Label services. *Music Week*. Available at: (accessed 10 October 2024).
Immonen, V. (2020) Questions on artist management. Interview by Allan Dumbreck [Zoom].
Kickstarter (n.d). Available at: www.kickstarter.com/learn?ref=nav (accessed 8 December 2024).
Kirkwood, S. (2023) Questions on artist management. Interview by Allan Dumbreck [Zoom].
Koeijvoets, S. (2023) Questions on artist management. Interview by Allan Dumbreck [Zoom].

Live-DMA (2021) Impact of COVID 19 on music venues and clubs on Europe. Available at: www.live-dma.eu/wp-content/uploads/2021/10/Impact-of-COVID19-on-music-venues-and-clubs-in-Europe-Live-DMA-Oct-2021.pdf (accessed 10 October 2024).

Mariuzzo, F. and Ormosi, P. (2022) Independent v. major record labels: Do they have the same streaming power (law)? *SSRN*. Available at: apers.ssrn.com/sol3/papers.cfm?abstract_id=3729966 (accessed 9 December 2024).

Mills-McLaughlin, C. (2020) Questions on artist management. Interview by Allan Dumbreck [Zoom].

MMF UK (Music Managers Forum UK) (n.d.). Available at: www.themmf.net (accessed 16 November 2024).

MMF US (Music Managers Forum US) (n.d.). Available at: www.mmfus.com/ (accessed 16 November 2024).

Moon, B. (2020) Questions on artist management. Interview by Allan Dumbreck [Zoom].

Naveed, K., Watanabe, C. and Neittaanmäki, P. (2017) Co-evolution between streaming and live music leads a way to the sustainable growth of music industry – Lesson from the US experience. *Technology in Society* 50, 1–19.

Nielsen, K. (2024) Questions on artist management. Interview by Allan Dumbreck [Zoom].

Paine, A. (2021) How COVID wiped put 70,000 jobs and £2.7 bn of economic value from the music industry. *Music Week*. Available at: www.musicweek.com/live/read/how-covid-wiped-out-70-000-jobs-and-2-7-billion-of-economic-value-from-the-music-industry/084388 (accessed 10 October 2024).

Paine, A. (2024a) BPI and MPA join forces again on LA trade mission. *Music Week*. Available at: www.musicweek.com/labels/read/bpi-and-mpa-join-forces-again-on-la-trade-mission/089899 (accessed 10 October 2024).

Paine, A. (2024b) Field work: Festivals facing up to a 'difficult market' as artists explore live options. *Music Week*. Available at: www.musicweek.com/analysis/read/field-work-festivals-facing-up-to-difficult-market-as-artists-explore-live-options/089799 (accessed 10 October 2024).

Paine, A. (2024c) CISAC reports global music collections up 7.6% to new high. *Music Week*. Available at: https://www.musicweek.com/publishing/read/cisac-reports-global-music-collections-up-7-6-to-new-high-but-digital-growth-rate-drops/090726 (accessed 13 May 2025).

Patel, R. (2024) Questions on artist management. Interview by Allan Dumbreck [Zoom].

Scougall, L. (2023) *Practicalities of Artist Management [Lecture]*. University of the West of Scotland.

Sentric (n.d). Available at: www.sentric.com/what-we-do (accessed 9 December 2024).

Trubridge, H. (2020) Questions on artist management. Interview by Allan Dumbreck [Zoom].

Vliet, H. (2019) *Festivalatlas 2018*. MXStudio/Cross-media Research Group, Amsterdam University of Applied Sciences, Amsterdam.

Webb, A., Bonham, P., Harmon, A., Coldrick, A. and Dethekar, M. (2022) *Essentials of Music Management*. Music Managers Forum, London.

Webster, E. (2014) Association of Independent Festivals Six-year Report 2014. Association of Independent Festivals. Available at: uklivemusiccensus.org/wp-content/uploads/2018/03/UKLiveMusic-Census-2017-full-report.pdf (accessed 10 October 2024).

Wray, D.D. (2024) *The Working Class Can't Afford It': The Shocking Truth About the Money Bands Make on Tour*. The Guardian, London.

6 External Factors and Conflict

Allan Dumbreck

Introduction

Having already examined the start-up and mid-term development of a management company in Chapters 4 and 5, this chapter examines some elements within the broader working environment which are likely to impact the artist–manager relationship over the longer term. While aware that we are considering the wider sphere of business management more generally, these issues have been identified by our interviewees as having significant bearing on the work of the manager and are not considered to be peripheral; they directly impact artist management in music and so need to be considered. We have grouped these responses into three key subject areas: government intervention; adapting to change; and the growth and influence of artificial intelligence. Finally, we consider the potential clashes and conflicts that can threaten or terminate the artist–manager relationship to allow better understanding between parties and possibly assist in resolution.

Government Intervention

Government involvement (national, regional or local – directly or indirectly) in the arts can often be subject to criticism for a variety of reasons. In the UK, key issues such as cuts to arts funding (Thorpe, 2024), the impact of the EU withdrawal on touring acts crossing the Channel (Paine, 2023a), and limited support for venues during the pandemic (examined in Chapters 4 and 5) have given rise to concerns that government does not take the music industries sufficiently seriously. Beyond these issues, our interviewees raised a diverse range of points which they felt the relevant authorities could assist with. Firstly, funding. Chris Chadwick, for example, would like to see more investment, specifically to support those who are talented but not best placed to develop their careers:

> There's a real problem in the music industry that, you know, it skews massively towards people who have the resources to be able to dedicate the time, to take a chance on being a successful musician. I'm thinking particularly about people from less-well-off economic backgrounds and I think that there's a massive representation [issue] within that. There are some amazing schemes in the UK. There are some people doing great things within funding, whether it's PRS or the BPI or help [for] musicians. But I don't think there's enough, and I would love to see that improved in the next five years, and more funding put into that.
> (Chadwick, 2023)

BPI and PRS support mechanisms include assistance during COVID, support for export growth and the PRS Members' Fund (BPI, 2020; Music Support, 2025; PRS for Music, 2025).

Brendan Moon generally agrees with Chris Chadwick but focuses more on required support for music enterprises: 'One thing that I don't think we really get enough support in is pure business' (Moon, 2020).

As we have already seen, funding support for the arts has been cut in the UK over the last 15 years (Higgins, 2024). More specifically, funding support in particular regions, including Scotland where Moon is based, has been subject to localised reductions due to the economic climate (Creative Scotland, 2024). Levels of support internationally are obviously dependent on individual national governments. Support for businesses is offered by the Department of Commerce in the USA, for example (US Deptartment of Commerce, 2024). In the UK, the government has recently invested a further £1.6 million in MEGS, the music export support scheme for UK artists at a critical growth level (UK Govt, 2025). In The Netherlands, the performing arts support fund is another example of investment in the creative industries (NL Govt, 2025); however, are these systems proportionate or sufficient?

Steijn Koeijvoets, based in The Netherlands also picks up on government support relating to international activity, comparing policy in his own nation to the French approach:

> Talking about France, specifically, you have the Bureau d'Exportes, which is the music export bureau. They even have funding or help programmes for French companies who work with foreign artists. So, for instance, if you're a Dutch artist, and you use a foreign company or there is a French company, then there is funding to be requested. But [in] France, for instance, we have Michelle David and True Tones. They just played Jazz Café [London] last week and Craig Charles of BBC Radio 6 is a big supporter. They're doing well so we're building [an audience in the] UK, but they're doing very well in France. So for us, [with government support from the host nation], France is an important market.
> (Koeijvoets, 2023)

The French government has established the National Centre for Music (CNM), which effectively includes an office for music exports (CNM (Centre National de Musique), n.d.). They provide support for French artists working internationally. This is what Steijn is referring to. He continues, citing the advantages experienced by better organized (better managed?) artists who are well placed to meet the required criteria:

> I think France and Canada are exceptions. There is funding available. But there have been cutbacks, or cuts on funding. It's harder to get the funding, but it also means that the [higher] quality bands or artists get the funding because they have a plan. So, in a way, I think we can improve as an industry [as] a whole by educating the managers [how to take advantage of the support systems].
> (Koeijvoets, 2023)

However, echoing Brendan Moon, Stein also sees a need for investment elsewhere. Not just in developing the careers of the acts but also in supporting the managers themselves:

> One thing I would like to see is [funding for managers]. There's a lot of funding for the artists, for the creators, but the industry [side], management companies, there's nothing, because, you know, we're the commercial guys. But I think that without management, artists would have a really hard time. So I think if there is some economic funding for management companies, so we can train younger managers, [that would be beneficial].
> (Koeijvoets, 2023)

His logic here relates to the period of time it takes for a manager to learn the business and then the timescale of developing the artist to the point where they are generating income:

'Obviously, management in art is an investment in artists. So sometimes you have to wait 2 years to get some money back. Same goes if you have a young manager or a trainee who you educate, and then after six months he, she or they are gone. So I would like to see – and this can be national or European – for [those working in] the commercial creative industry, such as managers, a funding programme; that would be good, I think, to keep a healthy music industry. In this way we can professionalize and at the same time do more for more artists.'

Ellie Giles, on the other hand, felt that if additional funding was available, then the live events sector (which at the time of our interview was still recovering from over a year of lockdown restrictions) needed support:

> I think that we need government help; that's ultimately what I think. The live industry needs government help. We need a very, very clear financial package, I think, from the government for the arts and the creativity sector, both in theatre, music, anything that involves a live audience. I think the record labels have a lot to answer for and need to look at how their business is and whether it is fair, instead of looking for tax breaks which, to me, are just immoral right now [immediately

post-pandemic]. They should be helping the live sector.

(Giles, 2022)

Tackling a different problem, which might benefit from government intervention, Steven Braines would like to see some kind of vetting or approval process (a type of certification?) for those working with young performers eager to join the industry:

> One of my personal things [which] I've always tried to pursue [with] the MMF was that we should have some kind of kitemark. You have the British Psychological Society, which I belonged to when I was a psychologist. You couldn't be a practising psychologist in the UK without being a part of it. So, therefore, if you'd abused a kid or something like that, or committed grand fraud or whatever, you wouldn't be able to work with kids, the same way you can't if you [want to be] a football coach or something like that.
>
> (Braines, 2023)

This might not be too different from the Disclosure and Barring Service checks (DBS) for employment in certain professions in England and Wales (UK Govt, 2024) or the Protection of Vulnerable Groups (PVG) certification required in Scotland for the teaching and community work sectors (Scottish Government, n.d) . These existing systems could perhaps be extended to include areas such as the arts where young persons could be in danger of being exploited. Seeing the parallels between artist management and the field of psychology makes this a key problem for Braines:

> I have a big issue that something like this [being a performer] is a massive carrot of dreams to someone. I feel that people are very open to being exploited and [they] don't do CRB [background] checks. I feel that if you had that kitemark system, and that some people haven't actually [been checked], you would know. If you were getting someone [as a possible manager] who had been through the kind of rigours [background checks], everyone would feel safe.
>
> (Braines, 2023)

While not being universally endorsed, support for some form of regulation in this area can be seen elsewhere. The deposition made to the UK government committee investigating the music industries by X-Factor contestant Rebecca Ferguson is one example (Ferguson, 2023). In her statement she expresses great concern for the way that she and other artists were managed and argues for licensing for artist managers as a first step towards greater transparency within the sector.

However, there does appear to be some debate surrounding this topic with other management voices expressing concern that certain groups or individuals might be dissuaded from becoming involved. The MMF response to the same inquiry (MMF, 2022) included a series of very specific and valuable recommendations on how the UK government could begin to address difficulties including misogyny in the music industry, including the creation of an independent standards authority (CIISA (Creative Industries Independent Standards Authority) (n.d)), currently being set up. However, their submission did not include calling for management licences or background checks.

Government policy which fails to take the creative industries into account (which could consequently be commercially detrimental); the lack of higher levels of support generally and in times of need specifically; the absence of professional background checking systems similar to those required in education; and regional variations in funding support appear to be key concerns in this area. The question we asked was admittedly quite open-ended, but that was intentional. The diversity of response here perhaps demonstrates the different experiences our interviewees have had in their careers. Generally, however, managers certainly felt that more could, and should, be done by government at all levels in supporting the music industries.

Adapting to Change in the Music Environment

Whatever the model for the manager, or their company, the business needs to be flexible and responsive to change. This is particularly true in the music industries, with new sales charts and playlists appearing every week. As the music environment increasingly switches to become more online and digital-based, many companies have been forced to adapt their operating practices. More recently, as we have seen, the lockdown effectively shut down live music completely. This has affected artist management companies significantly. Ross Patel started by explaining his company's background:

> Whole Entertainment [was] set up in 2016, with a very diverse roster of various music and entertainment clients. We've also, since the pandemic, started doing a lot more retainer/consultancy work, helping brands reach people in the creative industries. So [we're] joining the dots between organizations that want talent on board with whatever initiatives they're doing, and we [are] kind of the intermediary in those instances. That's one of the hats [we wear].
> (Patel, 2024)

He then explained the original business model and how they managed to adapt and overcome the barriers thrown up by the COVID pandemic in more detail:

> 2017, 2018, 2019 [and] 2020 all looked really good. It was a period of steady growth, and then, obviously, 2020 [COVID/lockdown happened] and everything just dropped off the side of the cliff. So those two years really did hit us and we had to make some quite drastic changes in how we operate as a business, and actually by the second year, by 2021, we had our best year financially because we were doing a lot more retainer work and consultancy work and a lot of stuff outside of traditional music management. Then those contracts all ended. We had three 12-month contracts, and it was [getting] us through the pandemic, and then everything started to return to normal, so we lost that and got back to more traditional management. So that became the focus again.
> (Patel, 2024)

Ross then elaborated further on what this actually means on a day-to-day basis for the company, specifically in relation to the return of the live events market:

> But currently, live band touring is not profitable. We're seeing a lot more activity across all of our clients and we've grown our roster. The workload has gone up, but the money that we're making has halved. So it's a really, sort of, strange dynamic to be in, [although I am grateful] to have the return of live music and, you know, for me, especially, being at festivals, that's where I network. That's where my community is. It always has been for the last 15 years. Having lost that, I'll never take it for granted again. Same with touring and travelling, but there are so many new obstacles and challenges that come with that now it's a different landscape.
> (Patel, 2024)

Patel has clearly been left with an awareness of the vulnerability of key aspects of his business model, however, he has proved that his company is able to adapt to change. Finding creative solutions to issues which affect your income is obviously important when the economy takes a downturn, but it is equally, if not more, critical to keep an eye on what might be happening further down the road. Looking to the future, Ross was considerably more optimistic, believing that the work they had invested in their artists was beginning to pay off:

> I do think that, moving forward, when we get to, hopefully, a place of more stability in the business – which I'm expecting and forecasting to have by the end of this year, which would be great – from that point [things] will be a little bit firmer because all of the clients are now at a point where they are self-sustaining. We've worked hard to get them to that point and now we can be a little bit more firm about what is owed to us as a business, because at the moment we've let a lot of things slide as I think a lot of managers do. But without having done that we wouldn't have been able to get them to the point that they're now at. So it's a bit of a give-and-take, and I do think that we work with people that, for the most part, appreciate what we do. I don't think they'll ever have a full understanding of any of that, but I think they understand it enough that, hopefully, that conversation won't be too difficult.
> (Patel, 2024)

Allowing the artist to develop to the point where a realistic income can be drawn from their turnover rather than pinpointing every penny due gives the artist some space to grow in the earlier stages, which also benefits the manager. This is particularly true when the economic environment is pressurized. However, once the artist has reached self-sufficiency, the manager needs to be realistic about their own income.

In the post-pandemic business landscape, Chris Chadwick also sees change elsewhere and not necessarily negative change. Firstly, he drew attention to the basics, including organizing meetings:

> I think that post-COVID, the way that … work culture has shifted creates a challenge there. It's not as simple or it's not necessarily as easy to invite someone for a one-on-one Zoom chat as it is to go and say, "Hey, do you [fancy] grabbing coffee? I'm going to be in the building next week", and it's a lot less colloquial. Maybe that's a good thing. Artist management, and the music industry in general, has been built on being very informal, and I think now Zoom culture does force it to be a lot more formal. And that's an adaptation; that's an adjustment for people.
> (Chadwick, 2023)

Secondly, agreeing with Ellie Giles, he can see the pressures on the live events sector brought about by a combination of factors, and is already considering future change:

> The challenges on live are really difficult. I think there's going to be a lot of festivals that are going to disappear over the next couple of years, if they haven't already, due to poor ticket sales. And, yeah, I think, just in general, that's taking a lot of money away from the rest of the industry or from an artist to be able to invest in their music, you know.
> (Giles, 2022)

In the music industries, the saying 'The only constant in life is change' could be interpreted as a fundamental ground rule (as we saw in Chapter 2). As we shall see in Chapter 7, the changes brought about by the UK's withdrawal from the EU, the pandemic and the cost-of-living crisis which followed have had significant impact on artist managers (Paine, 2023a; Martin, 2023). Dealing with the difficulties which have arisen over the past few years, our interviewees have experienced the importance of flexibility, identifying emerging issues, and recognizing the need for change and adapting to it as quickly and efficiently as possible; in some examples demonstrating that it is perhaps better to be part of the change than to be affected by it; which leads us to the most recent technological change sweeping through business more generally and the arts in particular – AI.

Artificial Intelligence

Artificial intelligence (AI) is already changing almost every aspect of music:

> The use of AI in the music industry is progressing quickly. Start-ups and digital companies are offering a variety of services for music production, playlist curation, promotions, and engaging with consumers through machine learning algorithms, forecasting analysis and automatic genre classification.
> (Canyakan, 2024)

The technology has recently been accused of replacing creative roles in music, but equally, many cite it as a valuable tool to assist the creative and management processes (Music Week, 20242024). As we discovered, it is actively in use already. Almost all managers we spoke with have been utilizing AI in some respect over the last few years. Many can see valuable current and future possibilities. As mentioned already in Chapter 4, for example, the AI-driven BeatBread platform is offering financial support for artists based on projected growth generated by data analysis of their existing metrics (Paine, 2024a).

This generative technology is now involved in almost every aspect of the creative industries. Within music, there were initial concerns related to software taking composition out of the hands of songwriters (Anderton et al., 2022), but AI has now widened its applications to include all aspects of the business including production, marketing, promotion and distribution (Boateng et al., 2025). Increasingly, the ethical and legal debates are being brought forward in an attempt to manage AI within the existing industries (Canyakan, 2024), but can this make a difference?

Concerns relating to the artificial generation of songs, AI artists and 'unofficial', 'new', spurious material from existing successful artists have been sufficient to cause the major labels and other US-based music production companies (Universal, Sony, Warners and Disney, to name four) to co-operate with artist representative organizations (including US trade union SAG-AFTRA) to jointly negotiate 'a groundbreaking agreement establishing, for the first time, collective bargaining guardrails assuring singers and recording artists ethical and responsible treatment in the use of artificial intelligence in the music industry' (Crabtree-Ireland, quoted in Paine, 2024b).

Across the Atlantic, MMF UK focused its second managers' summit on AI in the music industries, with Annabella Coldrick, Chief Executive, stating: 'The ramifications of existing AI technologies are enormous, and especially so for music managers, who, on behalf of their clients, need to be across all commercial, legal and practical implications of machine-based innovation' (quoted in Paine, 2023b).

These efforts to inform and protect creators, performers and rights holders may indicate the way that AI is managed or controlled over the forthcoming years. Lyle Scougall, manager of emerging artist Joesef, addresses the fears of those who see it as a threat and identifies the positives:

> I suppose there's a lot of stigma about AI, isn't there? I know the first reaction is, "Oh, AI is going to take over all these jobs", and it probably will replace a lot of jobs. However – this might divide the room here – I'm not against AI. I do understand that it could be used for negative reasons. However, in terms of running a business, project management, I think AI has got its place in terms of automating a lot of really mundane tasks that take up time.
>
> (Scougall, 2023)

He then explains what he means by this, discussing in some detail how AI has been instrumental in developing his business:

> I've built a full music management system for my company, and I leveraged AI to do that. I asked Chat GPT how I would do this and it told me. I've done it; and, for instance, I openly encourage AI in terms of that. My assistant staff member was in the office a couple of weeks ago and I [asked], "What are you up to?" And she [replied], "Oh, I'm just building a system for demos so that when a demo comes in it filters it into the correct folders"; and I was like, "How are you doing that?" And she says, "On Chat GPT asking the code". The AI was showing her how to do it. She'd never coded before in her life. So AI has its place – I think more so in terms of business and project management and being able to scale effectively, because the system that I've built has transformed the way that we work.
>
> (Scougall, 2023)

Lyle also addresses arguments which are currently common talking points in music surrounding composition/arrangement of music where AI is being accused of potentially destroying human creativity:

> On the music side, there's no doubt that there are massive intellectual property issues there. I could use AI to generate a singer's voice that is already well established and put it on Spotify. However, Spotify has become a bit wise to that and they're starting to clamp down on it more. I think there's definitely also benefits for musicians. If you produce your own music, there's AI you can use in your DAWs to help you start ideas or develop ideas. So I think it has its place; however, it is scary, it's a scary prospect, but all change is, isn't it?
>
> (Scougall, 2023)

Steven Braines has an equally pragmatic, positive approach, seeing opportunities for the use of AI which could actually assist in certain situations:

> I think technology is like any tool. Apply it well and it can be a great agent for change. I love tools that allow people to sing melodies and they turn into instruments. Imagine you have a limb difference [or disability] and now realize you [can] work without anyone else or you live remotely, or you're introverted and don't want to be in a band. I do believe in the magic of humans; it's not about something being word-perfect, it's about emotion and those moments of true connectivity. Who knows if AI could ever replace them?
>
> (Braines, 2023)

He then reminds us that previous technological advancements have faced negative criticism:

> We forget something, though – pianos are a tool; keyboards were the devil, then the computer-programmed keyboards were the devil, but think of all the incredible music that wouldn't have been made without those breakthroughs. AI is really good for managing tasks, generating artwork, presentations, all sorts of things, and saves time and money. I'm here for it if harnessed well, responsibly.
>
> (Braines, 2023)

Scott Kirkwood also takes quite a balanced approach. He, too, has seen an example of AI being used in composition/recording where it could make a positive difference:

> I haven't implemented too much AI with my work so far but can see it coming to good use for companies around me. Companies using AI to help with admin – email responses, checking applications, calendar management and even for friends and colleagues with dyslexia to help with those. The main thing I've seen [which is] quite crazy with AI recently is with the writer/ producer Rory James [who] I manage. When writing songs for pitch now [to successful US artists, for example], they will write the song with the top line in the session's vocal and put it through AI to sound like the artist they are pitching to.
>
> (Kirkwood, 2023)

As with all of those who responded to this question, Denise Allan has at least experienced AI. She is more cautious as she has some concerns, but can see both sides of the debate:

> So, for example, somebody is asking you "Can you give me 500 words on blah blah blah?" and you have the core elements, you have a few sentences on what you want to do and then you put it into Chat GPT and say, "Can you make 500 words of this text?" It will create it, then you will refine it and refine it and refine it until it's shaped in your tone and what it is that you want to achieve. So there are definitely practical uses.
>
> (Allan, 2023)

She does, however, see the issues where AI is involved in composition of music:

> There is a worry that there is going to be competition with artists who have spent their lives creating and trying to express themselves, and there seems like some kind of shortcut with somebody [who] decides to take a bit of Drake and a bit of somebody else and then merge it together. And then there is the question of how [that] impacts the finances of an artist, and for record companies for market share as well. So there are lots of different implications. Generally, I feel quite wary about it just from my position, but at the same time I can't help but see massive benefits as well.
>
> (Allan, 2023)

Taking a slightly more critical line, Chris Chadwick can see the potential for artists/creators to lose opportunities and income. However, he believes this might depend on whether the industry is able to regulate the technology:

> I think that depends a lot on legislation and, you know, the work that's being done by some of the UK music bodies. I mean, being honest, I think it's already affecting our sector and has been for a number of years in ways that we were probably not aware of. There was a story I read a couple years ago – probably three or four years ago now – about [one of the digital music platforms] directly employing composers to create music that they then playlisted, but it was owned by them, and it was characterized as ghost artists who had profiles and sometimes, you know, thousands [or] hundreds of thousands of listeners, but really, truly, they weren't paid songwriters, they weren't artist projects. [The platform] wasn't paying out royalties; they were paying a flat fee for, you know, the composition, basically. You can totally see that ... AI is undoubtedly going to present opportunities for DSPs like that to, I guess, fill their platform with royalty-free material. That's probably something that is, sadly, already happening, something that ... legislation and artist companies, the major labels in particular, given their sway, are going to have to find ways of tackling.
>
> (Chadwick, 2023)

Similar to Denise Allan's concerns voiced earlier, Chris can see other potential difficulties for creators and therefore, ultimately, for managers, too. He echoes doubts cast by other managers in relation to what governments are capable of [or willing to do] if it is only within national boundaries when the digital service providers (DSPs)/online retail platforms operate internationally:

> Where it is challenging is when it comes to artists' rights and songwriter royalties. And I've got to be honest, I don't hold up a lot of hope for the short-term preventative measures that we'll be able to take, because experience has taught me that, particularly when it comes to technology and particularly in a global music industry, it's very difficult to legislate against these things. The UK government can do what they want but this has an impact on the 180 territories that are on Spotify [or any

other platform], so I think it's going to be a challenging period, and I think it will definitely push the bottom line [affect profits].

(Chadwick, 2023)

The imperative for legal protection highlighted by Chris Chadwick is recognized by researchers: 'As pervasive AI technologies spill into the music industry, there arises an immediate need for laws and regulations to ensure they are used in ethical and responsible ways' (Canyakan, 2024). Equally, governments are aware of the issues involved and are attempting to raise greater awareness in order to take action, notably in western territories (Billboard/Associated Press, 2024). In the UK, a cross-party government publication recently signalled support for legislation to regulate AI to protect the music industries (UK Music, 2024). However, reflecting Chadwick's concerns, this might take some time as law-makers are discovering that clarification of how the technology functions is necessary prior to passing the required controls (Dalugdug, 2025).

Chadwick also envisages certain possible advantages but doesn't believe that the discussion surrounding AI currently has a clear-cut, black-and-white outcome within the global marketplace:

> As with all these things I don't think it's binary. I don't think it's all terrible and I think, talking to some producers, there's quite a lot of excitement about the possibilities of how stuff can be used creatively, so that is exciting. Whether it's used within DAWs, whether it's used in the live setting to create effects that are beyond something that could be manually programmed; I think there are some really exciting applications.
>
> (Chadwick, 2023)

Karl Neilsen has the same reservations as Chadwick in terms of the outright ownership and/or artificial production of music/sound to avoid paying composers, producers and musicians, but has seen AI help him manage another aspect of his business in a more meaningful way:

> I think there's going to be pros and cons [but] I don't think that they're to be feared. One force that we've seen that's for good is that I've got a bit of a publishing catalogue and we're working on a better way of sifting through that, searching the catalogue for keywords and stuff like that for better syncs and TV opportunities, so in that respect it's working really really good. I think [companies such as] Meta [the company behind Facebook and Instagram] have, allegedly, been hoovering up all the data and the songs; they're [possibly] working towards a position where they don't have to pay music copyright, quite clearly. So that's the danger.
>
> (Nielsen, 2024)

He has also seen activity which would previously have been regarded as an anomaly in business, which could signal a new direction, again cutting off certain previously lucrative income streams:

> You've got some weird things [happening]. There was Disclosure [the artist] last month. They got AI to remix their latest track and they did over 1000 versions in one afternoon (NFT Now, 2023). They then just flooded the algorithms with all their different versions. Now I don't know if it's right or wrong, but if you were a remixer back in the day, [they] might have killed that game. If you ask AI to do the remix, why would you go and pay [a person to do it], you know? I used to get between £5K and £15K for Goldie for remixes and that's another income source [which could disappear]. So it's helpful in some ways [but] I think it's going to affect income streams in another way.
>
> (Nielsen, 2024)

Karl then joins a number of our interviewees in sounding the alarm on AI being used as a composition/songwriting tool which has the potential to impact songwriters and composers:

> Some people are looking to create whole new business streams, but, you know, creating virtual artists using AI, if you think that's a model for you, then by all means go for it, but it doesn't feel intuitively correct for myself; but I'm not there to deny anybody any income streams; the only problem is that [if] it's not music and artists that are at the forefront, then it's about wanting the AI.
>
> (Nielsen, 2024)

Ross Patel has mixed views, seeing the positive values but also expressing concern regarding the prospect of endless additional, fractionally different 'clones' of original content being generated:

> I think it's here, you know, it has arrived, it's affecting [business] today. I think that there are very powerful tools that we can use to help the creative process. What I'm hearing a lot is, whether it's generative image-based AI or helping people navigate writer's block, that seems to be a useful way of integrating [AI] into daily use or just being able to tap into that and help spark something. I don't know if that's a healthy way of doing it, you know? I still see more value in people collaborating in person, getting together and having that shared experience, or maybe that's how you overcome [replace] that, but obviously AI is now at your fingertips so it's far more accessible and it's far more convenient.
> (Patel, 2024)

There is, as we are seeing, a theoretical, commercial and possibly ethical dichotomy in this development, which Patel highlights, echoing Karl Neilsen's concerns:

> So, I think it's going to bring a lot more debate. I also think it's going to increase exponentially the volume of creative output because now literally anyone can create something. The objectivity of how valuable that piece of art is will kind of become more blurred than it already is, and it will be very difficult to discern what is really amazing from what is not and what sits in between, and then also trying to figure out what's real and what isn't. I think now AI has become so powerful, being able to replicate yourself and just edit that and then multiply that by however many versions [is concerning]. Having a live performance or shooting a music video, for example, once and then creating 20 iterations of that same music video, you just have unlimited content to pump out in reality and I think that'll be a very useful marketing tool for some people initially, but then everyone will do it and we will just be flooded with this kind of "nothing" content. I think it would be positive for a few people who are the early adopters [but then] everyone will have access to it. You won't be able to discern between what's real and what isn't, what's meaningful and what isn't.
> (Patel, 2024)

Essentially, then, if you can use AI to generate an almost limitless number of possible versions of a song, a video, a press release, then simply release them all in the hope that one of them strikes a chord with the audience, where is the quality control? Where is the human filter which selects the version which best represents the artist and their art? This is one of the questions which AI poses as new technology often does in the early years when its ultimate value/purpose has yet to be realized.

Ross then clarified that he is one of the managers who is *not* currently using AI professionally. There is a personal belief ethic at play here, as he explains; however, he has worked with it away from the office:

> I'm not [using AI at the moment]; I dabbled a bit, but currently I use AI on the day-to-day level, I use Chat GBT or Google to find cooking recipes and make things a little bit easier for myself on a very basic-living level, but I'm not using it in the creative process because I don't really want to. I tried it, it's really impressive and it's really powerful and that kind of put me off. I don't think everything in art should be this easy. Meaningful art is made through struggle, and you tell the story, and if all I'm doing is typing in the first thought that comes into my head and letting the machine somehow find a representation of that, it feels vacuous, and I don't want to create art with people where that is the output.
> (Patel, 2024)

At the other end of the spectrum, Stein Koeijvoets is already using AI extensively within his company and already sees future uses:

> Well, we as a company are investing a lot to use AI to further standardize processes so there are a lot of people who we work with that ask questions [like] "Where can I find this?", "Where can I find that?", and [with] AI, by building our own assistance, we can more easily outsource that type of task which still conserves everybody's needs for input and at the same time we have more time to invest in the personal matters – you know, listening to bands, helping them with the more soft side of things. So we are very much for AI, but when it's put to use in a good way. I think we can benefit. Developments go really fast, really quickly, so we just need to keep up with them and, so far, we can benefit from them as a more efficient company.
> (Koeijvoets, 2023)

Here he gives simple examples of the use and value of AI in everyday business. Similar to the functions developed by Lyle Scougall, this demonstrates how AI is becoming standard practice across artist management offices:

> One of our acts that's booked by a promoter... this person needs information on the riders [agreed hospitality at events] and a press kit, a bio [biography], all that stuff. Normally, he comes to us asking for this and then we would reply to the email with the different links. Now it's just a bot where if you type in "I'm looking for...", you know, you have certain options: "I'm looking for the EPK [electronic press kit] of artist X", and then he or she, or they, will get the information, but it also helps us internally to communicate more easily. We [also] have a news bot which is sending out important articles to keep people updated.
> (Koeijvoets, 2023)

Overall, then, the jury still appears to be out on the subject of AI within music, with much depending on which aspect of the industries is being discussed. Our interviewees presented a range of responses to our question, but generally opinion depended on what it was to be used for. To streamline business practices was acceptable; less so when it was to be involved directly in the creative process, where human creativity could be sidelined. As we have seen, many observers, including industry bodies, are voicing their concerns with the global independent music network (WIN) publishing guidance on the future of AI, for example (WIN (Worldwide Independent Network (WIN), 2024), notably raising a similar set of issues to those detailed by our interviewees. Perhaps the most significant outcome here was that most of our respondents were already using AI quite regularly in some respect in their daily activity and could see progressively more use for it as time progresses.

Conflict and Issues in the Artist–Manager Relationship. What Goes Wrong?

Accepting that both roles can be highly pressurized and occasionally at cross-purposes to each other (art vs commerce), it is perhaps not entirely surprising that artist–manager relationships can reach flashpoints. What are the most common causes of disagreement? How can they best be addressed and resolved? Can they be avoided? This final question raised a series of diverse responses from our interviewees.

In Braines's experience, finance can always be a catalyst, but getting a manager's full focus, or at least the perception of this, is also an issue:

> Money is the biggest one so always be overly transparent. The other one is a classic. It's two acts or more feeling another project must be getting your attention if they aren't doing well, which often is not the case, in reality.
> (Braines, 2023)

Scott Kirkwood agrees on the first point, again resonating with Polly Comber's stance on restraint (Comber, 2022) where the claiming of expenses is concerned. However, this may not prevent disagreement:

> I never really charge for anything, just travel and accommodation. What I normally do with the majority of my artists is, because we do so much development before we launch an artist, I normally invest in an artist pre-release. I've had artists on my payroll just to get them by. That counters the money situation a lot of the time.
> (Kirkwood, 2023)

He also addresses the attention problem Steven Braines identified but broadens it somewhat to encompass the personal proximity and depth of the relationship. This can be critical as your artist progresses and other players see an opportunity for intervention:

> Trust is always key in artist management, and something that both the artist and manager should be fully confident with from the get-go. Once trust is lost from either side it rarely ends well. When an artist starts to do well it's not uncommon for sharks [other music business personnel] to circle your artist and do what they can to manipulate you out of the equation in one way or another. This is where trust in your relationship is key. Distance can also be an issue as Scott explains: It can also be difficult to maintain a level of communication with your artist if they are touring, doing promo or writing at the other side of the world. I generally try to travel with my artists as much as possible and build key relationships with my friends, peers

and contacts globally to make sure my artists are always in good hands wherever they go and never feel excluded.

(Kirkwood, 2023)

Similar to both Braines and Kirkwood, Stein Koeijvoets also raised the potential artist (mis) perception of career development (or perceived lack of) but from a slightly different perspective:

The main issue is expectation versus reality. Obviously both artist and manager should be ambitious but sometimes you know people are over-ambitious or are expecting something more, which can cause a lot of frustration; and I think the second one is workload/mental health. Both sides experience a very intensive process; You know. Creating music is intense but managing it can be as well, especially when things aren't going smoothly, which might be a cause of expectation versus reality; you know, if you're both tired maybe you're not as reasonable as you should be. So I think those are the main issues. Those are the core and then all different derivations. An example would be that a lot of artists say, "Hey, this song, why am I not on the radio?", and the first question I always ask is, "OK, do you listen to this particular radio station?" "No, I don't". [So] it's the lack of knowledge.

(Koeijvoets, 2023)

Karl Neilsen evidenced similar difficulties he has experienced with the occasionally more flamboyant character of artists leading back to the trust issue:

Artists are very obviously headstrong, egotistical; it's really hard to call out their bad behaviour when they've got addictive tendencies, whether it be drugs or other issues. I've been in some very difficult situations and when they stop listening, that's the biggest issue. You can't have an artist that doesn't listen; the breakdown of trust, it's just gone. Anything you say, they're not listening to you, so what's the point of being there? It's when they don't want to listen because they think they know better.

(Nielsen, 2024)

Chris Chadwick returned to the art-versus-business dichotomy at the root of the relationship, which can cause tension between the two parties in practical, everyday situations:

I think it's difficult. The classic, delicate line that you have to tread as a manager is that kind of commercial versus creative challenge, and your role as a manager, I guess, is to help an artist navigate that line; and so whilst I think artist managers more recently have taken a much more active role in A&R, I think one of the challenges that that presents is that if a manager is getting involved in A&R then they're expressly being asked to state opinions on that balance between creative and commercial, and I think one of your challenges as an artist manager is balancing what an artist's ambitions are creatively with how they need to get there commercially or how they create a viable business commercially. If it's a video, [for example], balancing the creativity and a really pure idea that your artist has with the reality of how much you have budget-wise to spend on that project, but also how much you should spend on that project, [is difficult].

(Chadwick, 2023)

This brings us back to one of the points made in the first chapter, that of the manager being perceived as the deliverer of bad news, Chadwick recognizes the inherent difficulty but suggests a firm, straightforward approach:

One of the biggest challenges for me [is] that you need to be able to be truthful. One of the bits of advice that an older manager gave me very early on in my career was "You're an artist manager, you're not there to make the decision, you're there to guide the artist to the right decision". So I guess you have an obligation to disclose information to your artist to help them make those decisions and sometimes that information is bad news. Not that I think it's always a big challenge, because you have to be able to be comfortable enough with an artist that you're going to be the face of bad news, you're going to be the bringer of bad news as well as good news. So there are ups and downs, and also to be tough enough to know that your artist is probably going to be reacting directly in the moment to that news to you, and it can be painful, it can be tough, it can feel personal. It's not, it's a reaction to maybe something that someone else has said or someone else has done, but you're going to be the person that takes that initial gut response, so that's really challenging.

(Chadwick, 2023)

This is part of the broader, day-to-day picture of managing artists, individuals, creatives, where identifying the correct approach to conveying information becomes vital to maintaining that relationship. Disarmingly, Chris also accepts that this is an imperfect art that requires ongoing self-reflection:

> I think that feels like the core challenge to me and it's all about fostering a relationship where it's honest and up-front without being cruel. I've been doing this coming up to ten years and I still don't know that I've found that perfect balance but it's something that I will continue to work on.
>
> (Chadwick, 2023)

Denise Allan is in a slightly different position due to being related to the band members. This has certain advantages but also creates different tensions, as she explained:

> I suppose I avoid some tricky water because I'm female for a start, but I guess, you know, thinking about Glasvegas, it's a wee bit more unique because the lead singer is my brother [so] the boundary there is crossed and we just can't help it. We're sitting at Christmas dinner and we're talking about music and my mother's involved because she's excited about it and everybody wants to hear about it. So sometimes it's more of an effort to not actually talk about it; and there's a cousin, Robert, as well, so the boundaries there are really quite difficult at times to maintain.
>
> (Allan, 2023)

She went on to identify the creation of realistic personal/professional limitations as an important mechanism to prevent friction and conflict:

> But having a healthy relationship, I think, starts from you as a person and having a healthy relationship to music and your work, because in music, especially the live industry, it's 24/7 unless you put those boundaries in; and one of the problems with managers is their burnout rate. It's really quite high because artists think, maybe up until recently, that they should be able to access you 24/7, but I think if you, through time, can gently let them know that "these are my limits and also I would like these to be your limits as well", then you're actually building in some kind of framework for a working relationship. For me, I don't really like people contacting me at night by either email or phone or text or anything, and I don't really like them contacting me at the weekends either. There [are] only two things that surpass that and [they are]: (i) if it's a big, big problem that cannot wait, that's an emergency – but I'm speaking about an emergency-emergency, not just, "We can't get this logo quite right" – then I don't mind; or (ii) if it's really, really, really good news, then I don't mind, but nothing in-between. Most things are in-between, so those are my boundaries.
>
> (Allan, 2023)

She then progresses to consider the problems involved due to the range of roles the manager must adopt:

> The other thing why it's really quite tricky is because as a manager you wear lots of different hats. You are in a business relationship with the person but you're also their friend. You're also their confidante, you are their counsellor, their teacher, you know, you almost have a parental role, so there's all these layers and these kinds of roles you play but sometimes things can get a wee bit blurred and that is a wee bit tricky for you to find your way, and for them to find their way as well. I think that having certain boundaries is where it starts.
>
> (Allan, 2023)

On Denise Allan's key point of drawing a line between working life and personal time and space, Patel agrees, making the key point that clearly explaining where the lines are and how and when they might change can be critical to retaining professional distance:

> Boundaries are the primary issue. If we're talking between an artist and a manager, I think the main thing which causes issues is having healthy boundaries between them. The manager's role is unfortunately ever-evolving, ever-changing and relies always on expectations. Also, the role is so undefined that anything can end up becoming the manager's job without any increase in value of their time and equities. I think setting boundaries around things is really difficult in the type of artist–manager relationship; that dynamic is very unique in that there is no real definition around it. What you already have is when you remove something and say, actually these people are going to do your PR now, these people are going to do [another part of the work], it defines their role, but it doesn't really define what the

manager does. That's probably something which still needs to be explored.

(Patel, 2024)

The final point in this section is made by Patel addressing the somewhat delicate issue of a written agreement:

The other thing is a piece of paperwork, bit of a contract in place, I think that's always something that creates some tension in a relationship that, generally, up until that point, feels really good, and then people are presented with a contract and artists don't expect to be paying for certain things they really should be, because of the nature of the relationship and what the demands are on the manager.

(Patel, 2024)

This was almost the only mention of a contract between the artist and the manager in over 20 hours of interviews we conducted in the course of our research. Managers often start work on a 'handshake agreement' where they discuss and agree the basic objectives and working practices with the artist, then get on with the work for an unspecified length of time, but usually up to the point where a realistic income appears. Some managers never sign a contract with their clients and perhaps Ross Patel's point above is exactly why. While the written agreement may be a cause for concern for the artist, it does create a form of security for the manager [and, realistically, for the artist also, although they may not see it that way]. Once what you have agreed has been written down and verified by both parties it can be put to one side while the work progresses and consulted as a reference point at a later date. This should give both sides peace of mind.

Although these obstacles and situations may seem to be disparate elements, the underlying message from all our respondents was the importance of openness and transparency in the interaction between manager and artist. Whatever the difficulty might be, real or perceived, the ability to speak clearly and directly to each other is apparently what counts. The principles of honesty and trust were given as bedrock to the longevity of the relationship whether they manifest themselves within contractual clauses or the fencing-off of free time vs working hours. All the managers we spoke with had wrestled with a range of problems in their working relationships but all suggested mechanisms, approaches, initiatives which they had applied to the benefit of both themselves and their charges. This parallels the point raised at the outset of the book that there is rarely a hierarchy within modern artist–management agreements; 'this is a partnership and should be based on mutual respect' (Webb et al., 2022, p. 3). Conflict resolution, finding solutions, is part of daily life for artist managers negotiating with record labels, concert promoters and media personnel. This also applies to the communication they have with their artists.

Conclusions

While there was no real consensus from respondents on which aspect of government involvement was most critical, the overall feeling was that governments generally needed to do more to assist the creative industries and music in particular. Background checks, investment [in artists and managers] and assistance in export markets were noted as significant issues here but the overall impression was that some governments were still not taking the creative industries seriously. While there have been instances of recognition [Tony Blair's Cool Britannia moment in 1997; Campbell and Khaleeli, 2017), the lack of government awareness or even an understanding of the damage which the EU withdrawal or the limited [and tardy] support funding to balance business income lost by the lockdown demonstrate a limited awareness of/concern for music as an industry.

The business environment is continually changing. This is perhaps more so in music than other industries. Adapting to those changes can be challenging but vital. Having dealt with the immediate impact of the pandemic, the resulting cost-of-living crisis, Brexit and the emerging challenges of AI in just the last 4 years, many managers are still working to come to terms with the new economic business landscapes. Adjusting swiftly to these and future changes appears to be a cornerstone to progression.

AI itself is still a somewhat unknown entity. The managers we spoke with believed its full potency and direction have yet to emerge. Concern surrounds the removal of the human element within music; however, the first tools are impressive and eminently useable, so the future is likely to include further generations of this software in some shape or form. Coming back to point one here, governments could perhaps take further action to legislate AI and to mitigate against possible losses for creators.

The causes of friction between managers and artists/creators are many and various. Money was identified by many, trust by most. Transparency, communication and honesty repeatedly arose in our conversations with interviewees. Creating realistic boundaries in terms of what can be discussed and when, creating space and time away from the work, do also [understandably] seem to be essential. The manager, continually operating on fresh opportunities at the periphery of the artist's business world, must be continually aware of potential pitfalls which could upset the relationship. This only adds to the delicacy of the professional balancing act inherent in the role..

References

Allan, D. (2023) *Practicalities of Artist Management [lecture]*. University of the West of Scotland.
Anderton, C., Hannam, J. and Hopkins, J. (2022) *Music Management*. Marketing & PR. Sage, London.
Billboard/Associated Press (2024) Senators put $32 billion price on artificial intelligence policy suggestion. Available at: www.billboard.com/business/tech/senators-artificial-intelligence-policy-suggestions-1235683163/ (accessed 15 May 2025).
Boateng, R., Boateng, S.L. and Budu, J. (2025) *AI and the Music Industry: Transforming Production, Platforms and Practice*. Routledge, New York and Abingdon, UK.
BPI (2020) Music export growth scheme (MEGS). BPI, London. Available at: www.bpi.co.uk/news-analysis/music-export-growth-scheme (accessed 18 July 2025).
Braines, S. (2023) Questions on artist management. Interview by Allan Dumbreck [Zoom].
Campbell, T. and Khaleeli, H. (2017) Cool Britannia symbolised hope. *The Guardian*. Available at: www.theguardian.com/inequality/commentisfree/2017/jul/05/cool-britannia-inequality-tony-blair-arts-industry (accessed 20 November 2024).
Canyakan, S. (2024) The role of AI in creative processes: Ethical and legal perspectives in the music industry. *Journal of Music Theory and Transcultural Music Studies* 2(2). Available at: jmttms.com/index.php/jmmtms/article/view/19 (accessed 18 July 2025).
Chadwick, C. (2023) Questions on artist management. Interview by Allan Dumbreck [Zoom].
CIISA (Creative Industries Independent Standards Authority) (n.d.) Available at: https://ciisa.org.uk/ (accessed 20 January 2025).
CNM (Centre National de Musique) (n.d.) French national music centre/bureau of music exports. Available at: cnm.fr/en/uncategorized/our-missions/ (accessed 18 November 2024).
Comber, P. (2022) Questions on artist management. Interview by Allan Dumbreck [phone].
Creative Scotland (2024) Closure of open fund for individuals. Available at: www.creativescotland.com/news-stories/latest-news/archive/2024/08/open-fund-for-individuals-closure-of-fund (accessed 4 November 2024).
Dalugdug, M. (2025) UK government faces second house of lords defeat over AI copyright rules. Available at: https://www.musicbusinessworldwide.com/uk-government-faces-second-house-of-lords-defeat-over-ai-copyright-rules/ (accessed 15 May 2025).
Ferguson, R. (2023) Evidence given to DCMS inquiry into misogyny in music. Available at: committees.parliament.uk/writtenevidence/124421/pdf/ (accessed 18 July 2025).
Giles, E. (2022) Questions on artist management. Interview by Allan Dumbreck [Zoom].
Higgins, C. (2024) Arts funding has collapsed under 14 years of Tory rule. *The Guardian*, 2024. Available at: www.theguardian.com/commentisfree/2024/mar/19/arts-funding-austerity-collapse-tories-labour (accessed 18 July 2025).
Kirkwood, S. (2023) Questions on artist management. Interview by Allan Dumbreck [Zoom].
Koeijvoets, S. (2023) Questions on artist management. Interview by Allan Dumbreck [Zoom].
Martin, D. (2023) Questions on artist management. Interview by Allan Dumbreck [Zoom].

MMF (2022) Evidence given to DCMS inquiry into misogyny in music. Available at: committees.parliament.uk/writtenevidence/110061/pdf/ (accessed 18 July 2025).
Moon, B. (2020) Questions on artist management. Interview by Allan Dumbreck.
Music Support (2025) The BPI announces a further £270,000 funding for artists, managers & grassroots venues impacted by Covid-19. Available at: www.musicsupport.org/news/bpi-funding-covid-19/ (accessed 18 July 2025).
Music Week (2024) We are excited about the potential': How AI is impacting the royalties market. *Music Week*, 2024. Available at: https://www.musicweek.com/talent/read/we-are-excited-about-the-potential-how-ai-is-impacting-the-royalties-market/090514 (accessed 18 July 2025).
NFT Now (2023) Disclosure's bronze editions break new ground in AI music. Available at: nftnow.com/ai/exclusive-disclosures-bronze-editions-break-new-ground-in-ai-music/ (accessed 24 November 2025).
Nielsen, K. (2024) Questions on artist management. Interview by Allan Dumbreck [Zoom].
NL Govt (2025) Performing arts subsidy schemes. Available at: https://business.gov.nl/subsidy/performing-arts/ (accessed 18 July 2025).
Paine, A. (2023a) UK music survey: 82% of artists touring EU say Brexit has hit earnings. *Music Week*. Available at: www.musicweek.com/live/read/uk-music-survey-82-of-artists-touring-eu-say-brexit-has-hit-earnings/088472 (accessed 18 July 2025).
Paine, A. (2023b) MMF to host manager summit on AI in music with experts from TikTok, Simkins, Deviate Digital and more. *Music Week*. Available at: www.musicweek.com/management/read/mmf-to-host-manager-summit-on-ai-in-music-with-experts-from-tiktok-simkins-deviate-digital-more/088462 (accessed 18 July 2025).
Paine, A. (2024a) European music managers alliance teams with beatbread on advances for members. Available at: www.musicweek.com/management/read/european-music-managers-alliance-teams-with-beatbread-on-advances-for-members/089847 (accessed 22 October 2024).
Paine, A. (2024b) SAG-AFTRA reaches new deal with major labels covering "ethical and responsible" use of AI. *Music Week*. Available at: www.musicweek.com/labels/read/sag-aftra-reaches-new-deal-with-major-labels-covering-ethical-and-responsible-use-of-ai/089594 (accessed 28 November 2024).
Patel, R. (2024) Questions on artist management. Interview by Allan Dumbreck [Zoom].
PRS for Music (2025) Supporting music. PRS, London. Available at: (accessed 18 July 2025).
Scottish Government (n.d). Available at: www.mygov.scot/pvg-scheme (accessed 18 November 2024).
Scougall, L. (2023) *Practicalities of Artist Management [lecture]*. University of the West of Scotland.
Thorpe, V. (2024) Britain behind Europe in arts funding. *The Guardian*, Available at: www.theguardian.com/culture/article/2024/jul/21/britain-behind-europe-in-arts-funding-and-education-crisis-report-shows (accessed 20 November 2024).
UK Govt (2024) DBS checks. Available at: https://www.gov.uk/request-copy-criminal-record (accessed 18 November 2024).
UK Govt (2025) Major new funding for music acts that supercharged careers of BRIT award winners. Available at: www.gov.uk/government/news/major-new-funding-for-music-acts-that-supercharged-careers-of-brit-award-winners#:~:text=In%20January%2C%20the%20Department%20for,well%20as%20live%20music%20venues (accessed 14 May 2025).
UK Music (2024) Artificial Intelligence and the Music Industry – Master or Servant? Available at: www.ukmusic.org/research-reports/appg-on-music-report-on-ai-and-music-2024/ (accessed 17 November 2024).
US Deptartment of Commerce (2024). Available at: www.trade.gov/media-entertainment-music-sector (accessed 14 November 2024).
Webb, A., Bonham, P., Harmon, A., Coldrick, A. and Dethekar, M. (2022) *Essentials of Music Management*. Music Managers Forum, London.
WIN (Worldwide Independent Network (WIN) (2024) WIN calls for joined-up approach on GenAI. Available at: https://winformusic.org/win-calls-for-joined-up-approach-on-genai/ (accessed 28 November 2024).

7 Finance and International

Brendan Moon

Introduction

This chapter explores the practicalities of the changing landscape of artist management examined from the perspective of a manager currently active in professional music. In the following pages, the workplace environment, finances, international touring and visa complexities for musicians and managers in the post-Brexit/post-pandemic era, including working in the EU and the USA, as well as how they manage tax considerations and royalty collections in the new geopolitical climate (Thornhill et al., 2024), will be examined. Finally, we will consider the recent consolidation of music companies as a possible reaction to the current situation.

This chapter is written from the perspective of a mid-level music act (and their manager) who regularly tour venues with a capacity of around 800–1000, but the information provided is relevant and applicable to music artists at other levels of operation.

One point of clarification here – in order to be completely transparent, the data provided originate from recent live music tours and other activities which I have organized and managed as an active artist manager. The artists I have been working with are predominantly in the alternative/rock genre and the touring locations are generally in western Europe; however, the data should be relevant to other genres and broadly indicative of other territories. I am aware that recent changes have already negatively influenced the profitability of live performances for some of the artists I represent, with their profit margins significantly diminishing (see the example tour accounts on the following pages). The data examined here therefore highlight the real challenges music managers face in achieving financial equilibrium.

Overview: A Decline in Music Income Against a Background of Rising Costs

This section examines strategies for efficiently assisting artists or musicians in response to the declining music industry earnings and rising expenses which have been discussed in the previous chapters. Illustrating this is straightforward, if disappointing. This section will explore various methods of reducing some of those expenses.

It is evident that individuals (artists) who possess exceptional and unique musical talent, work in small numbers (solo/duo) and demonstrate a strong work ethic, can achieve substantial financial success in the music industry. Larger groups which employ tour managers and road crews will have higher overheads and therefore may only become financially viable once the act has achieved a level of success and ticket sales that warrant such expenditure.

For almost a century, the music industry primarily depended on the two most significant streams of revenue generation: recorded music income from physical products, including CDs and vinyl, and live performance income from event tickets and merchandise. Consequently, achieving a successful record or touring profile (or both) were critical factors in establishing a sustainable career.

However, due to the proliferation of streaming services over the last 20 years, with the well-documented reduced levels of revenue for artists from these platforms, the traditional sources of income have experienced substantial change. This trend is visible in the swift and significant transition towards digital consumption in the UK. To clarify, as of 2024, 88.8% of the music consumed in the UK is now acquired through streaming, as reported by the British Phonographic Industry (BPI (British Phonographic Industry), 2023; Paine, 2024a). This format did not exist 25 years previously. The primary factor contributing to this situation is the decrease in per-stream compensation compared to previous conventional sales of physical products (Gany, 2024) although the costs related to marketing and promotion of recorded products, crucial for raising awareness in a fiercely competitive market, have risen due to the advent of digital marketing platforms (Forde, 2023).

The release of a record, however, even if it achieves only moderate popularity and fails to generate profit by itself, remains a key driver of concert ticket sales and merchandise sales, which can represent a significant financial return for the artist.

There is one other opportunity. Due to the recent re-emergence of vinyl records, with decreased production costs (around £4 per unit) and a marketplace where each 12-inch album may now be priced at approximately £20, the maths is clear. If an act can sell 1000 albums, for example, manufacturing costs will be around £4000 (inc. VAT). Even with marketing and VAT costs taken into account (selling direct to fans at live events and grossing sufficient income to be VAT registered (currently £90,000 – Govt UK, 2024)), this leaves a resulting profit of £10,000. If sales are through retail outlets, then distribution and retailer costs also need to be deducted, but this still represents a considerable income boost for an emerging artist. Beyond this, merchandise, such as T-shirts, caps and other items, can also be a lucrative source revenue.

There are difficulties, however. In this instance, it is essential to acknowledge that you must have a tour or significant live performances (e.g. festivals) to engage directly with fans (the most effective method for selling items directly). Here is where it might become difficult as the expenses associated with live events, as previously explained, continue to increase. Founder of Famous Friends management, Chris Chadwick emphasized the scale of these financial difficulties:

> This is an extremely challenging situation. The overall expense of touring is a major concern, and the escalating costs, especially in Europe after Brexit, are not only due to the aftermath of the COVID-19 pandemic but also the current energy crisis, rising fuel prices, and increased flight costs.
> (Chadwick, 2023)

The overall cost of touring can be broken down into individual expenditures (accommodation, transport, food and drink, crew). The consumer price index (ONS) for restaurants and hotels (essential requirements for a touring artist) in the UK, for example, showed a significant 41.4% increase in the first quarter of 2024 compared to that of 2015. Indeed, the peak inflation rate for restaurants and hotels of 11.1% in October 2022 marked the highest percentage rate in four decades (Statista, 2024). Subsequently, the rate persisted higher than the Bank of England's desired rate of 2% until May 2024.

Another expense, the cost of hiring tour buses, has become unaffordable to many tour managers having risen to £1200 per day, partly due to the persistent increase in fuel expenses as identified in the quote below from a firm's owner (Bell, 2023). According to the Office of National Statistics report (ONS, 2020), the mean cost of unleaded fuel in the UK at the time of writing, 15 July 2024, is £1.44 per litre. In comparison, the price of diesel (commonly the fuel required by tour vans and buses) is £1.56 per litre. During this period, diesel costs consistently exceeded petrol/gasoline prices, while the difference between them varied. Collectively, these issues have had devastating effects on UK touring businesses: 'The closure of Star Rider, the largest tour bus company in Scotland, is attributed to rising fuel costs, a shortage of bus drivers, and concerns about operators' licensing' (Bell, 2023).

A touring artist will use a disproportionate amount of fuel over a two-week to four-week tour compared to the average driver, for example, often covering several hundred miles in a day. Although the fuel price eventually decreased, this cost reduction was not passed on to artists.

Other indicators of difficulty are also visible. Artists are reporting being unable to participate in festivals due to the rising costs involved in performance, which often exceed their remuneration. Some individuals asserted that they have been compelled to decline offers to perform or omit part of their live performance or production equipment to work within budget at festivals (Dunworth, 2024). Many musicians experienced financial setbacks amounting to as much as £17,000 for a solitary performance (Tapper, 2023).

As we have seen, managers like Ross Patel have noticed the drastic cost increase, especially for touring in Europe where previously unnecessary journeys are now required for (often empty) vehicles to ensure post-Brexit compliance. Patel explained:

> Obviously, [there are now] more costs for touring in Europe because of visas [and] deadhead drives with vans, now that you need to have separate van drivers taking you from the UK to Europe; they go back, and then you have to get another van to take you around Europe. Then you have to get the other van back to pick you up. It's just ridiculous. All of those [costs] have gone up. I would estimate looking at our last couple of tour budgets [this constitutes an increase of] between 30% and 40%.
> (Patel, 2024)

Other managers agree. The economics of touring in the EU have become questionable for many artists. Karl Nielsen projected an even grimmer scenario, stating: 'The challenges of Brexit ... at the beginning of it, I thought we would be looking at 15 to 20% increases on our chart and on touring, and now it's more like 50–60%. It's become unviable. Some [EU] markets are unviable'. (Nielsen, 2024)

However, it may be that larger management companies and established artists have a better capacity to absorb these increased costs. Co-founder of Black Fox management, Polly Comber, noted a disparity in resources between this group and emerging artists, stating:

> When it's Liam Gallagher or Coldplay, they can swallow up these costs because the tour manager has got eight assistants working for him ... but when you're an act that's playing 200-capacity venues all round Europe or even 1000-capacity venues, you're starting to get in a [financial] hole.
> (Comber, 2022)

Is it possible to get around these issues? Artist managers need to adopt innovative and strategic approaches to navigate these challenging financial landscapes. This includes leveraging digital platforms for further revenue generation, seeking alternative income streams, and employing cost-effective touring strategies. Doing so, they better support their artists through the current financial turbulence.

Streaming services, social media, and direct-to-fan platforms offer alternative income streams that can supplement traditional revenue sources. Engaging with fans through exclusive content, virtual concerts and crowdfunding campaigns can also provide financial support while strengthening the artist–fan relationship. The significant range of possible income streams from online sources has been commented on by many in the industry, notably MMF UK (Webb et al., 2022) and academic sources (Anderton et al., 2022; Allen, 2022).

Managers should explore opportunities such as brand partnerships, licensing deals and sync placements in films, TV shows and commercials. Merchandise sales and fan subscriptions are also lucrative avenues to consider. By diversifying their income, artists can mitigate the risks of relying on a single revenue source. Employing cost-effective touring strategies is essential in the face of rising expenses. Shorter tours with fewer dates, regional tours to reduce travel costs, and collaboration with other artists for joint tours can help manage expenses. Engaging local crews and resources can also save costs.

Building a strong online presence is critical for modern musicians. Consistent content creation, engaging social media campaigns and interactive fan experiences can drive engagement and revenue. Many of these elements are examined in more detail elsewhere in this book. They should be actively considered. From the practical experience of a working manager, they are all valid and relevant.

International Touring

Financial example: European tour accounts

To better understand the difficulties here, we can examine touring finances in further detail. The example tour accounts which follow represent a UK-based act comprising two principal members, two session musicians and three crew members touring in the EU. This budget analysis is informed by recent tours of a similar nature and underscores the financial strain experienced by touring artists, particularly in the context of escalating costs (Table 7.1).

For clarification, this example is based on recent tours where the act(s) were alt/rock, the locations were all in western Europe (Spain, France, Germany, Benelux), typically there were two travel days per week (no concert), and insurance costs are not included. The events took place during the spring or autumn touring windows and the exchange rate can be taken as €1 = £0.85.

Despite generating substantial income from shows, merchandise and VIP sales, the expenses incurred during the tour almost equalled the total revenue, resulting in a very small profit margin. Several factors contributed to this financial underperformance:

a. Cancelled show: cancelling one show resulted in a direct loss of approximately €3000.00, significantly impacting the overall income.
b. High transportation costs: the cost of the tour bus (€13,234.50) and flights (€4352.50) accounted for a significant portion of the expenses, reflecting the increased travel costs identified by industry professionals (inc. Chris Chadwick and Ross Patel).
c. Crew and session musicians: payments to crew members and session musicians totalled €10,760.00, indicating the essential yet costly support personnel required for touring.

To mitigate such financial challenges and improve future tour profitability, artists and managers could consider the following strategies:

- More detailed planning: thorough planning and budgeting can help anticipate potential losses and allow for adjustments. This includes potentially securing insurance for cancellations and exploring more cost-effective travel arrangements. Chris Chadwick, for example, highlighted the importance of understanding the additional expenses associated with Brexit and how it impacts touring costs.
- Optimize tour scheduling by minimizing transportation costs through the strategic planning of tour routes to reduce travel distances (in close discussion with the booking agent) and maximize the use of regional tours (playing all shows in one region at once to avoid returning later, thereby incurring exaggerated travel costs). As Ross Patel noted, the high costs associated with visas and transportation in Europe can be mitigated through careful scheduling, thereby optimizing tour logistics.
- Cost-effective touring involves exploring alternative strategies, such as partnering with other artists on joint tours to share costs and resources. As Polly Comber observed, larger management companies and established artists have a greater capacity to absorb increased costs, a strategy that smaller acts can adopt by forming partnerships and joint or collective tours.
- Negotiating better production costs and exploring new merchandise possibilities with higher profit margins can increase profitability. Merchandise sales are a vital revenue stream, and improving profit margins can significantly impact the overall budget.
- Monitor exchange rates: be mindful of fluctuations and consider using financial tools to hedge against unfavourable currency movements, thus reducing exchange rate charges. This is crucial for international tours, where currency fluctuations can impact profitability.

Table 7.1. Example tour budget - short European tour (four piece band) (BPI (British Phonographic Industry), 2023)

Income		Euros
Total tickets (10 shows instead of 11 – one was cancelled)		€33,000.00
VIP tickets (94) (estimate was 150)		€2470.00
Merchandise sales (cash)		€7980.00
Merchandise sales (credit card)		€1210.83
CD and vinyl sales (cash)		€6190.00
Total income		€50,850.83
Expenses		Euros
Cancelled Show (costs)		€3000.00
Crew 1		€2500.00
Crew 2		€2500.00
Crew 3		€1000.00
Tour bus		€13,234.50
Flights out		€3160.77
Flights back		€1191.73
Freight, inc. carnet		€2000.00
Taxis (planned)		€330.82
Merchandise Costs		€4011.49
Session musician 1		€2380.00
Session musician 2		€2380.00
PDs (daily cash allowance)		€2600.00
Float and misc. cash expenses		
	Taxis (additional requirements)	€401.65
	Soft drinks/refreshments	€120.32
	Additional crew subsistence	€187.19
	Spares (batteries etc.)	€189.00
	Load out food	€144.50
Band member 1		€2380.00
Band member 2		€2380.00
Hotels		€2735.81
Exchange rate charges – £432.87, £130.92		€670.91
Total expenditure		€49,498.69
Balance (profit before tax)		€1352,14

The cost of touring has been documented by many in the industry (MBW, 2022; Paine, 2024b). By adopting these recommendations, artists and their managers might better navigate the financial challenges of touring, ensuring more sustainable and profitable tours in the future. Planning and strategic management are essential to overcoming the economic hurdles of the current music industry landscape. Escalating expenses in the music industry exacerbate the problem of decreased revenue. The costs related to production and promotion have substantially increased. However, artist management can implement strategies to control these additional costs.

Brexit – The Impact of the UK's Withdrawal From the EU on Artists of All Nationalities

Having already identified some of the issues faced by managers in relation to Brexit we now take a more comprehensive look at the broader implications. A recent survey by UK Music, the umbrella organization representing the industry's collective interests, underscores the challenges music creators face since the UK's departure from the EU in 2020 (UK Music, 2023). According to the survey, which garnered 1461 responses from a cross-section of the music community, 30% of music creators have experienced an impact on their earnings post-Brexit. A significant 82% of these respondents have seen a decrease in income, with musicians, DJs and vocalists among the most negatively affected (Brown, 2023). This decrease in revenue is particularly telling, as 70% of those unaffected by Brexit are not generally active within the EU, suggesting that the impact is felt most acutely by those who engage in cross-border work (Brown, 2023). The survey illuminated the stark reality that for 43% of the affected music creators, touring the EU is no longer a viable option (reinforcing Karl Nielson's statement earlier in this chapter). Artists like Katie Melua have cited increases in touring costs of up to 30%, with additional complications arising from vague tax protocols and increased administrative burdens (Paine, 2023).

A worrying 65% of the music creators affected by Brexit reported receiving fewer invitations to perform in the EU, with 57% unable to accept invitations due to prohibitive costs (Brown, 2023). In response, UK Music has urged the government to prioritize a Cultural Touring Agreement with the EU to alleviate these issues (Healy, 2024). Emerging music creators, crucial to the sector's vibrancy and growth, are among the worst affected. The barriers they face in the formative stages of their careers – restrictions on visas, work permits and truck hire, coupled with the labyrinth of red tape – are making international exposure and success increasingly elusive.

The logistical challenges faced by musicians like Two Door Cinema Club under Colin Schaverien's management after Brexit, for example, are overwhelming. Schaverien regrets the decline in ease of travel within the EU. Previously, they could rent a van, pack their equipment, including some T-shirts for selling, and embark on their journey (Arlidge, 2023). Travelling has become an intricate and expensive undertaking because of the customs documentation required for every piece of equipment and merchandise and the strict cabotage regulations restricting the number of pauses within the EU. Managers such as Schaverien find themselves trapped in a complex network of rising administrative responsibilities and costs that have risen significantly.

As we discovered from our interviews with managers in the aftermath of Brexit, musicians face unprecedented challenges related to international travel and visa requirements. The withdrawal of the UK from the EU has introduced myriad complexities for managers of artists touring across Europe. As Steven Braines (2023) states, 'Brexit's more of a pain in the a*** than COVID, just getting visas.

These logistical hurdles are compounded by rising costs, as noted in our interview with Chris Chadwick:

> The cost of touring is hugely worrying… particularly post-Brexit when it's not just post-COVID and it's not just in the light of an energy crisis [or] fuel prices going up and flight prices going up. It's also the added costs of Brexit that I think people are only just getting to terms with.
>
> (Chadwick, 2023)

David Martin at the FAC paints a broader, longer-term but relatively dark picture of the immediate future:

> It's made it far, far harder for our sector. We know the effects, and we are seeing the effects. On a macro scale, I don't think government ministers who don't spend all day every day in the music industries will see that for another 5 or 10 years.
>
> (Martin, 2023)

This sentiment is echoed by managers who see Brexit as a new barrier to EU touring that UK artists have previously enjoyed, as we have already seen with Karl Nielson, for example, identifying dramatic cost increases of 50–60% *and* Ross Patel's statement that it is 'just ridiculous'.

To be completely clear here, we did not encounter a single positive voice in support of the UK withdrawal from the EU in any part of our research. The above represents a small sample of the responses which we received.

UK acts touring in the EU – visas, additional paperwork and costs

This section explores the impact of these travel and visa complexities on musicians and their management teams, examining strategies for effectively navigating this new landscape. This analysis provides insight into the significant hurdles and offers practical solutions for maintaining successful international tours in the post-Brexit era.

The UK withdrawal from the EU has further complicated international travel for musicians, leading to a labyrinth of regulatory changes since the withdrawal in 2020 that require meticulous planning and compliance. This section analyses these complexities, focusing on the requirements for UK and Irish citizens and non-EU members touring within the EU and other international destinations such as the USA.

The cultural tapestry of the UK's music tradition has historically been woven with threads from across Europe, echoing John Donne's 'no man is an island' sentiment (Donne, 1624). This interconnectedness is exemplified by the shared musical heritage between the UK and its European neighbours. The exchange of artists across the North Sea alone, for example, has fostered a rich, diverse musical culture on the British Isles, influenced by Irish, Breton, Danish and broader Scandinavian traditions, amongst others (Blanche, 2019, p. 4).

Brexit has presented a formidable challenge, erecting new barriers in the form of visa restrictions and fresh bureaucratic complexities for touring artists. Recent reports underscore the impact of these new regulations on musicians' livelihoods. An Independent Society of Musicians (ISM, 2024) and Musicians' Union survey revealed that most musicians anticipate a decrease in earnings due to the additional red tape and costs associated with working in Europe post-Brexit (MU, 2024). *The Guardian* highlighted the stark reality faced by UK musicians, with average salaries plummeting, exacerbated by the newfound difficulties in securing EU income (Healy, 2024).

The following paragraphs will attempt to explain the mechanisms and associated documentation which are now required by touring acts.

The introduction of ATA carnets and Goods Movement Reference Numbers (GMRs) as part of the Goods Vehicle Movement Service (GVMS) has added considerably to the touring logistics (MU, 2024). An ATA carnet (Admission Temporaire) or Temporary Admission Carnet is a customs document that allows for the temporary movement of goods between the UK and other countries (Govt UK, 2019). A Goods Movement Reference (GMR) is a document that links multiple declaration references together for a single crossing of goods by a vehicle. GVMS links the Movement Reference Numbers (MRNs) for all pre-lodged declarations in a shipment to a single Goods Movement Record (GMR) that specifies the truck/trailer licence plate (Customs for Trade, 2024).

The ATA carnet is a crucial document for securing temporary export of professional equipment, trade fair goods and commercial samples to the EU (European Commission, 2024). However, UK artists must now navigate a more complex framework to confirm ATA carnet and visa requirements for international touring, with different requirements from each EU nation. Visas are typically unnecessary for EU citizens travelling between EU nations (European Commission, 2024). However, the situation for UK musicians is markedly different, requiring thorough checks and preparation for documentation and visas (MU, 2024). This does not mean that the problem is necessarily any easier for EU artists wishing to tour the UK. Acts from mainland Europe are now required to meet 'opaque and confusing' post-Brexit rule changes. This has caught out many international acts wishing to tour the UK (MU, 2024). The Musicians' Union has taken proactive steps to clarify these requirements and provide resources, such as webinars and discounted carnets, to assist artists in adapting to these changes (MU, 2024).

The dual impact of Brexit and the pandemic has significantly constrained the free cultural exchange that once thrived between the UK and Europe. The resulting insularity threatens not only the economic viability of musicians but also the essence of a shared musical heritage. As the UK conservatoires and the domestic music industry strive to maintain their global relevance and appeal, there is an urgent need to reassess and reformulate strategies to navigate these challenges. The freedom to tour visa-free within the EU remains intact for EU artists. Irish musicians and those from other EU member states are exempt from visa and ATA carnet requirements when touring within the EU, but not for those wishing to cross the Channel to work.

Crossing the Irish Sea to tour is, however, a little different. Post-Brexit, UK and Irish customs authorities have been working to simplify procedures. Irish customs have implemented an Oral Export Declaration for certain classes of goods, including portable musical instruments (MU, 2024). The Oral Declaration for Temporary Admission is now more frequently used for goods imported and exported from the UK, significantly helping solo musicians (Revenue, 2025).

If all you need is one instrument per person, there may be another solution. As reported by the MU, the then DCMS Minister, Caroline Dinenage MP, stated, 'Musicians travelling into and around the EU with portable musical instruments (those which you can carry yourself) are not required to obtain a Carnet'. When flying with instruments, however, checking individual airline policies is also critical, as stipulations and allowances vary widely (MU, 2024). Many musicians have been forced to buy a second airline seat to avoid their instrument ending up in the hold.

Musicians should consider an export declaration rather than an ATA carnet when travelling solely to the UK for merchandise such as T-shirts, vinyl and CDs, which are likely to be sold or distributed during tours. However, if touring extends from the UK to other European countries, merchandise can travel under an ATA carnet, with VAT applicable upon re-importation for goods sold (MU, 2024). It should also be noted that many music artists have their merchandise manufactured in an EU country and delivered to their first EU show to avoid crossing the Channel with unnecessary goods. Musicians working and touring in the EU or in European non-EU countries like Switzerland, Norway, Iceland or Liechtenstein should also ensure their European Health Insurance Card (EHIC) is current. However, it does not replace the need for comprehensive travel insurance (MU, 2024).

Tax considerations and royalty collections

Musicians should seek advice from tax experts to minimize liabilities and ensure they reclaim any amounts due. IMRO (the Irish Music Rights Organisation) and MU members must report their foreign performances to ensure royalties are accurately collected by affiliated societies in the territories where they perform (IMRO, 2024). Musicians are urged to promptly notify their local collection agency of foreign performances and provide comprehensive details, including venue information and set lists, to facilitate accurate royalty collections. Submission deadlines align with those specified under the Tours and Residencies Scheme (IMRO, 2024).

Similarly, the timescale on visa and work permit procurement has emerged as a critical issue, with 59% of respondents identifying it as a significant obstacle. Other barriers highlighted include administration, transport, production costs and cabotage restrictions – limitations on domestic and commercial transport by foreign vehicles –impacting hauliers (Brown, 2023).

In light of these findings, UK Music advocates maintaining a music exports office to bolster British talent and enhance their international presence, a model successfully implemented in other countries such as Germany, Australia and Canada (Brown, 2023). Artists have voiced the need for a tailored approach from the government to support the unique demands of the music industry. Amongst other protesting voices, Paul Smith, lead singer of Maximo Park, and Jennifer Johnston, a mezzo-soprano and creative producer, have both stressed the cultural and economic imperatives of reducing bureaucracy for UK musicians to thrive post-Brexit (Arlidge, 2023).

The 90/180-day travel rule

The 90/180-day travel rule applies to non-EU individuals, including UK musicians who tour within the free-travel Schengen area post-Brexit (25 of the 27 EU nations are included within the open-border Schengen area; European Commission, 2025). It permits these persons to remain in a country for a maximum of 90 days within a 180-day timeframe without requiring a visa. The 180-day period is a continuous timeframe that examines the preceding 180 days to calculate the number of days spent in the Schengen Area (Ward et al., 2023, p. 11). Non-compliance with the rule may result in monetary sanctions, restrictions on entrance, or other punitive measures. Travellers, especially touring artists, must diligently monitor their duration of stay in the Schengen area to adhere to the restrictions and prevent any legal complications arising from exceeding the allowed time limit. The financial impact on income can be substantial, as evidenced by a survey performed by UK Music, which revealed a 32% decline in the number of UK musicians undertaking tours in the EU compared to the pre-Brexit years (Ward et al., 2023). This can significantly affect artists' financial profits, as live performances may account for up to 80% of their income (MMF, 2019).

Although the UK government recognizes the problem, it has yet to discover a complete solution (Ward et al., 2023). The UK music industries persist in pressing for modifications to facilitate the touring process. There have been requests for the government to appoint a touring minister to serve as a central point of contact for the cultural sector dealing with these difficulties (All Party Parliamentary Group on Music, 2022). An agreement for cultural touring is a possible solution to alleviate UK musicians' regulatory and financial challenges. An agreement of this nature may encompass provisions for waivers for carnets and an exemption from cabotage limitations.

Let the music move report

As a first step to acknowledging the issues created by Brexit, the report *Let the Music Move*, published by UK Music and the All-Party Parliamentary Group (APPG) on Music on 19 July 2022, addresses the challenges facing the UK music industry, particularly in light of the post-Brexit Trade and Cooperation Agreement (TCA) between the UK and the EU. It makes several recommendations to alleviate the difficulties musicians and industry workers face when touring in the EU.

One key recommendation is for the UK government to negotiate an exemption for music workers, allowing them to support cultural performances under the TCA. Currently, the restrictions limit the ability of musicians and their support teams to work freely across the EU. The report suggests extending the working limits for musicians to 90 days within a 180-day period in all EU countries, thereby providing greater flexibility for touring musicians.

The report also highlights logistical concerns, such as the need to expand the number of UK border crossing points equipped to manage the paperwork required for international touring. This includes handling carnets and CITES (Convention on International Trade in Endangered Species) Music Instrument Certificates, which regulate the transportation of instruments made from protected materials.

Additionally, the report calls for exemptions for road haulage related to cultural touring. Currently, UK-based haulage companies are limited by EU rules when operating in the EU, which can make it more difficult and costly to transport equipment for tours. To address this, the report suggests negotiating a broader agreement that reduces bureaucratic hurdles and provides specific provisions for specialist event hauliers, who transport staging, lighting, and other essential music touring equipment.

Although the UK government has tried clarifying some of the arrangements with individual EU member states, the report argues that this results in the rules being more complex, leading to costly adjustments and frequent errors. As a result, UK Music workers are at a competitive disadvantage compared to their EU counterparts who do not face these same barriers (UK Music, 2023).

UK (And EU) Artists Planning to Tour in the USA

The following section is intended to give the reader an overview of the complexities of touring in the USA. However, this is not a comprehensive or exhaustive guide to the paperwork and activity necessary to complete such work. If you are intending to perform professionally in the USA, it is necessary to secure the services and advice of a relevant specialist legal expert.

Navigating the visa requirements for touring within the USA is complex and subject to frequent changes for non-US citizens. Musicians (and managers) are advised to consult experts and organizations like Tamizat, Artists from Abroad and Covey Law for advice and assistance regarding different types of US visas a considerable length of time before any planned touring there (MU, 2024).

A non-immigrant work visa is required for temporary employment in the USA, for which you will receive financial compensation. Acquiring a visa for temporary employment in the USA can be a protracted and costly endeavour. Fees, procedures and timelines are subject to alteration; therefore, it is essential to consult a skilled US-based immigration attorney for current guidance. Additional costs are likely, particularly if an interview is required at the US embassy in London or Belfast. There are many sources which provide the necessary detail for those considering this undertaking. One such valuable reference is Showcase Scotland, which is listed at the end of this chapter. Some overview data and suggestions follow.

The MU and Webster (2024) explain that the majority of expenses will pertain to the submission of the petition; hence, ensure that all necessary individuals are included. Incorporating other names is preferable to lacking a visa for a substitute or additional individual if required. Historically, all applicants were mandated to attend an interview at a US embassy; however, this is no longer universally applicable. A visa may be approved without the necessity of your physical presence, especially if you possess a prior US visa. Application can also be made to Belfast instead of London if you reside in Scotland (Showcase Scotland, 2023): [Regarding the US embassy in Belfast], they are generally more accommodating, and it is likely more economical for you to travel there if an interview is necessary. All shows [must be] booked and contracted before you can submit a petition. Then, allow plenty of time for visa processing.' (Showcase Scotland, 2023).

A work visa is not required for an unpaid showcase performance in the USA such as South by Southwest (SXSW). Theoretically, this can done through the easier-to-manage ESTA mechanism (Electronic System for Travel Authorisation), but generally, the advice is to get a B1 visa (Showcase Scotland, 2023). This visa allows an artist to enter the USA to carry out business activities such as attending conferences or meetings. Examples of difficulties include artists being turned away at immigration when attending showcasing events such as SXSW and trying to enter with only an ESTA. To obtain a B1 visa, an artist or manager must first complete a DS-160 form online here (https://ceac.state.gov/genniv/ [accessed 21/7/25]). Once this has been completed and the visa fee of $160 paid, an appointment needs to be scheduled at the US embassy in Belfast or London (Showcase Scotland, 2023). Some companies specialize in providing visa services to artists touring the USA (Showcase Scotland, 2023). Further contacts are provided at the end of this chapter.

US tax for non-US performers

Earnings in the USA will be subject to a withholding tax of 30% unless a Central Withholding Agreement (CWA) is secured with the IRS (https://www.irs.gov/Individuals/International-Taxpayers/Central-Withholding-Agreements

[accessed 21/7/25]). Essentially, this means obtaining a waiver to reduce the rate of tax based on a budget for the tour and expected net profit (or loss). For those who have worked in the USA before, filed tax returns will be needed to obtain a CWA (if this was not done at the time it will need to be done now for the years in question). A return for the current tax year will also need to be filed (Showcase Scotland, 2023).

The artist will need a central withholding agent to arrange all this. These professionals are authorized to negotiate CWAs with the IRS. Their services might cost around $750 but they could save much more in tax throughout a tour. A visa attorney can probably recommend someone, and it is a good idea to start on both fronts as early as possible. Copies of events contracts will need to be provided and a detailed budget for the tour's income and expenditure. When the CWA is granted, the IRS will provide a letter of confirmation, which can be distributed to each venue or festival on the tour. The letter confirms they do not need to withhold 30% of your fee (Showcase Scotland, 2023).

Artists will also need a social security number (SSN) or individual tax identification number (ITIN) to file the tax return. Applying for one of these requires a visit to the relevant tax office in person, so if you do not already have one, you will need to make time to do so while on tour in the USA. You will need to give a US address for your SSN or ITIN to be posted to; this will be the address of the central withholding agent you have hired (Showcase Scotland, 2023).

Consolidation of Prominent Management Companies and Portfolios

One final development here might be a way of overcoming many of the difficulties examined in this chapter. While the rank-and-file musicians in the music industry grapple with the financial turmoil induced by shrinking margins, one salient response has been the consolidation of music companies and the growth of large international management portfolios. This trend is not merely a reaction to the current crisis but also a strategic evolution that aims to stabilize and future-proof the sector. The impetus for consolidation is multifaceted. On the one hand, it is a defensive manoeuvre – companies seeking shelter from the storm of market volatility. Conversely, it is also an opportunistic play, a chance to acquire assets at a reduced cost during a downturn (Puziak and Martyniuk, 2012).

The Water and Music website has been tracking these developments for several years (Hu, 2025), mapping the growing interconnection between labels, tech companies and private equity firms in considerable detail. Equally, Crunchbase data present an overview where many music companies have recently been acquired, amounting to 697 entities with aggregate funding of $6 billion in transactions (Crunchbase, 2024, p. 1). This activity highlights a strong merger and acquisition environment, demonstrating the music industry's ability to adapt and endure in the face of unprecedented challenges – from bottom to top. This trend has extended to touring companies from the music tech sector, with Landr, Native Instruments and Splice all engaging in mergers and acquisitions (Tencer, 2023).

Investment banks have also shown a growing interest in the music industry's potential, as evidenced by Goldman Sachs' *The Show Must Go On* report (Yang et al., 2020, p. 59). It is expected that the value of the worldwide music industry will experience significant growth by the year 2030. Global live concert revenue has constantly increased from 2000 to 2019, with a compound annual growth rate (CAGR) of between 5% and 14%. This sustained growth has driven the events market beyond expectations with the result that in 2013, for the first time (and projected again post-COVID by 2024/25), live music revenue surpassed total recorded music. 'Spending on the UK live music sector and associated businesses has hit a record £6.1bn as a wave of huge acts from Elton John to Beyoncé cashed in on the pent-up demand to attend shows in person' (Sweeney, 2024).

The shift to touring as the primary source of artist revenue (above a certain level of artist success) has provided a tailwind to concert supply growth, which is likely to continue. It would appear that medium-scale and major artists now derive a large part of their income from touring (Sweeney, 2024).

Beyond this, the field of music publishing and collections of original music compositions (catalogue) has also seen significant change in the last decade or so. The investment landscape has expanded to include these music catalogues, with many A-list stars cashing in on their publishing portfolios (Ingham and Wang, 2021). Warner Music's establishment of a $650 million fund dedicated to catalogue acquisitions (Paine, 2019) and Kobalt's $600 million acquisition fund (Paine, 2017) exemplify a strategic shift towards owning more content. This content-driven approach indicates a longer-term vision where the value lies in intellectual property ownership.

Conclusion and Recommendations

In conclusion, while the music industry faces substantial financial challenges, artists and managers can overcome these hurdles through planning and innovative strategies. By better utilizing digital platforms, diversifying income streams, employing cost-effective touring strategies, building a solid online presence, and remaining adaptable, they can ensure sustainable and successful careers in the ever-changing music landscape. Live performance, the highest income-generating sector of the music industries for artists and managers, remains a cornerstone of artist careers, providing financial stability and critical fan engagement. Ross Patel stated: 'For all of our clients, I would say it's pretty crucial, and we rely on that direct fan connection [through live events]'.

The UK's departure from the EU has brought about visa and logistical obstacles that greatly complicate the touring process as evidenced by many of our interviewees. There will be long-term consequences. As David Martin emphasized, the current situation has significantly exacerbated the challenges facing our industry in the years to come.

Brexit has affected the financial sustainability for artists. As many interviewees pointed out, the impact of Brexit has been more significant than initially anticipated. Initially, tentative projections of a 15–20% increase in touring costs have been swept aside by the real increase, which may be closer to 50% or 60%. The situation has grown economically unsustainable below a certain level of success. More popular acts can more easily cover these expenses; less developed acts performing in smaller venues are at risk of falling into financial deficit.

Artists and managers can play a crucial role in advocating for policy changes that benefit the music industry. Engaging with industry bodies and government agencies can be advantageous in driving these changes forward. Furthermore, establishing a cultural touring agreement (CTA) with the EU could alleviate many of the current challenges faced by the industry.

The creative sector should utilize resources and support from music organizations. This would involve taking advantage of opportunities being provided by organizations like the Musicians' Union, which offers webinars, discounted carnets and other tools to help artists adapt to new regulations.

Once a global powerhouse, the UK music industry faces a critical juncture. The government's response in the upcoming renegotiation of the EU–UK Trade and Cooperation Agreement will be pivotal. As Elton John and other industry leaders advocate for change, there is still hope that the UK can reclaim its esteemed position on the international music stage (Ward et al., 2023).

Further contacts for touring the USA

Viva la Visa – contact Andy Corrigan: hello@vivalavisa.co.uk

Tam Ray Touring – contact Katie Ray: katie@tamraytouring.com

Tamizdat – contact Matt Covey: matt@tamizdat.org

References

All Party Parliamentary Group on Music (2022) *Let the Music Move – A New Deal for Touring*. APPG on Music/UK Music, London, p. 6. Available at: https://www.ukmusic.org/wp-content/uploads/2022/07/APPG-on-Music_Let-the-Music-Move_A-New-Deal-For-Touring.pdf (accessed 22 August 2025).

Allen, P. (2022) *Artist Management for the Music Business: Manage Your Career in Music: Manage the Music Careers of Others*, 5th edn. Focal Press, New York.

Anderton, C., Hannam, J. and Hopkins, J. (2022) *Music Management, Marketing & PR*. Sage, London.

Arlidge, J. (2023) How Brexit crippled touring for UK musicians. *The Sunday Times* July.

Bell, F. (2023) Frazer Bell interview 2023. Starliner tours.

Blanche, R. (2019) *Working as a traditional musician in Scotland*. Tradional Music Forum, Edinburgh. Available at: https://tracscotland.org/wp-content/uploads/2019/08/TMF-SUMMARY-REPORT-WORKING-IN-TRADITIONAL-MUSIC-final-JUNE-2019.pdf (accessed 21 July 2025).

BPI (British Phonographic Industry) (2023) *The New Music Democracy*. BPI, London.

Braines, S. (2023) Questions on artist management [Interview by Allan Dumbreck [Zoom], 5 December].

Brown, D. (2023) *A Manifesto for Music*. UK Music, London.

Chadwick, C. (2023) Questions on artist management. Interview by Allan Dumbreck [Zoom], 15 December.

Comber, P. (2022) Questions on artist management. Interview by Allan Dumbreck [phone], 19 September.

Crunchbase (2024) Music acquired companies. Available at: https://www.crunchbase.com/hub/music-acquired-companies (accessed 21 July 2025).

Customs for Trade (2024) What you need to know about Goods Vehicle Movement Service (GVMS). Available at: https://www.customs4trade.com/blog/what-you-need-to-know-about-goods-vehicle-movement-service-gvms (accessed 21 July 2025).

Donne, J. (1624) No man is an island. Available at: allpoetry.com/No-man-is-an-island (accessed 20 January 2025).

Dunworth, L. (2024) Nadine Shah explains decision not to play Glastonbury over low fee: 'Sorry to break it to you but music is my job'. Available at: https://www.nme.com/news/music/nadine-shah-explains-decision-not-to-play-glastonbury-over-low-fee-sorry-to-break-it-to-you-but-music-is-my-job-3763638 (accessed 2 February 2025).

European Commission (2024) Customs transit: ATA – Temporary admission. Available at: https://taxation-customs.ec.europa.eu/customs-4/customs-procedures-import-and-export-0/what-customs-transit/customs-transit-ata-temporary-admission_en#:~:text=The%20ATA%20carnet%20has%20also,to%20the%20point%20of%20exit (accessed 21 July 2025).

European Commission (2025) Schengen area. Available at: home-affairs.ec.europa.eu/policies/schengen-borders-and-visa/schengen-area_en (accessed 20 January 2025).

Forde, E. (2023) What will Spotify's price rise mean for its recording artists and songwriters? *The Guardian* 28 July. Available at: https://www.theguardian.com/music/2023/jul/28/what-will-spotify-price-rise-mean-for-its-recording-artists-and-songwriters#:~:text=%E2%80%9CAn%20increase%20in%20subscription%20fees,of%20music%20per%20paid%20user%E2%80%9D (accessed 21 July 2025).

Gany, E. (2024) How Technology is Shaping the Music Industry. Available at: https://ericgany.com/how-technology-is-shaping-the-music-industry/ (accessed 22 August 2025).

Govt UK (2019) Apply for an ATA Carnet. Available at: https://www.gov.uk/guidance/apply-for-an-ata-carnet#:~:text=You%20can%20buy%20an%20Admission%20Temporaire%20or,to%20countries%20where%20you'll%20use%20them%20temporarily (accessed 21 July 2025).

Govt UK (2024) Increasing the VAT registration threshold. Available at: https//www.gov.uk/government/publications/vat-increasing-the-registration-and-deregistration-thresholds/increasing-the-vat-registration-threshold (accessed 21 July 2025).

Healy, R. (2024) UK music industry presses government to solve post-Brexit limits on touring. *The Guardian*. Available at: www.theguardian.com/business/article/2024/sep/08/uk-music-industry-presses-government-to-solve-post-brexit-limits-on-touring (accessed 20 January 2025).

Hu (2025) *Music tech ownership ouroboros*, 2025 edn. Water and Music. Available at: www.waterandmusic.com/music-tech-ownership-ouroboros-2025#private-equity-doubles-down-on-music (accessed 2 February 2025).

IMRO (2024) IMRO – International Touring Guide. Available at: https://imro.ie/music-creators/international-touring-guide/ (accessed 21 July 2025).

Independent Society of Musicians (ISM) (2024) Travelling with instruments and equipment. Available at: https://www.ism.org/advice/travelling-with-instruments-and-equipment/ (accessed 21 July 2025).

Ingham, T. and Wang, X. (2021) Why superstar artists are clamoring to sell their music rights. *Rolling Stone*, 15 January. Available at: https://www.rollingstone.com/pro/features/famous-musicians-selling-catalog-music-rights-1114580/ (accessed 21 July 2025).

Martin, D. (2023) Questions on artist management. Interview by Allan Dumbreck [Zoom], 22 December.

MBW (Music Business Worldwide) (2022) *With touring costs spiralling, artists mustn't dismiss how much they're wasting on FX payments*. MBW, London. Available at: www.musicbusinessworldwide.com/with-touring-costs-spiralling-artists-mustnt-dismiss-how-much-theyre-wasting-on-foreign-exchange-payments/ (accessed 16 June 2025 (accessed 16 June 2025).

MMF (2019) *Managing Expectations: An Exploration into the Changing Role and Value of the Music Manager*. Music Managers' Forum, London.

MU (2024) Flowchart Guide to Working in Europe. Available at: https://musiciansunion.org.uk/working-performing/working-overseas/working-in-the-eu/flowchart-guide-to-working-in-europe (accessed 21 July 2025).

Nielsen, K. (2024) Questions on artist management. Interview by Allan Dumbreck [Zoom], 25 January.

ONS (2020) Consumer price index (CPI). Office for National Statistics. Available at: https://www.ons.gov.uk/economy/inflationandpriceindices (accessed 21 July 2024).

Paine, A. (2017) Kobalt capital closes $600 million investment fund. Available at: www.musicweek.com/publishing/read/kobalt-capital-closes-600-million-investment-fund/070382 (accessed 2 February 2025).

Paine, A. (2019) Warner music group and providence target catalogues with £500m acquisition fund. *Music Week*. Available at: https://www.musicweek.com/labels/read/warner-music-group-and-providence-target-catalogues-with-500m-acquisition-fund/078369 (accessed 21 July 2024).

Paine, A. (2023) Red alert: how red light's expanding UK operation is taking over the charts. *Music Week*. Available at: https://www.musicweek.com/interviews/read/red-alert-how-red-light-s-expanding-uk-operation-is-taking-over-the-charts/088053 (accessed 21 July 2025).

Paine, A. (2024a) BPI: UK recorded music market up 10% in 2024 with first increase in physical sales for 20 years. Available at: https//www.musicweek.com/labels/read/bpi-uk-recorded-music-market-up-10-in-2024-with-first-increase-in-physical-sales-for-20-years/091134 (accessed 2 February 2025).

Paine, A. (2024b) FAC & musicians' union publish open letter to government and live sector on cost of touring crisis. *Music Week*. Available at: www.musicweek.com/live/read/fac-musicians-union-publish-open-letter-to-government-and-live-sector-on-cost-of-touring-crisis/090751 (accessed 16 June 2025).

Patel, R. (2024) Questions on artist management. Interview by Allan Dumbreck [Zoom], 25 January.

Puziak, M. and Martyniuk, M. (2012) Defensive strategies against hostile takeovers: the analysis of selected case studies. Journal of International Studies 5(1), 60–69.

Revenue (2025) Temporary admission by oral customs declaration. Revenue. Available at: https://www.revenue.ie/en/customs/businesses/temp-admission-exports/rules-procedures/admission-oral-customs-declaration.aspx (accessed 22 August 2025).

Showcase Scotland (2023) Advice for Scottish artists planning to tour in the United States of America. Available at: http://www.showcasescotlandexpo.com/artist-support/touring-in-usa (accessed 21 July 2025).

Statista (2024) Average gasoline and diesel retail price in the United Kingdom at the beginning of each week from July 18, 2022 to July 15, 2024.

Sweeney, M. (2024) Economic impact of UK live music industry hits record £6.1bn. *The Guardian* 4 September. Available at: https://www.theguardian.com/business/article/2024/sep/04/economic-impact-of-uk-live-music-industry-hits-record#:~:text=Spending%20on%20the%20UK%20live,to%20attend%20shows%20in%20person (accessed 21 July 2025).

Tapper, J. (2023) I can't keep making a loss': Bands shun UK festivals as touring costs rise. *The Guardian* 2 July.

Tencer, D. (2023) Private equity loves music tech: Meet the music creation platforms backed by deep-pocketed funds. Music Business Worldwide. Available at: https://www.musicbusinessworldwide.com/private-equity-loves-music-tech-meet-the-music-creation-platforms-backed-by-deep-pocketed-funds/ (accessed 21 July 2025).

Thornhill, T., Goebbel, M., Bullock, A., Masse, M., Molenaar, D. et al. (2024) *The Touring Business Handbook 2024*. IQ Magazine.

UK Music (2023) Eight out of ten Brexit-hit music creators say their earnings have plunged since UK left EU. UK Music, London. Available at: www.ukmusic.org/news/eight-out-of-ten-brexit-hit-music-creators-say-their-earnings-have-plunged-since-uk-left-eu-uk-music-survey-reveals/ (accessed 16 June 2025).

Ward, M., McKinney, C. and Jozepa, I. (2023) *Touring artists and the UK-EU economic partnership*. House of Commons Library, UK Parliament.

Webb, A., Bonham, P., Harmon, A., Coldrick, A. and Dethekar, M. (2022) *Essentials of Music Management*. Music Managers' Forum, London.

Webster, D. (2024) Visa updates for musicians working in the US. Musicians' Union. Available at: https://musiciansunion.org.uk/news/visa-updates-for-musicians-working-in-the-us#:~:text=In%20better%20news%2C%20US%20immigration,airline%20advice%20and%20information%20here (accessed 21 July 2025).

Yang, L.P., Terry, H.P., Mubaye, P. and Bellini, H. (2020) The show must go on. Goldman Sachs, New York. Available at: https://archive.org/details/report_202109 (accessed 21 January 2025).

8 Equality, Diversity and Inclusion (EDI)

Clare K. Duffin

Introduction

> Diversity is not an option for music. It is a necessity.
>
> (UK Music, 2024)

Equality, Diversity and Inclusion (EDI) has become a hot topic of late. There has been a rise in EDI initiatives that have gradually swelled across the music industries. But has it come far enough; and how exactly have EDI policies, initiatives and advocacy impacted on artist managers? The increasing popularity in EDI is, of course, very welcome. However, it has, arguably, not developed sufficiently nor moved at the pace or with the urgency it perhaps could have done in recent decades. On a more positive note, there is a great deal to celebrate in terms of the EDI work being conducted, which has a direct influence on artist managers in the UK and beyond. Key organizations such as, but not limited to, the Music Managers Forum (MMF), UK Music, Keychange, Black Lives in Music, Independent Society of Musicians (ISM), and The F-List for Music and Parents in the Performing Arts (PiPA) have been advocating for a fairer and more inclusive music playing-field in music industries practice, most notably over the last ten years. These are groups of people commanding action for change to make the music industries a fairer, more equitable field in which careers can flourish.

Thus, in this chapter, an overview of the current issues, practices and initiatives pertinent to EDI will be addressed, considering how these impact on artist managers in the music industries. There will be close reference drawn from interview material with a selection of artist managers within the music industries, conducted especially for this publication. Furthermore, using Joan Acker's notion of inequality regimes, which are 'the interlocked practices and processes that result in continuing inequalities in all work organisations' (Acker, 2006, p. 441), a brief analysis of the long-standing and fundamentally embedded 'ways of doing' artist management will be addressed to present the most prevalent issues. The focus will first be on gender and we will subsequently address key issues pertinent to disability, age, sexuality, race and mental health – and intersections of these categories.

Let us look first at membership diversity. According to the MMF, 38% of its membership in 2022 of over 1 200 managers were female (UK Parliament Committees, 2022). Given the recent upward trajectory of female representation, this figure is likely to be higher now (in 2024), since overall membership has been declared at 1 500 on the MMF website (MMF, 2024a).

Whilst UK Music has reported an overall increase in gender representation, up from 49.6 to 52.9% (UK Music, 2022), there remains work to be done on inclusive practices pertinent to age, ethnicity and disability to facilitate a more equitable music industries workforce. UK Music's 'Ten Point Plan' (UK Music, 2022) has driven some positive change on the EDI agenda, calling for trade bodies to align with their action plan.

However, whilst lobbying for change has driven more awareness, conversation and a reasonable degree of positive change in the music industries, there are wider cultural shifts that are needed. Some of these shifts require support at government level before we see any noticeable impact, particularly with a view to creating meaningful enforceable policy.

Issues

In July 2022, a letter to the UK Parliament committee of written evidence produced by the MMF outlined a number of issues that, they believed, were contributing to misogyny in the music industries. Misogyny, in particular, has been a recurring problem within the scope of EDI, explicated across reports both in the UK and across the globe (Kahlert et al., 2021; UK Music, 2022, 2024; UK Parliament Committees, 2022). Press and media coverage of misogyny, bullying and harassment in the music field has been more prevalent since the '#MeToo' movement came to prominence in 2017, where women affected by sexual harassment in Hollywood, commencing with the Harvey Weinstein case, saw a surge in social media posts from those (mainly women) using the #MeToo to share their story. Black activist Tarana Burke was the first to use the hashtag in 2006. Since then, the #MeToo movement and the term itself have grown to become synonymous with gender inequity issues across a multitude of workplaces in music, the creative industries and beyond.

The MMF's written evidence to the Women and Equalities Committee (2024), who later produced the Misogyny in Music report, indicated continuing EDI issues around female managers experiencing bullying and harassment, stating:

> We also especially want to spotlight the often-overlooked instances of female managers who have reported being bullied, and in some cases abused, by their male clients as well as others within the industry and feel that there is a need for better support structures and a culture change to address this behaviour.
> (Committees Parliament, 2024, p. 2, written evidence supplied by MMF)

Bullying and harassment tend to germinate, at least in part, within systemic power dynamics, ingrained in such a way that social interactions and the positioning of people (within a typically capitalist, hierarchical system) are left fighting for 'a place at the table'. The COVID-19 pandemic further exacerbated and 'exposed the inequalities inherent in existing structures' (Taylor et al., 2021, p. 19), affecting those at the self-employed, grassroots level marginally more than those within more secure, salary-based roles.

Female music managers with young children also have challenges with artists'/colleagues' expectations in regard to the demands of always being available/on call 24/7 for their clients or in consideration of short-notice travel requirements. Many women drop out of music management and move into other more flexible professions at this stage (Committees Parliament, 2024, p. 2, written evidence supplied by MMF).

There is also the issue around the negative appearance of assertiveness and control when attached to women vs men in the music industries (Berkers and Hoegaerts, 2019). In research conducted on women music managers in the Flemish music industry, conclusions drawn by Mullens and Zanoni (2019) suggested that the 'music industry is organised around practices that reflect hegemonic masculinity' where 'women managers mimic many of these practices to fit the ideal manager' (Mullens and Zanoni, 2019, p. 7).

Two of the managers interviewed also draw attention to similar issues pertinent to gender dynamics. First, with Ellie Giles of Step Management:

> I feel like it becomes women against men and a blame game, you know? I'm on a f***** board full of a bunch of men who are probably twenty, thirty years older than me, but I can hold my own, I ain't f***** scared of them. I don't see my gender affecting me .... Men can be a little bit, you know, weird. But I'll hold them to account, and I'll say that to them, I'll say 'Look mate, like, what the f*** are you doing?' in a nice, diplomatic way, but I'll hold them to account.
> (Giles, 2022, interview transcript)

In terms of calling out some of these behaviours and considering the notion of individuals taking responsibility to be more 'EDI aware', Steve Braines (He. She. They. Management) elaborates:

> Humans are humans and there will always be some people being idiots. I feel that you can't ignore it. You can't ignore or pretend that it just doesn't exist. So, therefore, you're complicit in it if you don't call it out. I sometimes feel that people [act as if] they're almost from separate

worlds and they're not, they're just all people, all just trying to make some money and perform.
(Braines, 2023, interview transcript)

The Independent Society of Musicians (ISM) has produced several reports since 2018 on discrimination within the music sector, with key findings from the 2022 report indicating 66% of survey respondents reporting that they have experienced discrimination at work, 70% of which occurred in the past 5 years (Williams and Bain, 2022, p. 4). It was stated that this is up from 47% of respondents who reported having experienced discrimination in the 2018 Dignity at Work report (Williams and Bain, 2022). Ninety per cent of those identifying as non-white and as having a disability were reported to have experienced discrimination. (Williams and Bain, 2022).

The participants in the ISM Dignity at Work 2 survey (Williams and Bain, 2022) were predominantly musicians and not specifically artist managers in the music industries. However, given the prevalence of discrimination within the music sector – in which artist managers operate – there will, nonetheless, be elements of discrimination embedded into working practices that managers must look to effectively and appropriately navigate. In the same report (Williams and Bain, 2022), the ISM called for more government support comprising a list of recommendations. Ross Patel, manager at Whole Management, had a less than hopeful outlook in terms of what might be expected from UK government support for the music industries in general based on his experience:

> I expect to see, sadly, little to no support from the UK government for the music industry, which will lead to less opportunities for upcoming artists, venue closures, licensing conditions on certain types of events, certainly LGBTQ plus-related events, councils coming down on them pretty hard for no reason.
> (Patel, 2024, interview transcript)

Fundamentally, Patel's views in combination with the ISM's findings underline that discrimination remains a sticky problem in the music industries, with little support coming from the UK government. Employment laws and supporting policies are largely linked to 'workplaces' and contract types that fall outside of freelancers' working practices, meaning their engagement with music work can be more precarious and thus more open to exploitation.

Precarious Labour and Discrimination

The concept of precariousness is 'one that involves instability, lack of protection, insecurity, and social or economic vulnerability' (Rodgers, 1989, p. 3). Within precarious labour, there is often a 'lack of awareness about and access to benefits and protection' (Hennekam and Bennett, 2017, p. 68) which is intrinsically linked to 'casual' or 'informal work'. Informal workers are workers without access to labour protection or social protection through that work (McQuaid et al., 2021). Places of work and the notion of 'the workplace' in the creative industries can be seen as problematic. Enforceable legal and policy-based procedures are not covered nor managed in the same way for freelance workers, on whom the music sector heavily relies. Kuhn, 2016, p. 158) defines freelance work as: 'short-term employment relationships with a number of different clients and compensation on a project basis, and it has historically been associated with writing and creative occupations'. Freelancers are classified as independent contractors.

It is here, arguably, that a great deal of the regulated workplace protections, including those supported by relevant unions subsequently reduce the number and level of EDI policies which can be effectively implemented. Hesmondhalgh and Baker (2011) echo this with respect to the lack of stable workplaces in the creative economy.

Given the often precarious nature of employment in the creative industries and certainly within music (see also UK Music, 2021), there are at times blurred lines on professional working relationships – some of which can become skewed to the point of negative impact on perceived professional music roles. In other words, the level of uncertainty in roles (for example, musician only; musician *and* songwriter; self-managing artist; music artist manager to other artists *and* self-managing artist; record label manager, musician, artist manager *and* songwriter), when distinct roles overlap, can result in inadvertent discrimination. This is often aggravated by a lack of diversity in prominent roles: 'Female managers also reported being regularly mistaken by promoters/stage crew/senior industry figures for assistants, girlfriends etc., rather than artist managers' (Women and Equalities Committee, 2024).

Ultimately, the notion of being 'regularly mistaken' by key gatekeepers in the music industries is arguably symptomatic of female music managers being poorly represented. Subsequently, such a lack of diverse representation in key roles fails to encourage the younger generation into these roles. Furthermore, identifying and mitigating barriers facing marginalized groups is crucial in encouraging diversity and enhancing inclusivity.

The embodiment of power and control within precarious labour markets are key factors in considering how the barriers might be eradicated, levelling the playing field of employment opportunities. Hooper underlines that gatekeepers often hold such power over individual careers (Hooper, 2019, p.137). Gatekeepers do not necessarily hold a single role. However, they will tend to assume a certain degree of power as a person that makes decisions regarding access. Examples include live music promoters (access to being booked for a show); booking agents (access to being on a roster that books musicians at all); record label personnel with authority over signing new artists (access to the administrative and sometimes promotional support when releasing music as a single, EP and/or album). Baym (2018) and Miller (2016) refer to 'boys club' notions of 'systematic favouring of men artists and creative workers' (Miller, 2016, p. 120), whereby gatekeeper networks can be seen as prohibiting inclusive hiring practices. Hanson and Pratt (1995) draw further attention to the role of personal networks in relation to jobs acquisition in this regard:

> Networks of personal contacts and information, norms, and values that are filtered through them do not respect the neat divisions scholars have drawn between the economic and the social, between production and reproduction, between work and home; they are the medium through which individuals develop aspirations and, often, acquire access to jobs.
> (Hanson and Pratt, 1995, p. 6)

Music artist managers may also be perceived as those with such power and control, dictated by and generally depending on the artist–manager relationship. Again, given the often casual nature of these relationships (those not registered with the MMF, for example) and lack of visibility as to how these relationships are governed, both precarity and misuses of power can present themselves in contrast to equal, diverse and inclusive practices.

One of the nuances to freelance work that further accentuates discrimination and feeds into problematic power dynamics within the scope of precarious labour, is 'loneliness', particularly 'when [artist–manager relationships] can become confusing and confused, and changes over time' (Musgrave and Gross, 2020, p. 102). Arguably, loneliness can be seen as commonplace for many musicians and artist managers alike in the context of their employment status, the specific individual circumstances of that employment and lack of 'regular' working hours. Isolated working practices exist within the context of freelance music work as does a lack of self-belief 'with reference to the glass ceiling effect and lack of diversity in or access to 'gatekeeper' roles' (Black Lives in Music, 2021, p. 52). Managers may find themselves working days or weeks on end in isolation, researching opportunities for their artists, building social media assets, writing funding applications and/or juggling these types of activities with non-music jobs to produce a sustainable income for themselves. It is at such times, perhaps more so at the grassroots level, that loneliness may be more prolific and equal opportunities less apparent.

(Christou and Bloor, 2021, p. 2) define loneliness as:

> ...a social phenomenon experienced by individuals, groups and families within certain complex socio-economic circumstances, exacerbated by policies, belief systems [such as those which create racism or sexism], opportunities including income, life situations, all of which intermesh to reduce opportunities and wellbeing in those individuals and groups.

Thus, loneliness may be considered a fundamental issue borne of precarious labour that feeds non-inclusive practice and behaviours with respect to the 'complex socio-economic circumstances' it brings. Whilst the social status of artist managers can also be at the opposite end of the spectrum, depicted more so as 'socialites' in music documentaries, autobiographies and the media, there is evidence to suggest that isolated working practices will diminish the reporting of discriminatory incidents with freelance working conditions continuing to suffer from a comparatively poorer infrastructure (in employment law and EDI policy terms) to that of organiszations operating with the support of human resource management personnel. The ISM report (Williams and Bain, 2022) highlighted that the most common reasons for not reporting instances of bullying and harassment were 'it's just the culture' in the music sector (55%), followed by 'no one to report to' (48%) and 'fear of losing work' (45%). Similarly, on the non-reporting issue, music artist managers were grouped within the 'executives' category alongside music agents, music publishers and record labels, reported to have a 72% rate of discrimination and a 56% level of non-reporting of discriminatory issues (Williams and Bain, 2022, p. 22).

A freelance music manager based in the UK, wishing to remain anonymous to avoid any negative repercussions on their comments, also highlights the different ways she was treated during the course of email communications using a non-gender-specific sign-off. She elaborates:

> I noticed that different language was used when people were speaking about or to males versus females. For example, due to having a unisex name, I noticed that people would use different language with me via emails, referring to me as 'mate' or using more colloquial language. When they found out that I was a female, the language and attitude towards me would change. I found this, and still find it, really interesting because sometimes it appeared that things would get done quicker or to a higher standard when people thought I was a guy, but I could never understand why that was the case.
> (Anonymous freelance music manager, 2024, interview transcript)

It is not surprising that the lack of a qualified person, department or industry body to whom discrimination can be reported – with a straightforward start-to-finish procedure – has rendered a feeling amongst music sector workers as one that is 'just the culture' (Williams and Bain, 2022). There is no clear, consistent, reliable set of protocols that one can follow with any confidence to mitigate problems with discrimination. Whilst representative bodies provide important guidance to members (such as, but not limited to, the MMF, Musicians' Union and ISM), they cannot command the same gravitas in processual outcomes for offenders governed by employment law compared to organizations with employees taking a salary.

Precarious labour and discrimination are also themes in the landmark Black Lives in Music report published in 2021, which further emphasises the discrimination faced by black music creators and professionals. Eighty-eight per cent of all black music professionals in the 2021 report agreed that there are barriers to progression and 73% of black music professionals have experienced direct/indirect racism in the music industry; and more (80%) have experienced racial micro-aggressions (Black Lives in Music, 2021, p. 17).

> Being a Black female and a working mum literally puts me at the bottom of the hierarchy. The industry consists of mainly white cliques at the top. There are subgroups that have a greater ratio of ethnic professionals, but if you've been caught in a white corporate bubble, you're not with the in-crowd in either scenario. Visibility for Black professionals is a priority, not only for progression and recognition but so we can connect and grow together. We need to champion each other.
> (Black Lives in Music, 2021, p. 46)

Intersectionality is also important to highlight given the compounding effects of marginalization experienced by individuals. Intersectionality is defined as 'the interaction of multiple identities and experiences of exclusion and subordination' (Davis, 2008, p. 67). Intersecting characteristics such as black female music professionals with children evidence a compounding effect for those experiencing multiple aspects of marginalization. There is therefore a reduction in opportunities to meaningfully participate in music industries practice when these factors are combined. The culture of precarious labour and discrimination thus wields greater non-inclusive practices and behaviours in terms of intersectionality.

Initiatives

To tackle EDI issues, a few notable initiatives have been driving positive change. Keychange and the MMF Accelerator Programme are two such examples. Keychange is a not-for-profit organization that lobbies for gender equality in the music industries. It was initiated in 2015 by Vanessa Reed, former CEO of PRS Foundation (Keychange, 2024) and launched officially in 2017 with key partners Musikcentrum Öst, Reeperbahn Festival, BIME, Tallinn Music Week and Iceland Airwaves (Keychange, 2024).

Keychange is 'supported by the Creative Europe Programme of the European Union' (Keychange, 2024), a global network focused on changing how the music industries operate in order to reach what they call full gender equality (Keychange, 2024). Similarly, but for music managers specifically, the MMF Accelerator Programme has made an impact on driving forward the diversity agenda. The programme is backed by YouTube Music, Arts Council England, Creative Scotland, PPL and the Scottish Music Industry Association (MMF, 2024b) and is designed to provide 'a combination of financial and educational support – including 12-month grants of up to £12,000, alongside expert-led professional development training' (MMF, 2024b).

Since the end of 2023, 'the programme will have supported more than 100 managers from across the UK with 40% of participants from nations and regions outside of London, 43% from black or ethnic backgrounds, and 44% women or gender minorities' (MMF, 2024b). Furthermore, as an organization, the MMF also promotes the work of organizations such as Love Music Hate Racism and Pride in Music (MMF, 2024c).

In a wider industry context, lobbyist groups such as Parents in the Performing Arts (PiPA) have championed programmes of activity to better include parents and carers in performing arts practice. There is a growing body of research on 'mothering' in particular, to spark gender-inclusive initiatives. Mothers, for instance, assume more of the unpaid domestic work and tend to be the primary caregivers (Zhou, 2017), thus putting them in a further disadvantaged position and subject to the downfalls of 'gender gapping' (Duffin, 2023, 2024). The notion of mothering as being central to 'gender gapping' where multiple and repeated gaps such as in pay, or in work or practice, as time taken out of creative industries work to rear and care for children reflects intersecting barriers to participation for mothers, is evidenced in low female representation in most roles across the music sector.

Activist groups such as Hen Hoose, Women in CTRL, Pop Girlz and Help Musicians vary in their official status as established organizations, but share a focus on raising awareness on equality, diversity and inclusion in the music sector – most focusing on creating a better gender balance and supporting LGBTQIA + communities in terms of representation and participation in music industries practices.

Hen Hoose, for example, supports women and non-binary artists in their music careers through a variety of funded or partially funded initiatives. In 2024, Hen Hoose received funding from Creative Scotland to continue such work within EDI, rolling out the likes of the Beldina Odenyo Bursary, which provides production support and a studio session for artists with no previous professional recording experience.

Analysis

Whilst there is evidence that such initiatives are creating impact in moving the music industries towards a more equal, diverse and inclusive operation, representation remains a prevalent problem. Denise Allan, manager of Glasvegas, describes not being taken seriously in part due to the poor representation of women in artist management at the earlier stages of her career, stating:

> When I said that I was the music manager he just didn't believe me because he doesn't see enough people like me. Not seeing enough people that are representatives, they are small challenges and barriers that you come across. When you go into the live world it's ten times worse.
>
> (Denise Allan, interview transcript)

Similarly, Cara Mills-McLaughlin of Kingdom Management (the company known for bringing Lewis Capaldi to rising fame), highlights an experience at renowned Glasgow music venue The Barrowlands, where a tour manager was unwilling to 'deal with [her]' on an artist's fee settlement and insisted upon speaking with her male co-manager:

> ...the tour manager of the other band just did not want to deal with me at all, he would always go to Louis to deal with the fee or anything and Louis would [say], "no no, you deal with Cara, she's the manager, like you go to her", and he just point-blank did not want to have anything to do with me, which did feel like "I'm a young girl, he doesn't take me seriously".
>
> (Mills-McLaughlin, 2020, interview transcript)

In these examples, there are two points of discrimination: gender and age. Within artist management, being or appearing to be, 'younger' is presented here as a disadvantage – and interestingly at odds with perceptions of female artists. For artist managers, combining this notion of being 'younger' with being female, has been seen to have a negative compounding effect. Denise Allan draws attention to such issues, commenting on the poor representation of females of the so-called 'younger' age having less power and influence:

> I think there is also another inequality and that's age and it works mostly against you when you're young. I don't think you're really taken as seriously and that's something that's not really picked up on.... I remember being in my late 20s and just looking a wee bit younger and being with my business partner, Dean, who I mentioned at the very beginning, and being in record companies, and I don't think it's because I was female, I think it was just because I was young that they would tend to gravitate towards him to ask questions, but we knew we'd been through situations so many times he would just [say] "Denise, what do you think?" and I'd [say] "Right, OK, this is what we're doing here" and then it would change the dynamic a bit. I don't think that's recognized, especially in business. There is gender inequality for sure, racial inequality, and I think a lot of it is to do with representation and just, like, helping people actually come through that represent different sectors of society, and I just don't think it happens enough, which makes our job really quite difficult, to be honest, at times.
>
> (Denise Allan, interview transcript)

Data from the 2024 *Seat at the Table* report tell us that 52% of board members across the UK Music trade bodies are women, an increase from 32% in 2020 and 42% in 2021' (Women in CTRL, 2024). Sixteen per cent of board members across the organizations are women from a global majority background, an increase from 3% in 2020 and 7% in 2021. Over 55% of organizations have achieved 50% gender representation on their boards (Women in CTRL, 2024). However, not all artist managers in the music industries are members of the MMF and thus, the reality could be somewhat different.

For example, in an interview with CEO of the MMF, Annabella Coldrick, conducted in 2020, Coldrick states that there are music managers she was aware of at the time that had not joined the MMF and saw themselves more as 'lone entrepreneurs' adding, 'it's difficult to know' (Coldrick, 2020) how many non-MMF members are out there managing artists. This was particularly those at the grassroots level.

In 2012, the MMF launched their Equality and Diversity Charter (MMF, 2012). Five years later, in 2017, the MMF indicated: 'We have much to be proud of – our membership is 35% female and 15% Black and Ethnic backgrounds and we are aiming to increase this as we expand year on year' (diversity statement; MMF, 2017).

Thus, whilst the increase in MMF membership presents a positive upwards trajectory in terms of diversity, it is not absolute. Non-members – some of whom are 'DIY', self-managing artists – will be attempting to navigate a challenging terrain of relationship-building with, for example, promoters, record labels, independent record stores, social media influencers, publishers, tour managers, and more. Notwithstanding, entering into negotiations with such industries, personnel that do not take full cognisance of the nuances pertinent to the protected characteristics as set out by the Equality Act 2010. As diversity increases, so too must the industry working conditions, in terms of being adaptable and generally suitable for those who operate within it.

The representation of female, disabled, black and ethnic-background artist managers remains below expectations insofar as reaching a 'fully balanced' workforce in concerned, and this can be linked to certain barriers to participation. Intersections of these groups can also see compounding issues. Within (particularly larger) organizations, issues on equality can be dictated by those in power as 'systematic disparities between participants in power and control over goals, resources, and outcomes' (Acker, 2006, p. 443). Thus, when those with power – as is the case often in the music industries across all sectors – are able, white, middle-aged males, there requires to be a bigger focus on initiatives geared towards people of colour, females and those with disabilities in order to enhance diversity.

Neurodiversity – comprising the broad spectrum of differences in individual brain function and that 'there is no one "right" way of thinking' (Baumer and Frueh, 2021; see also Ali et al., 2024) – is equally important here. Diversity in any workforce or industry is deeply valuable in maintaining a balance in cultural views and in cultivating positive inclusive practices. Esta Rae, a black neurodivergent events manager and creative who provided the foreword in Black Lives in Music's most recent report, states: 'The subject pertaining to intersectionality and diversity is one that is ongoing, but it can be said that many barriers faced by individuals in the form of discrimination are based on multiple identities such as disability, gender, race, ethnicity, class to name a few' (Rae, 2023, p. 2).

However, according to research conducted by the ISM, Musicians' Union, UK Music and Black Lives in Music, there continues to be recurring non-inclusive practices existent within the music industries. If we consider how Acker's 'inequality regimes' definition extends to 'workplace decisions such as how to organize work; opportunities for promotion and interesting work; security in employment and benefits; pay and other monetary rewards; respect; and pleasures in work and work relations' (Acker, 2006, p. 443), we can also identify within such regimes a set of cultural factors particular to the music industries that must exercise an understanding of 'best practice' pertinent to equitable opportunities and inclusivity. The levels of discrimination highlighted in music industry reports published over the last 5 years suggest the 'ways of doing' or how we organize this work and related opportunities suffers greatly from lack of governance in freelance work. In other words, precarious labour.

One such example highlighted earlier in this chapter is the notion of 'mothering' which brings with it a set of socially prescribed expectations. As Spelman (1988) states: '...as long as it is only women who mother, in the social context in which they do, these differences in women and men will continue to exist. Change or put an end to such differences, the institution of mothering has to change.' (Spelman, 1988, p. 84).

Fundamentally, the example provided here serves to draw attention to inequities embedded in wider culture and society that must first be acknowledged by music sector gatekeepers before noticeable change will take effect. The most recent *Balancing Act* report from PiPA shows, for example, that 'women and freelancers face the brunt of unpredictable, precarious and unstainable working conditions' (PiPA, 2024) and where 'women continue to be the primary caregiver (77% of women vs 21% of men). Furthermore, that 'they were far more likely to reduce working hours or give up work altogether' (PiPA, 2024, p. 16). Thus, the lack of flexible childcare (PiPA, 2024, p. 8) to coincide with "core" music industry operations such as touring creates additional barriers.

UK Music has produced an extensive list of EDI policies and individual roles across sectors with reference to the "Five Ps" – the outcome of UK Music's Diversity Taskforce having conducted a "theory of change" exercise to take forward the aims of the aforementioned "Ten Point Plan". Fundamentally, the "theory of change" process reviewed how and where positive EDI impact could be developed and sustained. In a sense, the Five Ps (People, Policy, Partnerships, Purchase and Progress) provide a means to strategically respond to Acker's (2006) definition of inequality in the workplace in organizations.

The policies listed by UK Music cover the following areas:

- Disability
- Neurodiversity
- Pregnancy, miscarriage, parental rights and menopause
- Mental health
- LGBTQIA+
- Ethnicity/race
- Religion/belief
- Bullying, harassment and discrimination
- Intersectionality

What remains uneven is the support for freelance music artist managers conducting their business predominantly outside of an organization, which thus relies on representational bodies to broker industries-wide change – in culture and in attitudes – towards minority groups. From the UK Music list of policies, those mapping more so to music artist managers are the Parents and Carers in the Performing Arts (PiPA) and the forthcoming new body the Creative Industries Independent Standards Authority (CIISA), whose purpose will be 'to uphold and improve standards of behaviour across the creative industries and to prevent and tackle all forms of bullying and harassment' (UK Music, 2024). In addition, the key body providing guidance and support is the MMF, stemming in part from their Code of Practice.

Making Artist Management Equitable

Thus, how can music artist management in the UK and beyond be more equitable? The initiatives outlined above provide a reasonable degree of confidence that the culture may well be shifting within the music sector – out of the days of misogyny and lack of diversity into those that are more inclusive and supportive towards marginalized groups. However, as the recent survey data from ISM, Black Lives in Music and the Musicians' Union suggest, discriminatory behaviours have not disappeared. In fact, they remain quite prevalent, suggesting quite strongly that more action is required across the sector to improve the culture, conditions and protections for music industries workers.

Quota setting may be one way to mitigate poor representation of marginalized groups (see Hooper, 2019, p. 137), particularly on female artists being consistently behind male artists in festival line-ups (Mansfield et al., 2022); however, the implementation of this may be less straightforward outside of the live sector. Improving representation in artist management, more specifically, requires changes to the working culture as a whole.

As highlighted by the ISM in 2022, a key forward-thinking approach would be the reintroduction of rights on third-party harassment back to the Equality Act 2010 to protect freelance workers, for which ISM CEO Deborah Annetts has been lobbying. Such protections were removed on 1 October 2013 (Williams and Bain, 2022, p. 32) but an amendment, Worker Protection Act (Amendment of Equality Act 2010) 2023, is now making its way through parliament for consideration. As Annetts put forth in a letter issued on behalf of ISM members on 22 May 2023 addressed to the Right Honourable Kemi Badenoch MP:

> Many musicians' workplaces include public places such as concert halls, clubs, wedding venues, and theatres. Performances often take place at night and in licensed premises where alcohol is served. Harassment – particularly of a sexual nature – is rife in these environments. As it stands, employers, service providers, and fixers can distance themselves from liability in circumstances where preventative measures would have protected the workers.
>
> (Annetts, 2023)

Music managers are not separated from these issues, and given the data presented in recent reports discussed earlier in this chapter, it seems quite likely an artist manager will experience the same in their own professional practice directly, or vicariously through artists and clients with whom they have a working relationship.

Conclusion

This chapter addressed several of the EDI issues, policies and initiatives within the music industries, most of which are predominantly UK-focused. Nonetheless, the key points raised serve to underline that there is still work to be done to improve the working culture and conditions for music artist managers to make the music sector more welcoming and inclusive. There is a great deal to celebrate with respect to the advocacy, progress and greater sense of awareness pertinent to equality, diversity and inclusivity policies – and related practices – within the music industries overall. Organizations such as, but not limited to, the MMF, ISM, Keychange, Black Lives in Music, Pop Girlz, Hen Hoose, Musicians' Union, Women in CTRL, F-List, UK Music, and more, have collectively conducted considerable work to make booking, hiring and employment practices more equitable.

The evidence in the industry reports and academic research provided in this chapter highlights positive aspects and strides forward being taking in relation to a better gender balance being achieved in key music industry roles, propelled mainly by the Keychange 50/50 initiative. This, alongside UK Music's 'Ten Point Plan' is a demonstration of the extent to which change can take place to enhance equality, diversity and inclusion and perhaps mitigate the 'systematic disparities between participants in power and control' (Acker, 2006, p. 244).

However, the levels of discrimination and cases of harassment revealed in the Black Lives in Music 2021 report (Black Lives in Music, 2021) and ISM's Dignity at Work 2 report (Williams and Bain, 2022) suggest strongly that the volatile nighttime culture and precarious labour conditions synonymous with music sector work require government intervention to better protect music workers. This is key to building a better foundation upon which perpetrators of discrimination and harassment are held accountable. The call to amend the Equality Act (2010) as a vehicle to enhance accountability is one that may serve EDI policies and create a better, more inclusive music sector. The combination of heightened awareness of 'good practice' that is supported by legislation – and funded (arguably) by the most influential representative bodies – is fundamental to driving forward the equality, diversity and inclusion agenda.

References

Acker, J. (2006) Inequality regimes: Gender, class, and race in organizations. *Gender & Society* 20(4), 441–464. DOI: 10.1177/0891243206289499.

Ali, M., Grabarski, M.K. and Baker, M. (2024) An exploratory study of benefits and challenges of neurodivergent employees: Roles of knowing neurodivergents and neurodiversity practices. *Equality, Diversity and Inclusion* 43(2), 243–267. DOI: 10.1108/EDI-03-2023-0092.

Annetts, D. (2023) Letter to the Rt Hon Kemi Badenoch on behalf of ISM. Available at: www.ism.org/wp-content/uploads/2023/08/Letter-to-Kemi-Badenoch-May-2023.pdf-2.pdf (accessed 24 May 2024).

Anonymous freelance music manager (2024) Questions on artist management. Email correspondence with Clare Duffin, 23 May.

Baumer, N. and Frueh, J. (2021) What is neurodiversity? Available at: www.health.harvard.edu/blog/what-is-neurodiversity-202111232645 (accessed 15 May 2024).

Baym, N.K. (2018) *Playing to the Crowd: Musicians, Audiences, and the Intimate Work of Connection*. New York University Press.

Berkers, P. and Hoegaerts, J. (2019) Music, gender, inequalities. *Tijdschrift Voor Genderstudies* 22(1), 1–6. DOI: 10.5117/TVGN2019.1.001.BERK.

Black Lives in Music (2021) Being black in the UK music industry. Part 1 – Music professionals. Available at: s3.us-east 1.amazonaws.com/nadworks.streaming/BLiM/BLiM-report-industryprofessionals_21 09v01.pdf (accessed 23 May 2024).

Braines, S. (2023) Questions on artist management. Interview by Allan Dumbreck [Zoom], 5 December.

Christou, A. and Bloor, K. (2021) The liminality of loneliness: Negotiating feminist ethics and intersectional affectivity. *Journal of Cultural Analysis and Social Change* (1), 1–18. DOI: 10.20897/jcasc/11120.

Coldrick, A. (2020) Questions on artist management. Interview by Allan Dumbreck [Zoom], 7 April.

Committees Parliament (2024) Written evidence submitted by the music managers forum (MMF) (mim0017). Available at: committees.parliament.uk/writtenevidence/110061/pdf/ (accessed 28 February 2024).

Davis, K. (2008) Intersectionality as buzzword: A sociology of science perspective on what makes a feminist theory successful. *Feminist Theory* 9(1), 67–85. DOI: 10.1177/1464700108086364.

Duffin, C.K. (2023) Gender gapping: an analysis of mothering and freelance music practice in Scotland. Doctoral thesis, University of the West of Scotland.

Duffin, C.K. (2024) Mothering: The epicentre of gender gapping. In: Arditi, D. and Nolan, R. (eds) *The Palgrave Handbook of Critical Music Industry Studies*. Palgrave Macmillan, pp. 97–117. DOI: 10.1007/978-3-031-64013-1_7.

Giles, E. (2022) Questions on artist management. Interview by Allan Dumbreck [Zoom], 29 March.
Hanson, S. and Pratt, G. (1995) *Gender, Work and Space*. Routledge, London.
Hennekam, S. and Bennett, D. (2017) Creative industries work across multiple contexts: Common themes and challenges. *Personnel Review* 46(1), 68–85. DOI: 10.1108/PR-08-2015-0220.
Hesmondhalgh, D. and Baker, S. (2011) *Creative Labour: Media Work in Three Cultural Industries*. Routledge, London.
Hooper, E. (2019) The gatekeeper gap: Searching for solutions to the UK's ongoing gender imbalance in music creation. In: Raine, S. and Strong, C. (eds) *Towards Gender Equality in the Music Industry*. Bloomsbury Academic, New York, pp. 131–144.
Kahlert, H., Thakrar, K. and Das, S. (2021) Be the change report. Available at: change-women-making-music.pdf (accessed 22 June 2022).
Keychange (2024) About us. Available at: www.keychange.eu/about-us (accessed 25 July 2025).
Kuhn, K.M. (2016) The rise of the 'gig economy' and implications for understanding work and workers. *Industrial and Organizational Psychology* 9(1), 157–162. DOI: 10.1017/iop.2015.129.
Mansfield, M., Lynch, P. and Woodfield, L. (2022) Music festivals: Only 13% of UK headliners in 2022 are female. *BBC News* 24 May. Available at: www.bbc.co.uk/news/newsbeat-61512053 (accessed 23 May 2024).
McQuaid, R., Rand, S. and Webb, A. (2021) After COVID-19: What is the future for those working in the informal sector? Available at: www.emeraldgrouppublishing.com/opinion-and-blog/after-covid-19-what-future-those-working-informal-sector (accessed 24 May 2024).
Miller, D.L. (2016) Gender and the artist archetype: Understanding gender inequality in artistic careers. *Sociology Compass* (2), 119–131. DOI: 10.1111/soc4.12350.
Mills-McLaughlin, C. (2020) Questions on artist management. Interview by Allan Dumbreck [Zoom], 19 May.
MMF (2012) UK music launches Equality & Diversity Charter. Available at: themmf.net/news/uk-music-launches-equality-diversity-charter/ (accessed 18 February 2024).
MMF (2017) MMF publishes diversity statement. Available at: https://themmf.net/news/mmf-publishes-diversity-statement/ (accessed 18 February 2024).
MMF (2024a) About. Available at: https://themmf.net/about/ (accessed 21 March 2024).
MMF (2024b) Resources. Available at: themmf.net/resources/accelerator-programme/ (accessed March 2024).
MMF (2024c) Advocacy. Available at: themmf.net/about/advocacy/ (accessed 25 May 2024).
Mullens, F. and Zanoni, P. (2019) Mothering the artist: Women artist managers crafting an occupational identity in the flemish music industry. *Tijdschrift Voor Genderstudies* 22(1), 7–26. DOI: 10.5117/TVGN2019.1.002.MULL.
Musgrave, G. and Gross, S.A. (2020) *Can Music Make You Sick? Measuring the Price of Musical Ambition*. University of Westminster Press, London. Available at: www.uwestminsterpress.co.uk/site/books/m/10.16997/book43/ (accessed 23 May 2024).
Patel, R. (2024) Questions on artist management. Interview by Allan Dumbreck [Zoom], 25 January.
PiPA (2024) Balancing act 2024. Available at: ipacampaign.org/research/balancing_act_2024?referrer=/research24 (accessed 23 May 2024).
Rae, E. (2023) Unseen, unheard: Race and disability – black disabled experience in the UK's music industry. Black Lives in Music. Available at: blim.org.uk/report-unseen-unheard/ (accessed 22 May 2024).
Rodgers, G. (1989) Precarious work in Western Europe: The state of the debate. In: Rogers, G. and Rogers, J. (eds) *Precarious Jobs in Labour Market Regulation: The Growth of Atypical Employment in Western Europe*. ILO Publications, Geneva, pp. 3–16. Available at: www.ilo.org/public/libdoc/ilo/1989/89B09_333_engl.pdf (accessed 24 May 2022).
Spelman, E.V. (1988) *Inessential Woman: Problems of Exclusion in Feminist Thought*. Beacon Press, Boston, Massachusetts.
Taylor, I.A., Raine, S. and Hamilton, C. (2021) Crisis as a catalyst for change: COVID-19, spatiality and the UK live music industry. *Journal of the International Association for the Study of Popular Music* 11(1), 1–21. Available at: iaspmjournal.net/index.php/IASPM_Journal (accessed 24 May 2024).
UK Music (2021) UK Music urges music industry to break down employment barriers as survey reveals 1 in 5 disabled people face discrimination at work. Available at: https://www.ukmusic.org/news/uk-music-urges-music-industry-to-break-down-employment-barriers-as-survey-reveals-1-in-5-disabled-people-face-discrimination-at-work/ (accessed 12 May 2024).

UK Music (2022) UK Music Diversity Report 2022. Available at: https://www.ukmusic.org/equality-diversity/uk-music-diversity-report-2022/ (accessed 26 March 2024).

UK Music (2024) Equality across the music industry. Available at: https://www.ukmusic.org/equality-diversity/ (accessed 18 February 2024).

UK Parliament Committees (2022) Written evidence submitted by the Music Managers Forum (MMF) (MiM0017). Available at: https://committees.parliament.uk/writtenevidence/110061/pdf/ (accessed 19 August 2025).

Williams, K. and Bain, V. (2022) Dignity at work 2: Discrimination in the music sector. Independent Society of Musicians. Available at: https://www.ism.org/wp-content/uploads/2023/08/ISM-Dignity-2-report.pdf#page=4.06 (accessed 11 May 2024).

Women and Equalities Committee (2024) Misogyny in Music. House of Commons, UK Parliament. Available at: www.parliament.uk/site-information/copyright-parliament (accessed 25 July 2025).

Women in CTRL (2024) Seat at the table 2024 report. Available at: https://mcusercontent.com/3ce4dc5f13e86812160b00013/files/0fb70c51-6087-431f-af53-c38da862f3d7/Seat_at_the_Table_2024_Report_Final.pdf (accessed 16 March 2024).

Zhou, M. (2017) Motherhood, employment, and the dynamics of women's gender attitudes. *Gender & Society* 31(6), 751–776. DOI: 10.1177/0891243217732320.

9 Mental Health

Jayne Stynes

Introduction

This chapter explores how the working conditions of music management can negatively impact the mental health of a music manager as well as that of their artist(s). By considering specific aspects of the profession that can intensify poor mental health, it will discuss how factors including the complex power dynamics between the artist and manager, the intense pressure to succeed in a highly competitive music ecosystem, and the risk of financial insecurity can negatively impact the mental health and well-being of a manager and their clients. The final section will outline some of the ways in which music managers navigate these risk factors; in particular: the importance of establishing clear professional and personal boundaries with artists; and the value of music industry resources that provide support for music professionals in crisisMusic Manager Forum Code of Practice (n.d.).

Before delving into the main discussion, in the interests of transparency and setting the appropriate context, I outline my own position in relation to this subject. Before being involved in music education, I worked as a day-to-day manager for a London-based artist management company and, subsequently, acted as general manager for the UK Music Managers Forum (MMF). During my time at the MMF there were continuous conversations, workshops and panel discussions relating to mental health in a music industries context, and in that role I worked on two significant projects that spoke directly to these issues. Firstly, I co-ordinated and contributed to the revision of the MMF Code of Practice Music Manager Forum Code of Practice (n.d.), consulting with the MMF board, its membership, other music trade bodies, educators and lawyers to update the code, making it more accessible and representative of the current views of the industry. In addition, I project-managed and edited the revised Music Managers Forum (2021a), originally developed by my predecessor Fiona McGugan in 2017, alongside the charities Music Support and Help Musicians. I worked with one of the original authors, therapist Sam Parker, to update and refine the guide, incorporating more perspectives of music managers taken from interviews conducted during that time. This chapter draws from the pool of interviews conducted for this book, primarily with music managers based in the UK and internationally. It also includes some quotes taken from interviews included in the revised MMF *Guide to Mental Health* Music Managers Forum (2021a).

Having dedicated a notable portion of time at the Music Managers Forum exploring mental health-related matters, developing revised and accessible resources, communicating with dedicated music and mental health organizations, and, most important, listening to music managers as they shared their insights and experiences, I hope what follows is a snapshot of the growing awareness of supporting good mental health in the music industries. While much more extensive research needs to be produced on the complex dynamics between artist and manager (and how they might affect the well-being of both parties), this chapter highlights some of the key stress factors negatively affecting the mental health of managers (and their clients) and considers some of the practices and resources that managers are using to navigate this topic.

Growing Awareness of Mental Health Issues

Throughout our fieldwork speaking with professional music managers and related stakeholders, it was strikingly clear that mental health is a topic being recognized by the industry as a matter requiring urgent attention. Certainly, a shift in the way we speak about mental health and well-being has occurred in recent decades, with the 'sex, drugs and rock'n'roll' ethos of yesteryear no longer hailed as the 'must-have' accessory to a creative lifestyle, or indeed as a publicity hook to help sell records (Allen, 2022). That said, there are still specific working conditions, alongside professional (and personal) dynamics that make incidents of anxiety and depression prominent in the music industries (Gross and Musgrave, 2020; Musgrave and Lamis, 2025). While tales of impresario managers conducting business in questionable, sometimes downright criminal ways at the expense of their artists are less common today than those detailed in Rogan (1988) *Starmakers and Svengalis*, a number of high-profile deaths of artists in recent years have highlighted concerns about the duty of care owed to artists (Chaparro and Musgrave, 2021). We have only to think of the tragic losses of producer Avicii and rapper Lil Peep, both of which raised questions (and in the case of Lil Peep legal disputes) around what roles and responsibilities a music manager has relating to the health and well-being of their clients (Musgrave, 2020; Gross and Musgrave, 2020; Rouhani, 2023, p.130). While more discussions are taking place on the issue of artist well-being and what constitutes a duty of care from both a legal and moral standpoint, the question of how to effectively maintain the positive mental health of managers and their artists, alongside running a lucrative business, remains a complex and perplexing one.

Manager (Hardin, 2020) explains the importance of looking out for the mental health of an artist nowadays, recognizing the need for a reasonable work–life balance: 'That's a big part of management nowadays, more than ever, keeping an eye on mental health and making sure that that personal part of their lives is supporting the professional, and the professional has a healthy balance with that' (Chris Hardin, Hardin Bourke Entertainment).

This understanding that an artist needs time to maintain relationships, to rest, recuperate and, essentially, have a life beyond their artistic project seems increasingly common among managers. Furthermore, the correlation between supporting a healthy work–life balance and sustaining the long-term career of an artist is not lost on managers, emphasized by Chadwick (2023): '[As] a manager I'm very conscious that there's no artist business if you have an artist who has a breakdown or is suffering a mental health crisis. So it's really important to kind of recognize that danger.' (Chris Chadwick, Famous Friends Management).

How best to support this balance in light of the various pressures that affect an artist and manager will be discussed further below, but it was noted by manager (Patel, 2024) that despite the intense working conditions of running a successful release campaign, many UK artists appear to possess not only the required personality traits but are also fortunate to have the appropriate protective infrastructure around them:

> I think there are a few artists that have demonstrated that that is possible – Ed Sheeran and Adele being two, [also] Sam Smith. Actually, a lot of UK acts have achieved that level of success and had good management teams around them that have kept their feet on the ground through the process.
> (Ross Patel, Whole Entertainment)

What it means for management to keep an artists' feet on the ground, and indeed what it means to create conditions that support good mental health, can be infinitely elusive and complex. As no two human beings are exactly alike, each individual artist and band will have different needs and circumstances depending on their life experiences, their current and future success, their biographies, lifestyle choices and group dynamics, to name but a few elements. According to the (MMF Code of Practice, n.d.), however, managers do have an obligation to 'make reasonable efforts to address any issues around mental health and wellbeing…for both the artist they represent and themselves, signposting appropriate support resources where necessary' (MMF Code of Practice, n.d.). This requirement to signpost resources as well as to remain mindful not only of the mental health of the artist but also the manager as well is articulated explicitly by manager Ellie Giles (2022), who advocates for the value of counselling and therapy services:

> I take mental health seriously on all my clients, and myself. I took on [band name] and I said to the lead singer…"you need therapy", and I got him a number for Help Musicians, and within a week he was in therapy with Help Musicians, so, you know, that is important…. I think if everyone was in it [therapy], relationships wouldn't break down. So, yeah, I do take my mental health really seriously, I take my clients' mental health really seriously.
> (Ellie Giles, Step Management)

The services provided by music industry charity Help Musicians and other similar mental health resources play an integral part in fostering a culture that recognizes music professionals as human beings and not simply workers whose labour is to be exploited (Abfalter and Reitsamer, 2022). Giles's quote above illustrates the responsibility of a manager to signpost these resources to their clients, who often may not be aware what support exists. Furthermore, Giles's emphasis on valuing the mental health of the manager by not allowing themselves to be taken advantage of is an important one. Indeed, it is an issue championed by the Music Managers Forum in recent years.

The MMF *Guide to Mental Health* (2021a) marks a clear intervention in terms of recognizing the pressures music managers are under, highlighting the challenge of running the business of a client, while also looking out for their mental health, all without sacrificing or neglecting their own personal and professional needs. Speaking in the introduction to the guide, Biffy Clyro manager and MMF former chair Paul Craig acknowledges the progress that has been made in recent years: 'Increasingly, mental health is a subject we are no longer afraid to mention, and while a lot of work still needs to be done, fantastic organisations like Help Musicians, Music Support and others are providing resources and assistance for music professionals' (MMF, 2021a, p. 4).

Beyond recognizing the progress that has been made around issues of mental health and discussing some of the common issues that can affect artist managers and their clients, such as depression, co-dependency and addiction, the guide draws on the experiences of managers to convey how they are currently navigating the pressures of the job. Manager Shikayla Nadine, for example, affirms the need for managers to prioritize their own mental health:

> Managers are humans, too, that carry the pressure of their own career and their artists' careers on their shoulders. In order for us to perform our duties to the best of our abilities, we need to make sure our mental health is also right and being supported.
> (Music Managers Forum, 2021a).

This position is echoed, once again, by Paul Craig, who highlights the unique nature of artist management as a profession, where the needs of everyone except the manager generally take priority:

> Music managers tend to lead a strange life because they often spend 99% of their time worrying, caring, thinking about their artists, and very little time thinking, worrying, caring about themselves. They work under enormous pressure in a very uncertain landscape. If we say we value the mental health of all people, we should undoubtedly value the mental health of music managers, of ourselves. It's a simple fact.
> (Music Managers Forum, 2021a)

Having gathered perspectives from our interviewees, as well as drawing from perspectives shared in the MMF *Guide to Mental Health*, it is evident that the subject of supporting positive mental health and well-being is increasingly being considered and openly discussed. Managers understand that the nature of running an ethical, successful and well-rounded management business includes acknowledging artists as human beings who require conditions that take a healthy work–life balance into account wherever possible. Similarly, there is growing awareness that to be a good music manager and support one's artists and wider team, managers must take heed of their own mental health and well-being. Despite the growing awareness of the importance of supporting positive mental health in the music industries, running a successful management business in the competitive and fast-paced environment can make this extremely difficult. The following section examines some factors that can contribute to a poor working environment and exacerbate poor mental health for managers and artists working in the music industries.

Pressures of Music Management

While most careers in the creative industries require individuals to develop a sense of determined entrepreneurialism and resilience, alongside navigating the reality of a precarious and insecure workforce (McRobbie, 2016; Banks, 2017; Brook et al., 2020), the nature of artist management comes with its own unique set of challenges. The following section will examine some of the specific pressures and relationship dynamics music managers face, as highlighted by managers themselves.

Juggling multiple roles

Scholarship on music management acknowledges the multifaceted role of the profession (Bilton and Leary, 2002; Williamson, 2015), where duties and responsibilities cover everything 'from a planner and strategist to a form of guidance and a friend' (Chaparro and Musgrave, 2021). While the dynamic and versatile nature of music management is likely to draw people to the profession, as Martha Kinn (manager of Olly Alexander) notes, this can entail taking on duties that managers are not qualified or prepared for: 'As managers, we're constantly having to play roles that we're not equipped for, be it mum, dad, therapist, friend, business partner! We too need support and education, so we are able to give the best support.' (Music Managers Forum, 2021a).

This point is echoed by Glasvegas manager Allan (2023) when reflecting on the many 'hats' that must be worn to maintain a successful working relationship:

> You are in a business relationship with the person but you're also their friend. You're also their confidante, you are their counsellor, their teacher, you know; you almost have a parental role. So there's all these layers and these kind of roles you play but sometimes things can get a bit blurred and that is a bit tricky for you to find your way and for them to find their way as well.
> (Denise Allan, 677 Media Management)

Similar to the challenge of navigating a 'friend/confidante/counsellor/teacher' role, manager (Mills-McLaughlin, 2020) ruminates on the complex nature of being both a friend and a manager to an artist:

> I think being friends is a big part of it because... that's where the trust comes into things and obviously you have to trust your manager, because they're essentially taking your life into their hands to make it work for you. But then being able to have that relationship, where it's a working relationship – and sometimes, obviously, things aren't always smooth-sailing, so if you were originally friends, then it's obviously a tough conversation to [say], "Oh, what you've done is wrong", or "Things aren't going great, I really need you to pick up the slack" – [that] sort of thing, if you feel like they're not putting in 100% or whatever – having that kind of balance of serious but fun at the same time.
> (Cara Mills-McLaughlin, Kingdom Management)

That balance of 'serious but fun', as Mills-McLaughlin states, can bring with it a range of challenges linking to item 7 of the MMF Code of Practice: 'Make reasonable efforts to address any issues around mental health and wellbeing... for both the artist they represent and themselves' (MMF, n.d.). We can see how the lines between friendship and manager may become blurred in a range of scenarios when commerce, creativity and mental health interact. Take, for example, when a hectic touring schedule begins to take its toll on the physical and mental well-being of an artist. Without a doubt, the manager has a responsibility to signpost support; but what if the schedule won't allow adequate downtime? What if the artist continues to drink excessively to manage their anxiety and stress? Undoubtedly, each scenario needs to be dealt with accordingly, but in most cases there is no absolute right solution, and for that reason, the blurry relationship dynamics between an artist and their manager can create a highly stressful and sometimes detrimental situation.

Shifts in power dynamics

Leading on from the common expectation that managers wear many 'hats', fulfilling a wide range of responsibilities for their artists, the power dynamics between an artist and manager can shift over time, and indeed change under different circumstances. Morrow, 2018, page-prefix. 101) discusses how managers often have the power to choose which artists to work with, especially if that artist is at the early stage of their career. This may result in the artist feeling indebted to their manager, aware of the time and investment being put into their career, which has not yet become financially lucrative. If, however, an artist becomes successful but doesn't fully understand the copious duties the manager carries out behind the scenes, they may feel their manager is earning too much commission, not working hard enough, or is reaping the benefits of a success they didn't create (Jones, 2012, p. 78). In some cases, an artist might be in a position to negotiate down the commission of a manager based on the level of success they feel they have reached. In other scenarios, miscommunication around what constitutes fair remuneration for a manager can be a source of serious tension (O'Riordan and Gillon, 2021). While a manager may start out with a substantial amount of power and influence, ultimately, they are the ones providing a service to the artist, commissioning off the earnings of their clients. Morrow (2018) discusses the potential use of regulation to protect both the artist and the manager, highlighting how licensing or specific manager guidelines like a code of conduct could, in many instances, protect both artist and manager. Morrow warns, however, that if implemented poorly, these kinds of regulations could act as a restrictive measure, for example making the profession more challenging to establish a foot in due to costs associated with licences or qualifications (see also Chaparro and Musgrave, 2021 and their work on ethical decision making in music management). Another complexity that adds to the debate of how regulation might work is the fact that, often, at least until the artist begins earning a substantial income, many managers invest their time and energy without receiving payment for their services. The trust and collaboration necessary between artist and manager, as well as the ways in which this can begin as an informal relationship, makes the subject of regulation an ongoing conversation.

Questions regarding power dynamics in an artist–manager relationship, and indeed the subject of manager regulation and licensing, is a current, unfolding matter, with the *Misogyny in Music* report (UK Parliament, 2024) recommending that the newly formed, currently still in development, Creative Industries Independent Standard Authority (CIISA) explores mandatory manager accreditation with the UK Music Managers Forum. While this chapter does not allow for further exploration of management accreditation, there is undoubtedly a link between ethical work principles and supporting positive mental health, as well as the urgent need to facilitate clear and effective pathways to reporting incidents and meaningful accountability for exploitative practices.

Pressure to succeed

As discussed in earlier chapters, managers place an emphasis on the need for ambition, drive and a solid work ethic, with the same expected from the talent they work with and invest in. While these attributes may be instrumental to the success of a management business, the need to be 'always on' and driving the project forward must inevitably take its toll on the well-being of everyone involved. The pressure to succeed, to make an artist project thrive in a highly saturated and competitive market, alongside the many years of work required before a project is likely to receive external investment from a label or publisher, for example (Frenneaux, 2023), makes it unsurprising that this can affect the mental health of a manager and indeed the mental health of their artist. Of course, if the project is lucky enough to find any level of attention, the impetus to develop, grow and progress means that the workload is unlikely to get any lighter, as manager Hardin (2020) discusses:

> I've seen a lot of people burn themselves out there's that hunger – this is an industry that attracts people that want to achieve greatness. You can beat yourself up, you can burn yourself out, I don't know how I would deal with that, going on stage, the accolades and the adulation,

being bigger than life and then taking that off and putting that in a drawer somewhere and going, "OK, let me be a healthy husband, or a healthy father, or a healthy son, or brother or sister", you know, any of those things; [it's a] very challenging business when you start to break it down like that.

(Chris Hardin, Hardin Bourke Entertainment)

Manager and label owner Scougall (2023) stresses the need for music managers to protect their own well-being, highlighting how this is necessary to show up as the best manager possible for your artist:

You need to look after yourself, because if you're not as close to 100% as you can be, how can you give to anyone else? And that's one thing I didn't really take much heed of in the early days. I was just constantly, "Oh, we need to make this work", constant focus, focus, focus. And I ended up a bit burnt out, to be honest, in the first year. And that's because I wasn't prioritising my health.

(Lyle Scougall, Mañana Music Management)

Alongside the will to make a project monetarily successful are the pressures that an artist experiences as they promote themselves and seek to build an audience online. The remit of artists today requires them to invest time and energy into their digital personas in order to cultivate a fan base and promote their music (Baym, 2018). Managers are aware of the toll this can take on their artists. Chadwick (2023) discusses his concerns around the long-term impact of quantifying success through social media engagement, which may or may not translate into ticket sales or streams:

If an artist starts to measure their success in [terms of] likes and follows [on social media], that can be deceptive and doesn't represent genuine income for the artist's business; and [it is] also dangerous in the sense of the widely publicized challenges that social media poses, not just in music but for everyone, when it comes to mental health.... I don't know if we as an industry are yet fully aware of the impact that that has in terms of the pressure on an artist, day-to-day, and it's really important that we continue to educate ourselves when it comes to the impact of, I guess, validation through social media and music careers in general.

(Chris Chadwick, Famous Friends Management)

While a growing number of voices are advocating for more measured, controlled engagement with social media (Jones and Heyman, 2021; Music Managers Forum, 2022), the motivation to find consistent, new and engaging ways of connecting with an audience online is a core requirement for a release campaign; and for the vast majority of artists, an inescapable pillar of their multifaceted career. Before we begin exploring ways of mitigating or reducing these pressures, one further factor, that of financial insecurity, must be considered.

Financial insecurity

Despite the UK music industries generating £7.6 billion for the UK economy and employing over 216,000 people (UK Music, 2024), we know from MMF UK data that only 52% of managers are working full-time as managers, while the rest are juggling a freelance career or have another job alongside their management work (Music Managers Forum, 2019). Furthermore, the MMF members survey highlighted that while 25% of managers were earning above the national average, 56% were earning less than £10k per annum (Music Managers Forum, 2019). These figures highlight just how precarious a career in artist management can be; and, indeed, for many existing or aspiring managers, a huge amount of time, energy and resources can be dedicated to building the career of an artist without any guarantee of financial remuneration. Even for managers whose clients are beginning to see some level of success, artists need to be making upwards of £100k per annum for a manager to be earning the London living wage, based on a 20% commission set-up (O'Riordan and Gillon, 2021. p. 267).

As someone whose job it is to have an overview of the challenges music managers are facing, MMF Chief Executive Coldrick (2020) shares her thoughts around how the shifting industry has put managers in a more risk-laden position:

You will see how much the industry has shifted an awful lot of responsibility for artist development to the manager; partly because the industry, for probably the last ten years, withdrew in doing that early-stage talent development. So you would have managers, potentially, not only investing their own time but also their money in many, many places. Time is money if you work for nothing for two or three years. Managers need to know more than ever before and become bigger risk takers. It can be quite heart-breaking; you'll find someone who works for three years on something and then the artist gives up, and you're like, "Oh God! Nothing happened!"

(Annabella Coldrick, MMF UK)

For managers working on projects which are not yet generating substantial profits, they often juggle these responsibilities with other paid work. In some cases, this may be music-related, such as working at a label or marketing agency, but in many cases the work is unrelated and without a great deal of flexibility in terms of juggling these various duties. As music manager Steven Odufuye states:

> No one ever prepared me for the financial side of things, like the inconsistency of funds. I had worked up to two jobs at one given time just to make ends meet and that was hard for me mentally because I had to deliver shopping and still have label meetings that same day or week. The pressure for success kept building and building as I started to compare myself with other managers and artists that I looked up to, which led to a lot of stress and anxiety as well as a breakdown in my relationship at the time.
> (Music Managers Forum, 2021a, p. 24)

Similarly, manager Shikayla Nadine emphasizes the emotional toll placed on trying to accomplish success with an artist, putting managers at risk of poor mental health:

> The role of a manager is so diverse; for new managers or smaller managers it can be extremely difficult. You're working in the hopes of making someone else successful enough so that you can live off 10–20% of what they're earning. That is a huge pressure on your shoulders, extremely stressful and anxiety-inducing. The fear of being unsuccessful, not knowing enough and even not knowing when or how to plan for your future can lead to depression.
> (Music Managers Forum, 2021a)

Bearing in mind the financial precarity managers face trying to develop their business, the costs associated with supporting an artist in the early stages of their career can be vast. In some cases, this might require up-front investment from the manager, as highlighted by the 2021 *Managing Expectations* report, which showed that 75% of managers had invested their own money developing the talent they represented (Music Managers Forum, 2021b). Investment can vary from artist to artist, covering anything from studio time to promotional costs. It can also apply to the time invested by a manager – arranging meetings, seeking partners, co-ordinating activities etc. In some cases, staying on top of these expenses is only feasible by well-resourced management companies, and in other cases it may be an individual manager footing these costs up-front. In either case, problems can arise in terms of the realistic chance of recouping costs, not least because artists may wish to reinvest any income they generate into furthering their career. This is where the importance of having a management agreement which clearly outlines commissionable incomes and deductible costs is vital (O'Riordan and Gillon, 2021, p. 267). Artist management is a risky business and there is ample scope for misunderstanding or uncertainty around artists feeling indebted to their managers.

> [M]oney is a big, big aspect of it. I'm lucky that I get to work in a company that has had a successful artist, and that obviously helps with cashflow and launching other artists. But you need, I think, to have a successful act; it's expensive to develop a new artist... at that stage [it's] everyone's issue, it's not just solely on the manager that they have to have money to help launch the career, but I do think that is a massive barrier to launching yourself into the artist management world, to be taken seriously, that you have a successful artist, because obviously you need to get that successful artist first.
> (Cara Mills-McLaughlin, Kingdom Management)

As Mills-McLaughlin (2020) points out, managers employed by financially robust management companies have access to a level of investment that increases their chances of breaking a new artist. The reality, however, is that most managers operate independently (Music Managers Forum, 2021b), meaning that managers from less-well-off backgrounds will often lack vital support or infrastructure that would allow them to take professional risks and/or invest in their artists' careers.

While financial precarity and the challenge of making a management business viable is something that all managers need to navigate, structural inequalities relating to race, class, gender and disability (amongst other characteristics) can exacerbate this, as we saw in Chapter 8. With regards to the additional struggles facing certain managers, the Black Lives in Music (2021) shows that only 38% of black music professionals make 100% of their income from the music industry (compared with 69% of white industry professionals), meaning that a significant number of black music professionals are supplementing their career with work from outside the industry in order to meet their living costs (Black Lives in Music, 2021). Furthermore, considering the growing data around the gender and ethnicity pay gap that permeates the music industries, we must recognize how pay inequalities can present even more barriers to female managers, especially black women managers, and more generally to any manager of colour (as highlighted by Odufuye above). The Black Lives in Music report also shows that, on average, black women are paid 19% less than black men, 25% less than white women, and a shocking 52% less than white men (Black Lives in Music, 2021), indicating how black women trying to establish a career in music management will face far more precarity than their male and white female counterparts. Similarly, reports like *Dignity at Work* (ISM, 2022) highlight the prevalence of bullying and harassment (in particular, sexual harassment and racism) faced by music industry professionals, especially freelancers. Manager Chadwick (2023) draws attention to the challenges that burgeoning musicians and their managers face, highlighting the importance of funded programmes to help level the playing-field:

> I actually think there's a real problem in the music industry... it skews massively towards people who have the resources to be able to dedicate the time to take a chance on being a successful musician. So I'm thinking particularly about people from less-well-off economic backgrounds. And I think that that's a massive representation thing within that.... There are some amazing schemes in the UK. There are some people doing great things with funding, whether it's PRS or the BPI or Help Musicians. But I don't think there's enough, and I would love to see that improved in the next five years, and more funding put into that.
> (Chris Chadwick, Famous Friends Management)

Alongside the funding opportunities mentioned by Chadwick, there is the manager-specific programme run by the MMF, supported by Youtube Music, Arts Council England and Creative Scotland, known as Accelerator, which we first examined in Chapter 3. Running annually since 2019, the Accelerator programme (of which Chadwick is an alumnus) provides a year-long bursary and training for 'tipping point' managers, to help them develop a robust, sustainable management business. Ultimately, in light of the financial pressure of supporting a developing artist in the early years of their career, particularly for newly established managers, and the structural inequalities that make some creative industries workers more vulnerable than others, the importance of arts funding (for both artists and managers) has never been more vital.

Supporting Positive Mental Health as a Music Manager

Many of the managers interviewed were able to point towards good practice in terms of being sensitive to their own mental health and that of their artist. These included establishing and maintaining clear boundaries in a working relationship, emphasizing trust and open communication, as well as adhering to good ethical and business practices, such as having fair contracts, following the MMF Code of Practice, and utilizing resources from mental health organizations where necessary.

The value of boundaries was stressed by manager Giles (2022), as well as by MMF Chief Executive Coldrick (2020), in terms of how these specific parameters can support a healthy working relationship:

> Because I'm very boundary'd with my clients – you know, I make sure that they don't contact me after a certain time of night and I'm not emotionally invested in them – I'm business-invested in them. Probably [one specific artist]

> I'm probably most invested in because I've worked with him for eight years now, so we've come closer, but I still have a detachment there. So yeah, I think the ability to build and nourish a relationship but then also the ability to detach and not see when bad things happen to that artist, you don't go "Oh my God, the world's ended!".
>
> (Ellie Giles, Step Management)

> Internally, I think it's building trust but maintaining a professional relationship and being able to have boundaries that are professional [to what] the relationship requires.
>
> (Annabella Coldrick, MMF UK)

As discussed in Chapter 6, manager Allan (2023) elaborates on her interpretation of good boundaries, explaining that, for her, these are ground rules that need to be developed over time and which ultimately benefit all parties involved:

> Having a healthy relationship starts from you as a person and having a healthy relationship to music and your work because, in music, especially the live industry, it's 24/7 unless you put those boundaries in; and one of the problems with managers is their burnout rate. It's really quite high because artists think, maybe up until recently, that they should be able to access you 24/7, but I think if you, through time, can gently let them know that "these are my limits and also I would like these to be your limits as well", then you're actually building in some kind of framework for a working relationship. For me, I don't really like people contacting me at night, either email or phone call or text or anything, and I don't really like them contacting me at the weekends either. There [are] only two things that surpass that [and they are]: (i) if it's a big, big problem that cannot wait, that's an emergency – but I'm speaking about an emergency-emergency, not just "We can't get this logo quite right" – then I don't mind; or (ii) if it's really, really, really good news, then I don't mind, but nothing in-between. Most things are in-between.
>
> (Denise Allan, 677 Media Management)

Beyond the belief in having good boundaries with working relationships, as seen above with the example of outlining preferred communication times and clear understanding of what constitutes 'urgent' issues, interviewees also indicated the importance of maintaining open communication. On a basic level, as explained by Scougall (2023), communication is about sharing and listening to ideas in a respectful way:

> So, having a direct line of communication, open and honest. And that doesn't mean you can just be an [a***hole] and say "that's terrible", I don't agree with that; it's just all about being open, respecting their opinion, respecting their view. However, having a clear line of communication between all of it.
>
> (Lyle Scougall, Mañana Music Management)

While the quote above applies specifically to offering feedback on creative ideas, this advice extends to any exchange relating to an artist's project, campaign or release. More indirectly, however, managers indicated how important good communication is in terms of ensuring artists fully understanding the 'partnership' element of the working relationship and, indeed, recognizing the value of a manager's worth. Returning to manager Giles (2022), we see a call for more teamwork between the artist and the manager, something potentially quite challenging to accomplish for those who have established more of a 'parent–child' relationship:

> I think that we, as an industry, need to really realize that management value as well as the artist value – understanding how hard it is and how easy it is and work as a team. There's going to be times when, you know, your manager might need a week off and you need to take a bit of the reins, but you're a team at the end of the day, you're a business partnership, and the way I see it, if you were working in a restaurant – if you owned a restaurant together, someone takes slack one time and the other person takes some slack, that's what you do, you work together as a team. So yeah, I'm very conscious of that and making sure everyone's well and talking.
>
> (Ellie Giles, Step Management)

Following on from our discussion previously about how demanding it can be for a manager to make an artist business financially viable, and the plethora of unpaid duties a manager might carry out in the early stages of their working relationship, Patel (2024) highlights the needs of his own business. In the comment below, Patel expresses a desire to be more direct with artists around raising commission, particularly when a client is starting to see success:

> I think that our business has suffered as a result of leniency, despite contractual obligations that

are in place with all of our clients. I think that comes down to personal relationships. Again, it comes down to our moral stance and ethics, but I do think that, moving forward, when we get to hopefully a place of more stability in the business... I think that from that point we will be a little bit firmer, because all of the clients are now at a point where they are, you know, self-sustaining and we've worked hard to get them to that point. And now we can be a little bit more firm about what is owed to us as a business, because at the moment, we've let a lot of things slide as I think a lot of managers do.
(Ross Patel, Whole Entertainment)

Patel's indication that managers often 'let a lot of things slide' for the good of the artist–manager relationship, and Giles (2022) comments about the value of teamwork, highlights the importance of being flexible and suggests that everyone involved could benefit from clearer communication and education around the role and value of the artist manager. This is where the role of organizations like the Music Managers Forum becomes important, particularly in terms of providing educational resources relating to good business practices.

In terms of the educational resources managers are drawing from to establish and/or maintain a working relationship with their artist that encourages positive mental health, artist manager, entrepreneur and MMF board member Nielson (2024) identifies the MMF Code of Conduct as a form of 'self-policing' and boundary-setting mechanism:

> [B]eing a member of the MMF, you know, we put down a strict code of conduct. That would never have happened when the MMF was first at its inception, but now it's kind of self-policing. You really need to lay down a set of guidelines just so people are aware of what the boundaries are, but also you can explain it to your artist and it comes in with the organization.
> (Karl Nielson, Music Manager)

While there are more in-depth conversations to be had around how accountability operates with codes of practice created by music manager membership bodies (Morrow, 2013; Chaparro and Musgrave, 2021), in his comments above, Nielson identifies the tangible use of having guidelines for the artist–manager relationship which we can assume would help support the positive mental health of everyone involved.

More generally, the music industry is increasingly making resources available to encourage practices that maintain good mental health and, furthermore, provide support for those experiencing poor mental health or a mental health crisis. Manager Chadwick (2023) notes the enhanced attention on these issues: 'I think there's a lot more focus on education, and resources being passed around about mental health in the music industry, and I would love to love to see that continue, particularly in the face of things like virality on social media' (Chris Chadwick, Famous Friends Management).

Today, artists and music industry professionals have access to support offered by charities like Help Musicians, Music Support and Tonic Rider, offering access to emergency counselling, support groups, training and a range of other resources. Help Musicians is the most extensive in terms of the scale of its offering, not only crisis support for those experiencing poor mental health but also by providing grants and professional development opportunities to foster healthy and sustained careers for musicians and professionals in the UK. Help Musicians is also responsible for having established Music Minds Matter, a dedicated mental health phoneline providing support for music professionals and available 24/7. There are early indications that other music businesses are beginning to see the value of investing in mental health resources for their staff and artists, with Sony launching a 'wellness' programme for artists (Paine, 2021), and Universal Music (2020) an insightful report on neurodiversity (*Creative Differences Handbook*), amongst various other initiatives, events and partnerships. Overall, however, greater collaboration between commercial business, mental health charities and music trade bodies will be necessary to nurture a working culture that genuinely respects the needs and sensitivities of individuals alongside the business objectives of the music industries.

Conclusion

The realities of what a music manager must face in order to run a sustainable business, and keep their clients happy and healthy, creating a work environment that recognizes the pressures to succeed in a highly competitive music industry, the endless workload of producing and releasing music, maintaining a vibrant social media presence and nurturing a fan base, as well as securing investment and developing new partnerships, is a tall order for any standard 9-to-5 job. Of course, music management is far from an ordinary career choice. Beyond the specific issues discussed here, including the need to fulfil various roles as a manager, navigating power dynamics, the pressure to succeed and financial strain, there are additional factors such as experiencing economic hardship, or discrimination in the form of misogyny or racism that can affect the mental health of a music industry professional. As discussed above, work is being carried out to develop greater connectivity between resources that address bullying and harassment in the industry (such as the newly developed CIISA), and organizations like Help Musicians, Music Support and the PRS Members' Fund, who seek to support those with poor mental health or related issues. Looking ahead, there are more conversations to be had around how both individual dynamics and structural inequalities can be addressed in order to support good mental health for everyone in the music industries.

References

Abfalter, D. and Reitsamer, R. (eds) (2022) *Music as Labour: Inequalities and Activism in the Past and Present*. Routledge, Abingdon, UK.
Allan, D. (2023) *Practicalities of artist management [lecture]*. University of the West of Scotland.
Allen, P. (2022) *Artist management for the music business: Manage your career in music: Manage the music careers of others*, 5th edn. Focal Press, New York and London.
Banks, M. (2017) *Creative Justice: Cultural Industries, Work and Inequality*. Rowman & Littlefield Publishers, New York.
Baym, N. (2018) *Playing to the Crowd: Musicians, Audiences, and the Intimate Work of Connection*. NYU Press Scholarship.
Bilton, C. and Leary, R. (2002) What can managers do for creativity? Brokering creativity in the creative industries. *International Journal of Cultural Policy* 8(1), 49–64. DOI: 10.1080/10286630290032431.
Black Lives in Music (2021) Being black in the UK music industry: Music industries professional part 1. Available at: https://blim.org.uk/report/ (accessed 10 November 2025).
Brook, O., Taylor, M. and O'Brien, D. (2020) *Culture Is Bad for You: Inequality in the Cultural and Creative Industries*. Manchester University Press, Manchester, UK.
Chadwick, C. (2023) Questions on artist management. Interview by Allan Dumbreck [Zoom].
Chaparro, G. and Musgrave, G. (2021) Moral music management: Ethical decision-making after Avicii. *International Journal of Music Business Research* 10(1), 3–16. DOI: 10.2478/ijmbr-2021-0001.
Coldrick, A. (2020) Questions on artist management. Interview by Allan Dumbreck [Zoom].
Frenneaux, R. (2023) The rise of independent artists and the paradox of democratisation in the digital age: challenges faced by music artists in the new music industry. *DIY, Alternative Cultures & Society* 1(2), 125–137. DOI: 10.1177/27538702231174200.
Giles, E. (2022) Questions on artist management. Interview by Allan Dumbreck [Zoom].
Gross, S.A. and Musgrave, G. (2020) *Can Music Make You Sick? Measuring the Price of Musical Ambition*. University of Westminster Press. DOI: 10.2307/j.ctv199tddg.
Hardin, C. (2020) Questions on artist management. Interview by Allan Dumbreck [Zoom].
ISM (2022) Dignity at work 2: Discrimination in the music sector. Available at: https://www.ism.org/wp-content/uploads/2023/08/02-ISM-Dignity-2-report.pdf (accessed 10 November 2025).
Jones, M. (2012) *The Music Industries: From Conception to Consumption*. Springer.
Jones, R. and Heyman, L. (2021) *Sound Advice: The Ultimate Guide to a Healthy and Successful Career in Music*. Shoreditch Press, London.
McRobbie, A. (2016) *Be Creative: Making a Living in the New Culture Industries*. Polity, Cambridge, UK and Malden, Massachusetts.
Mills-McLaughlin, C. (2020) Questions on artist management. Interview by Allan Dumbreck [Zoom].

Morrow, G. (2013) Regulating artist managers: An insider's perspective. *International Journal of Music Business Research* 2(2), 8–35.

Morrow, G. (2018) *Artist Management: Agility in the Creative and Cultural Industries* [e-book]. Routledge, Abingdon, UK and New York.

Musgrave, G. (2020) Avicii: True stories (Levan Tsikurishvili, dir.). *Dancecult: Journal of Electronic Dance Music Culture* 12(1), 94–97. DOI: 10.12801/1947-5403.2020.12.01.15.

Musgrave, G. and Lamis, D.A. (2025) Musicians, the music industry, and suicide: Epidemiology, risk factors, and suggested prevention approaches. *Frontiers in Public Health* 13. DOI: 10.3389/fpubh.2025.1507772.

Music Manager Forum Code of Practice (n.d.) MMF Code of Practice. Available at: https://themmf.net/about/code-of-practice/ (accessed 16 May 2024).

Music Managers Forum (2019) Managing expectations. Available at: https://themmf.net/wp-content/uploads/2023/10/Managing-Expectations-MMF-2019.pdf (accessed 10 November 2025).

Music Managers Forum (2021a) MMF guide to mental health. Available at: https://themmf.net/wp-content/uploads/2023/10/MMF_Guide_to_Mental_Health_2021.pdf (accessed 16 May 2024).

Music Managers Forum (2021b) Managing expectations. Available at: https://themmf.net/wp-content/uploads/2023/10/MMF-Managing-Expectations-Report-2021.pdf (accessed 10 November 2025).

Music Managers Forum (2022) MMF digital burnout report. Available at: https://www.themmf.net/wp-content/uploads/2023/10/MMF-DIGITAL-BURNOUT-REPORT-FINAL-5.pdf (accessed 10 November 2025).

Nielson, K. (2024) Questions on artist management. Interview by Allan Dumbreck [Zoom].

O'Riordan, J. and Gillon, L. (2021) The artist/manager relationship. In: Harrison, A. and Rigg, T. (eds) *The Present and Future of Music Law*. Bloomsbury Academic, New York. Available at: https://bloomsburymusicandsound.com/encyclopedia?docid=b-9781501367809

Paine, A. (2021) Sony Music launches wellness programme with counselling and a hotline to address stress and anxiety. *Music Week*. Available at: www.musicweek.com/labels/read/sony-music-launches-wellness-programme-with-counselling-and-a-hotline-to-address-stress-and-anxiety/084252 (accessed 16 May 2024).

Patel, R. (2024) Questions on artist management. Interview by Allan Dumbreck [Zoom].

Rogan, J. (1988) *Starmakers and Svengalis: The History of British Pop Management*. Queen Anne Press, London.

Rouhani, N. (2023) Lil Peep's former label settles unlawful death lawsuit. Billboard. Available at: https://www.billboard.com/pro/lil-peep-mother-settles-wrongful-death-lawsuit-label/ (accessed 8 June 2025).

Scougall, L. (2023) *Practicalities of artist management [lecture]*. University of the West of Scotland.

UK Music (2024) This is music 2024. Available at: https://www.ukmusic.org/wp-content/uploads/2024/11/TIM-Report-2024-reduced.pdf (accessed 6 June 2024).

UK Parliament (2024) House of Commons Committee Report: Misogyny in music. Available at: ublications.parliament.uk/pa/cm5804/cmselect/cmwomeq/129/report.html (accessed 16 May 2024).

Universal Music (2020) Creative differences handbook. Available at: umusic.co.uk/Creative-Differences-Handbook.pdf (accessed 16 May 2024).

Williamson, J. (2015) Artist managers and entrepreneurship: Risk takers or risk averse. In: Dumbreck, A. and McPherson, G. (eds) *Music Entrepreneurship*. Bloomsbury, London. Available at: www.bloomsbury.com/uk/music-entrepreneurship-9781472525406/

10 Outcomes, Conclusions and Further Research

Allan Dumbreck

Introduction

As stated at the outset, our three objectives in writing this book were: (i) to make the case for the artist management sector being worthy of this type of study; (ii) to portray the nuance of the role through the various career stages of managers and artists, with the accompanying industrial and personal challenges this presents; and (iii) to contextualize and understand artist management in the contemporary music industries, casting new light on both.

In this concluding chapter, we will highlight twelve overlapping findings before returning to these objectives and suggesting some potential further research that was beyond the scope of this work. We believe that this is a substantial work of research which has addressed these objectives, and which seeks to add to the existing literature on the topic by drawing on the accounts of many active artist managers with different experiences and at different levels while recognizing what was realistically possible within limitations (timescale, politics and global pandemic to name but three).

These outcomes are not prioritized in any particular order, but links to chapters are given so that more detailed explanations and accompanying literature references can be found.

Key Outcomes

The artist–manager relationship is at the core of the music industries but needs further recognition, support and, possibly, regulation

To state the somewhat obvious first principle here, as examined in Chapter 1, without an artist there can be no music business. The part that is perhaps less obvious is that, in many instances, without the manager, their talent would often remain hidden, undeveloped, unpromoted, and therefore unknown. Furthermore, without the manager, the artist cannot grow or sustain the career which supports all other music sectors. Consequently, the artist and manager are interdependent and may be considered in some respects a single, core unit. Hence, we should locate the artist and the manager jointly at the centre of any map of music as a business.

Next, aligning with other recent research (Jones, 2012), the manager needs to engage directly with every aspect of the business (live events, record companies, studios, producers, music publishing, media, merchandise – the list continues) in a way in which no other role is required to replicate. Managers, therefore, are the critical link between all sectors of the music industries. As discussed in Chapter 1, the manager is 'akin to the blood supply or nervous system linking all theatres of music in a coherent and constructive manner' (Anderton et al., 2022), giving the manager a singular overall understanding of the music industries that is perhaps clearer, but almost certainly more complete, than other sectors. This is fundamentally inherent to the role and constitutes a 360-degree scope of operation which dictates working with all other relevant parties, but, consequentially, offers the manager an almost unique overview and understanding where most other roles have a narrower field of vision due to their work interacting with fewer associates.

Unsurprisingly then, networking is vital (as discussed in Chapter 5). While government support could make a significant difference here (see Chapter 7), could it be that, given that artist management representation has only arrived relatively recently in comparison to other sectors, this has perhaps allowed those sectors to get ahead (in terms of recognition and support); or is it simply because of the significant, highly visible economic scale of the live and recording industries? While managers are well connected with other parts of the music industries, the role can be quite solitary with managers often not working collectively (although this may no longer be the case with the emergence of larger management companies such as Red Light or Live Nation).

The recorded music, publishing and live sectors have historically appeared to have stronger voices and more leverage at the negotiating table, as per Annabella Coldrick's explanation of why CMM needed to be created (see Chapter 3). Could artist management benefit from better recognition? (To be clear here, this is not a criticism of the work of artist representation, merely a recognition of the fact that other sectors mobilized to secure a collective voice at an earlier point in time and are perhaps further developed and acknowledged (see outcome 2 below for further explanation).

This core-unit, pivotal relationship is not without its difficulties. We also examined conflict and issues within the artist–manager relationship. While the causes of friction between managers and artists/creators are manifold, the issue of finance was identified by many and trust by most. Transparency, communication and honesty repeatedly arose in our interviews, meaning, for example, that establishing realistic boundaries in terms of what can be discussed, and when, is vital. Therefore, creating space and time away from the work does also, understandably, appear to be critical in forming a healthy artist–manager relationship. However, it is to the advantage of the manager of a successful artist to sustain that connection. Therefore, the manager, continually working on the development of fresh opportunities at the periphery of the artist's business world, needs to be continually aware of potential pitfalls that could upset the relationship.

The final point here relates to responses on government intervention, which we examined in Chapter 5. This point currently remains somewhat open-ended. Many managers believe that other roles (creators, events personnel) benefit from government support in ways they do not. Business support (how to get started) and funding/advisory support on exports were identified as lacking, with some national governments doing more than others to assist. If the role of the manager was better recognized as central to artist development, would this open the doorway to business development support and financial investment? There could be significant benefits to all involved if industry bodies and government agencies would consider offering more robust training programmes and funding schemes for music managers who are developing emerging artists. Thresholds of growth for eligibility and potential returns could be introduced to control such initiatives and make them cost-effective. Many managers appear to believe that this could make a critical difference.

On the flip side, as suggested by Braines (2023), greater trust in managers might be established if the government introduced a professional background check system similar to that which already exists for teachers. With many artists being younger and/or coming from vulnerable groups, this form of regulation would give managers a 'kitemark, which could make the profession more secure. This could be mandatory for artists below a certain age working with managers.

While not being universally endorsed, support for some form of regulation in this area can be seen elsewhere. The deposition made to the UK government committee investigating the music industries by X Factor contestant Rebecca

Ferguson is one example (Ferguson, 2023). In her statement she expresses great concern for the way that she and other artists were managed and argues for licensing for artist managers as a first step towards greater transparency within the sector.

The MMF response to the same inquiry (MMF, 2022) included a series of very specific and valuable recommendations on how the UK government could begin to address difficulties, including misogyny, in the music industry, including the creation of an independent standards authority (CIISA, currently being set up). However, their submission did not include calling for management licences or background checks. This is an ongoing debate, with other voices within music suggesting further alternatives. As one observer told us, 'It's a complex issue, but it doesn't mean it can't be solved'. We hope that progress is being made with this issue; however, it may be some time before a specific, decisive outcome is agreed between all parties involved.

Global representation – Can an international organization for managers create positive change?

The development of a fully functioning and vocal global organization which represents the interests of the national MMFs (of all key markets) and artist managers, generally, at international level, could possible make a significant difference to the recognition of the role of the manager and the issues that affect him, and to the working lives of managers and artists worldwide. In Chapter 1, we saw that, perhaps due to being established earlier, the other sectors have stronger and more vocal representation, while in Chapter 3, we noted that certain key nations such as South Korea (a global presence in terms of native artists) do not currently have national MMF representation. This may be due to the way their domestic music industry is structured with artists signing to a talent agency rather than a manager (Hwang, 2024); however, given the example of Japan (see Chapter 3), it may be possible to establish some form of MMF in South Korea at some point in the future.

Collective representation is relatively recent; the artist management sector has only established national representative organizations in the last 30 years or so. Recorded music, music publishing, royalty collection and live events have benefitted from national and global representation beginning in 1851. The first MMF was formed in 1992. While significant advancements have been made in qualifying and, to some extent, quantifying the sector, the national MMF organizations and their collective network are still comparatively young and not so developed by comparison with the music industries more generally. There is still considerable scope for growth and integration.

However, we must also bear in mind that many of the issues we have identified require to be addressed at a national level, where legal systems operate, rather than an international level (although as we have seen in Chapter 3, EMMA was at least in one part created to raise awareness of artist management issues at European level). The value of global representation could therefore be limited as legal change tends to happen within individual nations rather than globally.

Unlike other music sectors (e.g. recorded music, music publishing), historically there is no single, visible and regularly active global representative organization that has been consistently vocal on behalf of artist management, although this may now change. To be truly representative on a worldwide stage, such an organization would require to unify and be recognized by all existing individual national MMFs (as at mid-2025, not all national MMFs are members of the IMMF or EMMA). The development of representation for artist managers in individual nations is an evolving process driven and controlled by various factors including, but not limited to, local political and economic conditions, the need for advocacy, growth of the sector in each individual nation, tangible benefits for members, and the commitment of individuals determined to create a single united voice. As examined in Chapter 3, other sectors took considerable time to reach agreement on unilateral worldwide representation. This might also be happening over time for artist managers and, once established, may eventually significantly strengthen their collective voice.

The IMMF might be the obvious organization to take this role (EMMA operates primarily within the EU although MMFs such as those in Australia and New Zealand are now members) but, to date (as many we spoke with pointed out), it has had limited visible activity and market profile (as they themselves have recognized) and so there is still work to be done in this field. A cursory check reveals that although the IFPI and CISAC have members in a similar number of countries as the IMMF, they are mentioned hundreds of times in music industry journals (*Billboard*, *Music Week*) where the IMMF is less frequently featured (to take one example of engagement/visibility). This could be in the process of changing, however. As we go to print, new management at the IMMF could lead to significant development of the organization's media profile and industry importance; but regardless of which organization takes this responsibility, the existence of a body to advocate for the interests of managers and their artists at a worldwide level could be transformational in an era of limited returns to performers from their recorded work and the difficulties live events might face in the near future given environmental issues. While many within the MMF organizations have worked to progress the role/sector significantly, it appears there is still some way to go for artists and managers to have a position at the discussion table commensurate with their relative importance (as discussed in outcome 1 above).

As we have seen, some key nations still lack a representative body – while there are now over 60 national MMF organizations (MMF UK/MMF Canada etc.), with around 50 of them being IMMF members, some countries with international relevance within music currently have no established MMF national representation. As discussed in Chapter 3, the IMMF has stated that it is 'helping to build new MMFs in places where there are not [currently] MMFs' (Ragoowansi, 2025), indicating that moves to establish further national MMF organizations (or national representation under a broader body) are progressing. This could create a broader base giving an international body greater legitimacy.

Activity elsewhere within the MMF network (e.g. MMF UK, EMMA) has shown that significant impact/change can be achieved when managers and artists have a strong, unified voice. Could a single global organization to represent managers and their artists, which is active and recognized by other sectors, make a critical difference in wider, more fundamental debates affecting managers and their clients. We will perhaps discover this in the near future.

Well-researched, credible data and statistics on the artist management arena would allow a better understanding of the sector

Although we have seen an increase in the number of surveys and the volume of qualitative/quantitative data being generated by individual MMF organizations (see Chapters 1 and 3), tracking the scale of artist management as a distinct theatre (in metrics) remains complex. Although industry research and data are growing (e.g. ROSTR/Chartmetric), there currently exists an incomplete set of published statistics on numbers of managers, management income, import/export value and sector growth/change, for example. This is an area for considerable further research which would benefit greatly from close interaction with the MMFs worldwide.

Recorded music, music publishing and live events appear to have gained credibility and recognition from collating and releasing data on their scale and value within national/global economies over decades (e.g. IFPI/CISAC). If these data were available for artist management, they could have a significant effect on the recognition of the sector (perhaps by government and other music sectors). Could awareness of the economic scale here also enable further leverage in negotiation for the sector? During our research it has been pointed out that difficulty in tracking these data is at least partly due to the confidentiality of agreements which managers *do* sign (we do not always have access to the figures within the contracts they negotiate); plus, there is an ongoing informality in the business dealings of artist management (some work is undertaken without a contract/formal agreement being in place). Hence, some of these statistics could be difficult to determine. However, if these data could be tracked, this might lead, over time, to the sector becoming more commercially transparent and possibly better positioned/recognized as a result.

We found a series of notable reports commissioned or undertaken by MMF organizations, which gave important insights into artist management (e.g. MMF UK, EMMA, MMF Australia – see Chapter 3). However, some fairly straightforward data (such as the number of members an MMF has or the percentage of professional managers who are members of an MMF within any one nation) were quite difficult to establish outside of the more high-profile organizations.

Another possible future research area might be to try to establish the key abilities and characteristics which managers require (operating nationally, continentally and/or internationally). This does not appear to be a static skillset and it could be almost undefinable due to differences in terms of genres managed and also between the working environments of different nations, as our research perhaps indicates (see Chapter 2). However, it appears there may be some basic similarities as examined in the analysis of our interviews (Chapters 4–6).

Investigation into EDI and mental health issues (Chapters 8 and 9) has also uncovered valuable data about the shifting demographics of the field (broadly indicating a more representative gender balance as well as an increase in minority representation within the ranks of professional managers) but as with other subject areas this research needs to be ongoing to determine change or improvement.

It is almost impossible to categorize management styles/roles; the delicate balancing act of maintaining the artist–manager relationship inevitably results in a wide range of interactions and behaviours that are not easily defined or grouped. However, the combination of education and experience within the wider spheres of music making and business do appear to be increasingly valuable assets when entering artist management.

Where do managers come from? It would appear, from existing evidence and our interviews, that there is no single pathway into artist/creator management but perhaps proximity to the music industries or musical creativity for those who discover a desire to be involved but do not feel that they could be the creator might act as a catalyst. Frequently identified previous roles included A&R (record label), live events and, of course, being active performers.

The opportunity to enter management in a situation where there is little to lose and possibly much to gain could be a further factor. Whatever the reason, many of those interviewed had transitioned into artist/creator management from other roles and sectors rather than having made an initial decision to start there. This is not to say that everyone who 'jumps ship' from other roles in music to become a manager will become successful or even have a better chance. A great deal may depend on how much was learned from whatever experience and/or education was gained whilst in the industry (see Chapter 4). Further research might bring greater clarity to this issue, and this leads to the next outcome.

There is no typical manager or route into artist management

Through the examination of the development of artist management in Chapter two and the interview analysis of Chapters 4–6, we can see that while there is some commonality to the way managers operate there is no single approach to the role, no unique mindset or skillset, for want of a better description. Although all wish to develop their artists professionally and commercially, managers can undertake their work in very different ways demonstrating a range of approaches, characteristics and personality traits.

Education and training offer an advantage, but provision could be more specifically targeted

As we examined in Chapter 4, knowledge and awareness of the business environment and the practicalities of working within the music industries appear to be becoming increasingly important. The relatively recent range of research we located indicated that, typically, over half of all managers were now educated to degree level, with that percentage appearing to increase over time.

Previous research into the scale and scope of the developing music education provision at college and university level (MED, 2024) shows near continual growth in numbers of programmes and students, at least in the UK (currently 2000+ music courses in 2024). While there still appears to be no universally accepted music-specific education which leads directly to guaranteed employment in most sectors of professional music, the research we have undertaken appears to indicate that there is a value in gaining an education at university level and also in music or business-specific subjects. The majority of those responding to the MMF (2019), EMMA (2023) and those we spoke with have studied at degree level (see Chapter 4). Many have completed programmes in areas related to their current position and have seen the benefits from that. While it can be stated that the music industries, at least in the artist/creator management sector, appear to be becoming more professional via an increase in the number of those working there having qualifications, further, more detailed research would be necessary to examine this more broadly and over a longer period of time.

Somewhat disappointingly, however, most of those we interviewed felt that they had not been taught all the skills required for the work they were undertaking daily in the music industries. While many had completed qualifications in relevant subject areas (broader music industries or general business subjects, for example), there appears to be interest in creating a qualification which is better tailored to the requirements of the professional music environment from a manager's perspective. The latest edition of the UK Music Education Directory shows programmes in music business and music entrepreneurship but very little which specifically examines artist or creator management within the 2000+ courses listed. To be clear, as Editor of the MED and a music course founder myself, I am aware that many programmes do have modules or classes specifically focused on artist management; however, it is possible that an education programme devoting a greater level of content to the necessary knowledge and competences which the manager needs could be a significant step forward. This would require completion of the difficult-to-define skills and abilities analysis already discussed as a prerequisite (see outcome 4).

There is also the question here as to whether an HE/FE establishment could support or sustain courses solely focused on artist management. This is quite a specific field, with limited numbers of possible applicants. Perhaps this is why the subject usually ends up being part of a broader qualification in music or creative industries.

Training initiatives, single-issue workshops, networking opportunities and short education courses being set up and run by the MMF organizations themselves *do* appear to be quite extensive and of significant value (as reported by the interviewees in Chapter 4). These have the advantage of being able to tailor the content and focus on what managers need as opposed to broader college or university programmes which are providing for a wider range of possible career trajectories (music business generally, performance and/or production). Potential further collaboration between MMFs and established education centres with existing music business programmes could perhaps pay dividends here.

Experience (and knowledge) count when developing an artist, even at the beginning

It is not particularly startling to hear that previous industry experience has a positive value for artist managers. Working in a parallel field allows the proto manager to see the pitfalls and springboards associated with that role and decide whether they wish to get involved, as well as allowing them to grow their network of professional contacts. Many other roles in music have limited or fixed incomes/turnovers where managers (often on a percentage of the finance they generate) have the potential to earn more (although they may often earn very little to start with). This could be a potential encouragement to switch tracks as we have already discussed (outcome 4).

When gaining experience, networking is key. Overall, our interviewees tended to agree that a broad network of industry connections was highly valuable and recommend working closely with those who already have experience, to learn from them, effectively as a form of shadowing or mentoring. Clearly, industry organizations, notably the MMF network, can be vital in supporting this role, too.

There is no single operating business model for managers although to take one rule of thumb, an approximate working ratio of 1 manager to three artists appears to be a functional average. Some work alone with a small group of artists/creators, others work in teams to manage larger numbers of artists or to engage with new media. However, even here there are different operational models. If the solo manager can grow their business, as Scott Kirkwood did, then it appears they can then decide whether they wish to bring in further managers/artists or remain working by themselves with just one act (Chapter 4).

Examining the selection of artists, we found that the managers we spoke with rarely identified specific characteristics as clearly as Hardin (2020) who identified 'great' and 'unique' as key criteria in Chapter 4. They tended to indicate that they were seeking an undefinable artistic quality which they believed they could recognize. Drive (i.e.ambition) and a uniqueness in their sound/look were as far as most would go in defining what they were looking for. The former, determination and a strong work ethic on the artist's behalf, was the factor which arose most frequently in our conversations and seemed to be the most important.

Live performance has returned to again become the primary source of income. It would appear from our interviews that while COVID severed the events income stream causing a significant revenue loss for artists and managers, the return to live performance has thrown up other difficulties including the shortage of experienced staff and a log jam of many acts trying to return to touring at once. Beyond these, the closure of many venues, particularly at the grassroots level, has only increased the congestion. The cost-of-living crisis has added to this, pushing up touring costs while causing fan bases to become more selective about their spending (Chapter 5). While a live performance can be a career-transforming step, bringing an act to the attention of record companies, the media and their growing fan base, the need to play live does depend on the genre of music and the nature of the artist. However, live events are still an important form of connection with music and with the artist from an audience perspective generally and remain financially attractive to artists and managers as ticket sales and merchandise are highly significant revenue generators once a significant level of success is achieved.

It would appear, however, that a record label is not necessarily needed at the start of the artist's career but is quite critical if/when they are ready to step up to international level. The value of their experience coupled with their global network of staff located in (and highly familiar with) the individual international marketplaces can be of crucial importance (Chapter 5). The availability of capital investment is also a key advantage, but many artists and managers are now choosing to work with label services rather than take on a full record label deal, at least initially. Finally, in relation to record labels, there are some difficulties with the loss of record company personnel at local level who had critical market knowledge, but generally the models still work.

Where artists are also composers/songwriters, music publishing (often considered to be the third most important source of income behind live events and recorded music, respectively) can be a steady and long-term source of financial security. This sector can generate revenue from catalogue assets (existing songs/compositions) without further artist activity. Managers should examine these possibilities as they can often provide income for managers and artists later in their careers.

Managers are (usually) poor. Should they get equity in their artist's business?

Remuneration for artist managers can be very limited, particularly in the early stages of their clients' careers. Investigation into the full range of income streams (Chapter 7) and fair rates of return from each of these, as well as support funding to avoid managers having to invest financially in the development of their artists, could make a critical difference to the sector.

Managers often earn very little, particularly when starting out. The sector suffers from generally low salaries for most participants: in the MMF UK's most recent survey, 76% of those surveyed earned less than £30,000 per year,

12% earned nothing, and 72% did not have a pension (Bonham et al., 2024).

Low income is a significant issue. In Chapter two we first encountered the limited earning levels managers have to deal with at the outset of their work when the artist requires investment and is not generating significant revenue. The commission which managers charge has generally settled in the region of 20% of gross income with some variation across the more developed territories, mostly within the range of 15–25%. In Chapter four we addressed the issue of variation of the commission rate across different nations and whether managers themselves thought it was fair (some believed that it was too low for the work required). This is an ongoing debate. Additionally, many charge directly related expenses above this but caution is advised in this area to avoid disapproval and potential conflict with clients.

Making a financial investment in the early development of their artists (Chapter 7) often appears to be a requirement in the absence of other sources but it also raises concern in the longer term when there is no guarantee of return. This is a sector-wide issue caused by a need for early investment in the artist and a lack of sources of finance. Funding schemes (such as the MMF Accelerator programme) can offset this but clearly the risk factors need to be assessed. There are no guarantees that the investment will be recovered, which increases the risk for emerging managers who do choose to make this financial commitment. Financial insecurity can also contribute to mental health issues (Chapter 9). Investment is therefore another aspect of the role which we believe would benefit greatly from further research/consideration.

Offline and broader diversification is therefore critical. These sources include, but are not limited to, brand partnerships, sync agreements, merchandise, sponsorship/endorsement and fan subscription possibilities. Online data sources on the artist's fan base generated from artist activity (which are becoming increasingly accurate and detailed) therefore provide vital mailing lists for direct marketing.

The 'sunset' clause, which defines the remuneration a manager is entitled to for the work undertaken in developing the artist (which continues to generate income for the artist after they have parted ways), is an essential element of longer-term financial security for the manager. Not dissimilar to royalties from successful compositions/recordings, which may benefit the writer/performer for years beyond the initial release period, this represents a possible line of sustainable income. Industry bodies could perhaps develop standardized guidelines for sunset clauses that are fair and reflect the changing dynamics in the music industries. These guidelines should be flexible and adaptable to individual artist–manager relationships and different genres of music.

However, is there another approach? A number of those we spoke with indicated an alternative perspective: could the manager be considered the CEO of the artist's business and gain some form of equity in that business, to be retained over time, almost as a shareholder? This would most likely run beyond the term of a sunset clause. This occurs regularly in other business sectors, so why not within music? If we consider that the manager was perhaps the key element in growing the artist's career in the crucial early years, then that investment should surely be recognized in their later career, which would not exist but for the original efforts of that manager. Should the manager therefore not benefit from the same income streams over the same time period as the artist? It is difficult to examine this issue in detail as contractual agreements in this field are not normally made public (see outcome three above). Further transparency might help here but artists and managers may well be reluctant to allow scrutiny of their interactions.

Across all the sources we investigated, it appeared that most managers were working for a level of remuneration below their national average level of employment income. However, given that the main source of income is currently commission, the success of the manager is directly related to the success of their artists. Is this a reflection of the poor returns artists are receiving from sources such as streaming? Additionally, what income there is does not appear to be evenly distributed, with certain groups experiencing lower returns (relating to gender and ethnicity), indicating that further work needs to be done in the EDI area (Chapter 8).

Overall, the financial landscape for artist management is somewhat limited. Only in the event of an artist sustaining a highly successful career over several years (and retaining the same manager) do prospects improve. This is an outcome experienced only by a minority.

Brexit has negatively impacted European music management

There was one area of our research where opinion was almost entirely unilateral. European managers were quite unanimous in claiming that the UK withdrawal from the EU has been of almost universal detriment to the music industries generally and to the artist management sector specifically. We did not find anyone working in music within our research or within the work of others who expressed a positive opinion on this matter. The damage caused to international touring (in both directions) due to the tightening of border controls as well as the working-abroad restrictions for non-EU performers in continental Europe is actually prohibitive, rather than simply restrictive, below a certain level of operation. Therefore, the longer-term impact on the development of future UK artists could also be significant (and the full impact still to be realized) if the experiential and career-building opportunity of growing a European audience over time has effectively been removed, as indicated by Martin (2023) and others in Chapter 7.

Examining these issues in Chapters 5 and 7 led us to believe that this could increasingly affect UK artist development more generally as some of the ramifications are only emerging over time. UK and EU law makers are having to adapt existing legal structures which can take months or years to process and additional time to implement. This results in a mechanism which appears, to those required to use it, to be becoming more restrictive as they progress. Fresh barriers, such as only being able to be in the EU for 90 days within any 180-day period (for non-EU members), or the carnet documentation required to transport equipment to and from the UK/EU, adversely affect those within Europe as well as those within the UK.

As a result, costs have increased against a background of recent national economic contraction with projections of the increased financial impact ranging from 15 to 60% more, depending on the genre of the act and their level of existing success (Chapters 6 and 7). While this item has slipped away from the news headlines due to greater crises taking precedence, it appears that the more significant long-term effects of the UK withdrawal from the EU could still be ahead of us.

However, now that we are perhaps seeing possibilities of more open interaction between the UK and the EU (Makortoff et al., 2025), might this be the time to reapply pressure to create a more empathetic agreement on cultural exchange? Recent communications from the EU appear to indicate a softening of attitudes towards the UK. Without reversing the withdrawal agreement, we could perhaps negotiate better terms for touring musicians which would be to the benefit of all involved.

In summary then, Brexit has negatively impacted touring and international income streams. Playing live in Europe for UK acts now requires considerable forward planning to control budgets, optimize touring schedules, examine alternative touring strategies (e.g. joint tours), and monitor exchange rates, thus maximizing income (where profitable touring is possible). The reverse is also true. The levels of operation where continental live performance is no longer financially viable include those for emerging acts trying to play abroad for the first time. Therefore, this is currently a barrier to international development for both UK and EU acts.

A constant state of flux: artist management is in continual change

As in many other sectors of music and the creative industries, change within artist management is constant, often sudden and usually irreversible. This includes the evolving skills and abilities required for the role as well as the shifting environment managers operate within. Chapter two examined the changing nature of the role of the manager from an authoritarian, Svengali-style approach (mid-20th century) to a more nuanced, understanding and supportive position. In Chapter six our interviewees themselves flagged up continuous change which they had experienced and the considerable adaptations to COVID and Brexit were examined in Chapter 7. Could these be areas where additional support for managers would be valuable? (outcome 1).

Those we interviewed identified several points where early engagement with new developments gave them a competitive advantage (Chapters 4, 5 and 6). These included adapting to the arrival of AI and the necessary awareness of other managers expressing interest in your acts once they achieve initial success.

The manager therefore does seem to operate in a landscape where practically every element (financial, regulatory, technological, logistical, creative etc.) is subject to change almost without notice and needs to be observed closely at all times. As we have seen, some of these factors exist within the music industries where the manager may have an element of influence (e.g. dynamic ticket pricing, controversy over streaming income) but many are environmental and beyond her/his control (e.g. Brexit, COVID, AI). Hence, while the manager may well be in the driving seat of their artist's career development they do not necessarily have complete control of the vehicle.

This could create an atmosphere of ongoing instability which would no doubt add to the psychological pressures examined in Chapter 9. Not for the faint-hearted, the work of managing the careers of individuals active in music presents itself as a continuous and precarious balancing act. Our interviewees stressed the importance of actively looking for change and adapting to it as quickly and efficiently as possible.

In so much as it is possible to define, given the diverse and often conflicting models we have examined, the role of a manager and the nature of management has changed. The importance of education and/or guidance on careers, managing vulnerability, health and well-being and the intelligent route to market have become central to the role of the manager. In the current century, managers, many of whom come from different and varied backgrounds, have more access to education and support than their predecessors (although this could still be greater) and they tend to be more protective and empathetic towards their clients (Chapters 4 and 9). The history of the role shows significant change and development not only in the operating environment but also in the mindset and actions of the managers themselves as their sector professionalizes, bringing collective representation and some regulation and definition.

Overall, change is therefore seen as an ongoing constant with potentially negative consequences if not recognized early enough, with recent geopolitical developments affecting the music industries (COVID/Brexit) having drawn this into sharp focus.

Work remains to be done to improve equality, diversity and inclusion in artist management

EDI (equality, diversity, inclusion) has seen some progress but requires further development. The music industries have indeed moved forward from the 1960s and 1970s when artist managers were accused of being 'a sleazy bunch of businessmen out to bilk their, often black, R&B clients for a few quick bucks, with little respect for artists as musicians or their rights in law' (Chapple and Garofalo, 1977), as John Williamson explained in Chapter 2. We found, in Chapter 8, that the artist management sector itself has demonstrated ability to develop in this respect with increasing numbers of non-male, non-white managers over the last quarter of a century, to take the UK as one example. However, a brief overview of the ownership, boards and management of some of the larger management companies shows that these remain largely the preserve of older, white, middle-aged men.

The live events and nightclub arena continues to pose challenges as reflected in the experience of female managers we interviewed. (Allan, 2023) and (Mills-McLaughlin, 2020) both reported situations at concerts where male staff at the venue initially refused to believe that they were managers, at times avoiding communication altogether (Chapter 8).

The relative scarcity of female managers in the mid-20th century, as examined in Chapter 2, has given way to a world where many breakthrough acts such as Last Dinner Party (all-female) have female representation. However, it should not be assumed that progress here is a natural development. Change has only been achieved through the perseverance of those driving it and continued progress depends on the sustained efforts of organizations, initiatives and individuals working at both local and national levels.

EDI progress is therefore ongoing. Significant effort remains to improve working cultures and conditions for music artist managers (and those in other roles) to make the music industries more welcoming and inclusive. Nonetheless, there is much to celebrate with respect to the advocacy, progress and greater sense of acknowledgement pertinent to the heightened awareness surrounding equality, diversity and inclusivity policies within music. To take the UK as an example, organizations such as, but not limited to, the MMF, ISM, Keychange, Black Lives in Music, Pop Girlz, Hen Hoose, Musicians' Union, Women in CTRL, F-List, UK Music, and more, have individually and collectively conducted considerable work to make booking, hiring and employment practices more equitable.

While diversity is improving, it still has some way to go. Although there is now a much more diverse workforce within artist management than there was even at the turn of the century, only 43% of managers identify as women and 29% as black, Asian or from an ethnic background (Bonham et al., 2024, p. 8). However, this research also notes a gender pay gap with 29.6% of male managers earn more than £30,000 per year but only 22% of women earning at the same level.

Discrimination, however, remains an issue. Cases of harassment revealed in the Black Lives in Music 2021 report (Black Lives in Music, 2021) and ISM's Dignity at Work two report (ISM, 2022) suggest strongly that the volatile nighttime club culture and, generally, the precarious labour conditions synonymous with music sector work may require some form of government intervention to better protect music workers.

Future progress requires systematic change. Amending the Equality Act (UK Parliament, 2010) as a vehicle to enhance accountability is one that may serve EDI policies well and create a better, more inclusive music sector. The combination of heightened awareness of 'good practice' that is supported by legislation – and funded (arguably) by the most influential representative bodies – is fundamental to driving forward the equality, diversity and inclusion agenda.

Music (and management) can be detrimental to your health

Similar to EDI, discussed above, awareness of mental health issues in music has grown, but more still needs to be done. Music managers nowadays do appear to be taking this issue considerably more seriously than those in the last century, but progress is not always universal or guaranteed. We first encountered this with Tara Richardson's self-reflection on anxiety in Chapter 2. We later examined the side effects of intensive online promotional activity, which many artists are required to generate (which can be overtly negative) in Chapter 5. Creating boundaries to protect space and free time within the artist–manager relationship (Chapter 6) is also fundamental to a healthy work–life balance. Chapter nine examined this area in considerable detail, and while we found general concern had triggered some action towards more healthy mindsets (as well as a range of support mechanisms that have been established), ongoing monitoring and preventative activity are essential for progress in this area.

The nature of artist management can put pressure on mental health – sustaining multiple roles, managing the power dynamics, balancing the pressure to succeed against financial insecurity – in effect, the realities of what a music manager must face daily to run a sustainable business (and keep their clients happy and healthy) – can exert considerable psychological pressure. Creating an employment environment which recognizes the impact of the drive to succeed in a highly competitive music industry, the endless workload of producing and releasing music, maintaining a vibrant social media presence and nurturing a fan base, as well as securing investment and developing new partnerships, could make a real difference to managers' (and artists') well-being.

Managers *are* now becoming more open to considering and discussing good mental health – our interviews with artist managers and the activities undertaken and progress made by organizations such as Help Musicians, Music

Support and the PRS Members' Fund, which seek to support those affected, show that the awareness of psychological well-being and the need for mechanisms to protect those working in this sector are visible and rising.

Research in this area is becoming more detailed and informative, with examples including the Black Lives in Music report, which reveals that 36% of black music industry professionals feel that their mental well-being has declined since joining the industry (Black Lives in Music, 2021, p. 55). This figure jumps to 39% when we look at black women alone. Similarly, reports like the ISM's Dignity at Work (2022) report highlight the prevalence of bullying and harassment (in particular, sexual harassment and racism) faced by music industry professionals, especially freelancers. Data of this nature clarify, qualify and quantify the scale of the issue, allowing us to better understand the problems, address them more realistically and monitor progress.

Hence, while work is being done to develop greater connectivity between resources that address pressures such as bullying and harassment in the industry (in particular, the newly developed CIISA), there is still more to do and more direct, in-depth conversations to be had around how both individual dynamics and structural inequalities can be addressed to support good mental health for everyone working in the music industries.

Managing technology

Along with the aforementioned challenges, the platformization of music and its attendant disruption has demanded an increasing amount of attention and resources from artists and managers alike as they have adapted to continual technological change. In the first part of this century, this has included (to name just a few) digital downloads, streaming, YouTube, TikTok and the advent of AI. As each of these has organizationally changed the music industries, managers and artists have had to learn and adapt at a faster pace than in the past, often taking up time that would previously have been allocated to either creative or other business activities. While these have brought many benefits to consumers, the outcomes on the production side must be viewed more ambivalently.

In particular, the mental health issues noted in the previous point (as with elsewhere in society) are often attributed to the omnipresence of some of these platforms and the devices on which they are devoured. Yet for artists and their managers, these are essential for market growth, generating engagement and gathering audience data. However, it is easy for all involved, not least the artist, to become overwhelmed. Our interviews reflected this, stressing the importance of developing online presence but ensuring that the artist does not over-stretch themselves generating the social media content audiences expect. This can become a serious health issue (Chapter 5).

It is also worth noting that, for some, the importance of social media can be overplayed. Hits and likes often do not convert to meaningful engagement with the artist or, ultimately, sales. Some major acts including Halsey, Doja Cat and FKA Twigs have highlighted the pressures and challenges of navigating TikTok (Fenwick, 2022) while others, often established in an era before social media, can sustain a career with distinctly limited online engagement. The other side of this, of course, is an unprecedented amount of data in the hands of artists and managers which can positively inform business decisions surrounding demand, choice of tour venues and set lists.

The advent of artificial intelligence (AI) is merely the latest iteration of this. Unsurprisingly, our interviewees recognized its importance and most admitted that they were using it to some extent in daily business activity but were worried about its future application and likely detrimental impacts on recording artists, including their potential redundancy. As with every previous technological advance (recordings themselves, radio, cassettes, CDs, downloads, streaming), there has been considerable noise from copyright organizations about impending doom with corresponding pleas for (rather than hope of) government intervention or regulation. And, like the past, the most likely outcome is one where an uneasy coexistence endures until the challenges posed are superseded by yet unknown technologies.

Coda

To end, we return to the original aims of the book and suggest some avenues for further research. We set out to take artist management seriously as a fundamental and essential activity across the music industries while presenting the many facets of the role and differences in how this plays out in individual circumstances. In doing so, we noted the multifarious commercial and personal issues that arose because of the underlying informality (despite the best efforts of sector organizations) of the role. Lastly, we sought to bring a fresh perspective by bridging the gap between the brief but insightful accounts of artist management within the wider music industries (like those in Frith, 1978; Jones, 2012 and Anderton et al., 2022), the anecdotal and sensational (e.g. Garfield, 1986) and the instructional (Allen, 2022; Webb et al., 2022).

In short, we have captured a snapshot of artist management in transition over a relatively short period in a range of predominantly European contexts. By taking this slightly more practical approach, we have deliberately foregrounded the voices of a range of managers (as both contributors and interviewees) which we have found to be conspicuous by their absence in many previous accounts. Allowing them to share their experiences, perspectives and concerns has helped us build a more accurate and complicated view of what is involved in managing creative people within the music industries.

This complexity is evidenced in the preceding examples, where we have seen how a group of managers with different backgrounds and skillsets have navigated the music industries on behalf of an equally diverse cohort of musicians working across a range of genres, markets and demographics. In this sense, our findings are unsurprising, and it is no easier to pithily define the role than ever: there is no single definition of what an artist manager does nor is there a single route into the role. Each manager is effectively unique in what they do and how they do it, and yet they are all trying to achieve the same outcome – success, however measured, for their artists. Nevertheless, while examining individual professional pathways, there are obvious commonalities, similar experiences and recognized concerns which most managers share. So, while there may not be definable 'models' for manager behaviour or career strategy, there is sufficient commonality to develop support strategies (especially around education, contracts, health and finances) for the role.

In addressing our third objective, we have presented the work of the manager as critical, central to artist development (and therefore to the entirety of the music industries) and perhaps undervalued or at least under-recognized. Their profile/reputation within popular culture remains caricatured and misunderstood at best and yet the reality of the actual work is that it is relentless, complex and multifaceted, requiring an agile and singular mindset and a particular resilience. The manager is required to be multi-skilled and multitasking, adapting to unexpected situations, identifying opportunities and finding solutions daily. Yet, in another familiar refrain from across the creative industries, the manager is often poorly rewarded (and in the early stages of artist development not rewarded at all) for such dexterity.

Throughout this research we have been able to add some detail and insight that helps build a broader and more detailed picture of artist management, but it is important to note that this is only a first step towards a fuller understanding of the role and that there are difficulties in overly generalizing as a result, for two main reasons. The first is that our interviewees and experiences offer a range of perspectives, but these represent only a tiny percentage of working managers in the industries. The second is the lack of transparency across the sector and music industries more widely. Of course, there are many valid reasons why financial and contractual arrangements are not made public, but the absence of such knowledge presents a considerable barrier to presenting a 360-degree view of artist management for researchers and educators.

Though these gaps will never be comprehensively filled, there are two broad areas that are ripe for further exploration. The first would focus on management contracts and their clauses, and the financial implications of these for both artists and managers would be at the top of any shopping list for future research around artist management. Further unpacking the working relationships between artists and managers and the basis on which these are undertaken would also offer the possibility of tailored, more specifically artist management-orientated programmes in higher and further education.

The second speaks to the study of different experience of artist management around the world and further exploring the tensions between the global and the local in the field. The pre-internet model would often see local entrepreneurs (in music or elsewhere) working with local acts with the aim of pursuing a recording contract. Often, these partnerships would fail with managers sacked or replaced, bands splitting up or solo artists quitting their pursuit of a musical career with no apparent audience. Even where successful in the short term, there are countless stories of the first manager being replaced, fairly or unfairly, as the stakes became higher. Now, in a global, online and increasingly corporate business, as we have seen, none of these cornerstones remains.

In the light of these changes, there is scope for further research around the business models and approaches of the large, transnational companies that now dominate the top end of the sector while also considering the possibility of a global, representative organization for managers in addition to the national ones. Such an organization – in much the same way that the International Federation of the Phonographic Industry (IFPI) does for record labels – would go some way to giving managers the stature and voice in the music industries that is often drowned out by the more effective lobbying of other interests within it. More generally, such an organization would provide an umbrella for the common aspects of artist management that we have identified while also reflecting specific local and national challenges around the world.

This notwithstanding, it would be remiss not to finish by returning to our own work and the aim of locating the artist and the manager at the centre of discussions of the music industries. In doing this, we have gained new insights into an increasingly complex, demanding and pressurized profession, one which is also increasingly professional and responsible for the welfare of musicians globally. These relationships are not universally consistent or always unproblematic, but the Wild West days of 1960s and 1970s management are long gone and it is important to remove the work of contemporary managers from such a context.

Throughout, we have noted that management in the music industries is often a thankless task due to the combination of high expectations and challenges both within and outside the control of the protagonists. In adding to the literature around it and recognizing that the role could be better explained, we have, hopefully, contributed to understanding it and, in a small way, recognized and thanked those who are doing the work.

References

Allan, D. (2023) Practicalities of artist management [lecture]. University of the West of Scotland, 17 November.
Allen, P. (2022) *Artist Management for Music Business*, 5th edn. Routledge, New York.
Anderton, A., Hannam, J. and Hopkins, J. (2022) *Music Management, Marketing and PR*. Sage, London.
Black Lives in Music (2021) Being black in the UK music industry. Part 1 – Music professionals. Available at: s3.us-east 1.amazonaws.com/nadworks.streaming/BLiM/BLiM-report-industryprofessionals_21 09v01.pdf (accessed 23 May 2024).
Bonham, P., Coldrick, A. and Webb, A. (2024) *Managing Expectations*, Workforce Edition. MMF, London.
Braines, S. (2023) Questions on artist management. Interview by Allan Dumbreck [Zoom], 5 December.

Chapple, S. and Garofalo, R. (1977) *Rock'n'Roll is Here to Pay: The History and Politics of the Music Industry*. Nelson-Hall, Chicago, Illinois.

EMMA (2023) Music managers in Europe. Available at: emma.community/wp-content/uploads/2024/01/EMMA_Music-Management-in-Europe-Report.pdf/ (accessed 26 September 2024).

EMMA (European Music Managers Alliance) (n.d.). Available at: https://emma.community/ (accessed 3 August 2025).

Fenwick, J. (2022) Musicians are suffering on Tiktok. Do they have a choice? *Vice Magazine*. Available at: www.vice.com/en/article/musicians-are-suffering-on-tiktok-do-they-have-a-choice/ (accessed 26 June 2025).

Ferguson, R. (2023) Evidence given to DCMS inquiry into misogyny in music (UK Parliament). Available at: committees.parliament.uk/writtenevidence/124421/pdf/ (accessed 3 August 2025).

Frith, S. (1978) *The Sociology of Rock*. Constable, London.

Garfield, S. (1986) *Expensive Habits*. Faber & Faber, London.

Hardin, C. (2020) Questions on artist management. Interview by Allan Dumbreck [Zoom], 29 April.

Hwang, A. (2024) K-pop management innovation changes global music industry. Available at: www.korea.net/NewsFocus/Opinion/view?articleId=254952 (accessed 2 February 2025).

ISM (2022) Dignity at work 2: Discrimination in the music sector. Available at: www.ism.org/images/files/ISM-Dignity-2-report.pdf (accessed 16 May 2024).

Jones, M. (2012) *The Music Industries: From Conception to Consumption*. Palgrave MacMillan, Basingstoke, UK.

Makortoff, K., Courea, E. and Stewart, H. (2025) EU trade chief says it 'could consider' UK joining pan-Europe customs deal. The Guardian. Available at: www.theguardian.com/business/2025/jan/23/eu-uk-europe-trade-deal-pan-euro-mediterranean-convention (accessed 2 February 2025).

Martin, D. (2023) Questions on artist management. Interview by Allan Dumbreck [Zoom], 22 December.

MED (Music Education Directory) (2024) Available at: https://www.jamesonline.org.uk/jamesresources/med_2024/ (accessed 3 August 2025).

Mills-McLaughlin, C. (2020) Questions on artist management. Interview by Allan Dumbreck [Zoom], 19 May.

MMF (2019) Managing expectations. Available at: themmf.net/resources/knowledge/?subject=managing-expectations&material= (accessed 16 May 2024).

MMF (2022) Evidence given to DCMS inquiry into misogyny in music. UK Parliament. Available at: committees.parliament.uk/writtenevidence/110061/pdf/ (accessed 3 August 2025).

Ragoowansi, N. (2025) Questions on artist management. Interview by Allan Dumbreck [Zoom], 7 January.

UK Parliament (2010) Equality Act 2010. Available at: https://www.gov.uk/guidance/equality-act-2010-guidance (accessed 16 May 2024).

Webb, A., Bonham, P., Harmon, A., Coldrick, A. and Dethekar, M. (2022) *Essentials of Music Management*. Music Managers Forum, London.

Appendices – Questionnaires and Further Possible Research

Appendix 1

Artist Management questionnaire (first round: 2020–2023)

1. Please give a short history of your experience/work within the music industries.
2. How would you define your role as an artist manager in the music industries?
3. What do you consider to be the most valuable attributes for an artist manager wishing to enter the music industries?
4. What education/qualifications did you have prior to working in music and how valuable do you believe education is to an artist manager?
5. How has artist management changed while you have been working in that role?
6. How important is social media and consumer analytical data to artist management?
7. Are traditional promotional methods (TV, radio, press) still important?
8. Do you need a record company?
9. How important is live performance to artist development?
10. What do you believe are the key issues currently facing artist management?
11. Which significant developments do you expect to see in music in the next five years?
12. If you could change/modify one aspect of your sector of music, what would it be and why?
13. What are the key ethical issues affecting artist management?

Additional questions (second round: 2023–2024)

1. How did you first become involved in artist management?
2. How do you think AI will affect your sector?
3. What are the key problems and issues which cause difficulties for the artist–manager relationship?
4. Do you think anything/enough is being done to address inequalities in the music industry? Have you encountered meaningful or effective efforts to address gender inequalities or racism, for example?'

Appendix 2

Possible future research

Further data and analysis on these topics would shed considerable light on the role of the artist manager, the work they undertake and the value they bring to our cultural and creative environments.

Possible further research directions – some potential lines of investigation

a. Further research into data on and analysis of MMFs and representative organizations to clarify their development and value.

b. Examination of possible FE/HE programme content specifically for managers.
c. Investigation of artist manager remuneration. What is a fair commission rate and why? Could/should managers be awarded an equity investment in their artist's business(es)?
d. Could a more equitable agreement be negotiated to more easily facilitate commercial cultural exchange between the UK and the EU?
e. Can a globally representative manager's organization be developed? What should its objectives be? Is it able to make significant change on behalf of creators and managers?
f. Given the key role of artists and managers, are they sufficiently recognized/ represented within the music industries, the broader creative industries and/or the global business environment more generally?

Index

AI-driven BeatBread platform, 93
Album band, 18–20
AMA France, 41
American Federation of Musicians (AFM), 32
Artificial intelligence (AI), 93–98, 102, 154
Artist management, 146–147
    change within, 151–152
    characteristics, 13–14
    equality, diversity and inclusion (EDI), 127, 152–153
    future research, 147
    historical development, 24–25
    mental health issues, 159
    overview, 1–5
Artist–manager relationship, 6–7, 143–145
    adapting to change, 81–93
    artificial intelligence (AI), 93–98
    conflict, 98–101
    government intervention, 89–91
    issues, 98–101
Artist managers
    artist, early funding, 66–67
    artists selection, 62–63
    business arrangements, 63–64
    commission rate, 67–70
    communication skills, 56
    education/qualifications, 56–60
    equity, 149–151
    experience, 52–53
    initial motivation, 51–52
    international organization, 145–146
    key skills, 54–56
    management skills, 56
    management teams, 65–66
    in 1955, 15
    in 1960, 15–18
    in 1970, 18–20
    pre-millennial tension, 20–21
    previous music industries experience value, 60–61
    previous music industry role, 53
    remuneration, 149
    rock'n'roll era, 14–15
    role, 54
    sole traders, 64–65
    21st century, 21–23
Artist & repertoire (A&R), 81
Association of Artist Managers (AAM) Australia, 5, 35, 41
Association of British Orchestras (ABO), 4
ATA carnet, 110, 111

Balancing Act, 126
Brexit, 109–110, 151
    90/180-day travel rule, 112
    Let the music move report, 112–113
    royalty collections, 111–112
    tax considerations, 111–112
    travel and visa complexities, 110–111
British Phonographic Industry (BPI), 4
Business models, 63–64

Central Withholding Agreement (CWA), 113, 114
Commission rate, 67–70
Communication skills, 56
Concert Promoters Association (CPA), 4, 31
Confédération Internationale des Sociétés d'Auteurs et Compositeurs (CISAC), 4, 30, 31
Council of Music Makers (CMM), 33

Index

COVID-19 pandemic, 1, 4, 9, 10, 32, 33, 37, 78–80, 87, 89, 92, 109, 120, 149, 152
Creative Industries Independent Standards Authority (CIISA), 127

Digital service providers (DSPs)/online retail platforms, 95
Discrimination, 121–123, 124–126
Diversity, 125

Equality, diversity and inclusion (EDI), 119–120
    age, 124–125
    artist management, 127, 152–153
    discrimination, 121–123, 124–126
    diversity, 125
    initiatives, 124
    mothering, 126
    neurodiversity, 126
    policies, 126–127
    precariousness, 121–123
    women, 120, 124–126
European Music Managers Alliance (EMMA), 5, 37–38, 67, 69, 74
European tour, 107–109

Finance, 66–70
Financial insecurity, 136–138

Goods Movement Reference Numbers (GMRs), 110
Government intervention, 89–91

Honesty, 54, 55, 62

IMUC Germany, 41, 42
Individual tax identification number (ITIN), 1147
International Federation of Musicians (FIM), 32
International management portfolios
    growth of, 114–115
International Managers Forum (IMF), 27–28
International Music Managers Forum (IMMF), 42–43, 45
International tour
    Brexit (*see* Brexit)
    budget, 108
    cost, 109
    European tour, 107–109
        documentation, 110
    financial underperformance factors, 107
    logistical challenges, 109
    profitability, 107
    United States (US), 113–114
        non-US performers tax, 113–114
        touring complexities in, 113

Intersectionality, 127
Investment banks, 114

Live performance, 78–80
Loneliness, 126–127
Manager, types of, 24
Marketing, 81
Mental health
    artist management, 153
    awareness, 132–134, 153–154
    music management pressures, 134
        financial insecurity, 136–138
        multiple roles, 134
        power dynamics shifts, 135
        success, 135–136
    support, 138–140
Mothering, 126
Music companies
    consolidation of, 114–115
Music income decline, 104–107
Music Managers Forum (MMF), 4, 27–28
    Australia, 5, 34, 35
    Canada, 5, 35, 39–41
    Finland, 42
    geographical representation, 43–44
    importance, 35
    New Zealand, 34, 35, 40
    objectives, 44–45
    Sweden, 42
    UK, 5, 9, 24, 27, 29–30, 32–37, 52, 67, 69
    US, 4, 34, 35, 38–40
    Zimbabwe, 5
Music Producers Guild (MPG), 33
Music Publishers Association (MPA), 4, 30
Music publishing, 84–86
Music representative organizations, 29
    artist management, 34–36
    composition/publishing, 29–31
    cross-industry representation, 33–35
    live events/performance, 31–32
    musicians/performers, 32–33
    music production, 33
    recorded music, 30–31

National Centre for Music (CNM), 90
NEMAA Norway, 42
Networking skills, 55, 57, 63
Networks/mentoring, 73–75
Neurodiversity, 126

Parents and Carers in the Performing Arts (PiPA), 126, 127
Performing Right Society (PRS), 4
Power dynamics, 135
Precariousness, 121–123
Promotion, 81

Record company, 80–84
Recording Industry Association of America (RIAA), 4
Resilience, 56

Social media/metrics, 75–78
Social security number (SSN), 114
Société des Auteurs, Compositeurs et Éditeurs de Musique (SACEM), 4, 28
Sunset clause, 150

Transparency, 54–56, 62
Trust, 54, 55, 62

UK Music, 33–35

Worldwide Independent Network (WIN), 98

www.ingramcontent.com/pod-product-compliance
Lightning Source LLC
Chambersburg PA
CBHW041410300426
44114CB00028B/2977